The Archaeology of Race and Racialization in Historic America

The American Experience in Archaeological Perspective

UNIVERSITY PRESS OF FLORIDA

Florida A&M University, Tallahassee
Florida Atlantic University, Boca Raton
Florida Gulf Coast University, Ft. Myers
Florida International University, Miami
Florida State University, Tallahassee
New College of Florida, Sarasota
University of Central Florida, Orlando
University of Florida, Gainesville
University of North Florida, Jacksonville
University of South Florida, Tampa
University of West Florida, Pensacola

The Archaeology of Race and Racialization in Historic America

Charles E. Orser Jr.

FOREWORD BY MICHAEL S. NASSANEY

University Press of Florida
Gainesville/Tallahassee/Tampa/Boca Raton/Pensacola
Orlando/Miami/Jacksonville/Ft. Myers/Sarasota

27 26 25 24 23 22   6 5 4 3 2

Library of Congress Cataloging-in-Publication Data
Orser, Charles E.
The archaeology of race and racialization in historic America /
Charles E. Orser, Jr. ; foreword by Michael S. Nassaney.
p. cm.—(The American experience in archaeological perspective)
Includes bibliographical references and index.
ISBN 978-0-8130-3143-9 (paper)
1. Archaeology and history—United States. 2. Race—Social aspects—
United States—History. 3. Ethnicity—United States—History. 4. Racism—
United States—History. 5. Social classes—United States—History.
6. Material culture—United States—History. 7. Historic sites—United States.
8. Excavations (Archaeology)—United States. 9. United States—Race relations.
10. United States—Antiquities. I. Title.
E159.5.O77 2007
973.'04—dc22   2007007774

The University Press of Florida is the scholarly publishing agency for the State
University System of Florida, comprising Florida A&M University, Florida
Atlantic University, Florida Gulf Coast University, Florida International
University, Florida State University, New College of Florida, University
of Central Florida, University of Florida, University of North Florida,
University of South Florida, and University of West Florida.

University Press of Florida
2046 NE Waldo Road
Suite 2100
Gainesville, FL 32609
http://upress.ufl.edu

Contents

Tables

Figures

Foreword

As a nation founded on the ideals of liberty and freedom, the United States has yet to extricate itself from a reliance on the racial categories that perpetuate social inequalities. The earliest European settlers in North America excluded indigenous peoples by racializing them, effectively severing them from history and justifying the doctrine of manifest destiny. This thorough and ongoing process of racialization was created and used to define a social hierarchy that became integral to the operation of colonialism, capitalism, and imperialism. Despite efforts by anthropologists since the time of Boas to discredit biological and scientific notions of race, race persists as one of the central conceptual inventions of modernity.

Racial classifications remain tenacious in the United States; they are imposed labels that agglomerate individuals based on real or perceived physical differences. Their manifest function is to create distinctions with social meanings that naturalize systems of hierarchy and inequality. In *The Archaeology of Race and Racialization in Historic America*, Charles Orser extends race and racialization beyond the color line that W.E.B. Du Bois so perceptively identified in the early twentieth century. While black and white has been the dominant metaphor for twentieth-century race relations and civil rights, Orser details how nativist Americans manipulated racial categories to apply to immigrant groups in the nineteenth century. Whiteness and membership in that category is as much a social construction as otherness is.

In the mid-nineteenth century, the Irish phenotype was excluded from whiteness when the masses of Irish immigrants that constituted a potential labor pool were arriving on American shores. Fueled by perceptions by nativist Americans that Irish immigrants were not skilled workers and fears about papist religious beliefs, racialization of the Irish took place in America through spatial segregation and the use of simian images to create and reinforce stereotypes. The process was extended to the Chinese in the West, where the willingness of Chinese immigrants to work for low wages and endure harsh living conditions threatened white privilege and access to historically white work. Parallels can be seen in contemporary debates over Mexican labor migrants. Throughout American history, immigrants have faced challenges and obstacles from nativists who saw it as their duty to keep America white. Not surprisingly, such racialized social conditions have a structurally institutionalized basis with material implications that are amenable to archaeological analysis. For social archaeologists, race and class are vectors that organize the material world in ways that reproduce racial practice, prejudice, and ideology.

Archaeologists have been slow to examine this pervasive process in American social life for various reasons. The hesitance of archaeologists to confront racism, which was initially studied under the guise of ethnicity, may stem from the fact that race is a formidable topic whose very investigation seems to essentialize it. In addition, most archaeologists have been socialized in a system that institutionalizes inequality based on racial categories; thus, race continues to shape archaeological practice today. Yet upon closer examination, archaeologists can reconsider and deconstruct familiar scenarios in which racialization played a role. For example, the New England town green with its white picket fences, churches, and public buildings stands in contrast to the pastel, multicolored buildings that were common in the early years of the Republic. The whitening of New England was an invented tradition that served to set old Yankees apart from the newer German, Polish, and Irish arrivals. It was only when these latter groups demonstrated that they were capable of accepting the values of white Anglo-Saxon Protestant America could they become incorporated into the melting pot. Assimilation was really the only proof.

In my study of changing cultural landscapes associated with pioneers in Battle Creek, Michigan, it became apparent that the first Euro-American settlers appropriated the land and forged an identity that they defended from newcomers. Racial difference was part of that strategy, which led to Indian removal in the 1830s. In the Yankee West, pioneer descendants were slow to accept immigrants from southern Europe in the early twentieth century. When an Italian family first rented and later owned the old Greek Revival house that had been built by Battle Creek's first schoolteacher, they naturally made some landscape and interior modifications that suited their Old World tastes. Archaeological, oral, and photographic evidence indicate that they removed the ornate and probably decaying Victorian porches on the house and planted two rows of grapevines to create a private arbor where they could play bocce and consume the fruits of their labor. Yet neighbors resented these changes and claimed they had "ruined the neighborhood" and were running a speakeasy during the Prohibition years. These are recollections of a woman who as a young girl likely heard her father's accusations at the dinner table and internalized them well into her eighties. Attitudes of exclusion continue into the present and are used to keep the newest groups of immigrants in their place, effectively denying them full participation in the American dream. This ideology of disdain for immigrants is rooted in racial theory but is expressed under the veil of concern for the native-born working class.

Excavated material culture, when linked with drawings, writings, and legislation, provides greater insight into the process of racialization. It can also illuminate the past in ways that can empower otherwise disenfranchised groups. Archaeology can reveal the subtle ways that groups accepted, rejected, negotiated, and accommodated to the social conditions that permeated their places of work, worship, and leisure. The challenge for historical archaeologists and other social scientists is to unravel the choices human agents made under the constraints of institutionalized racism. Given the limited attention archaeologists have paid to this dimension of the American experience, the archaeological record is a potentially fruitful entry point from which to observe racialized differences in the material culture of capitalism. Such an analysis will likely demonstrate that race has colored archaeological evidence in ways that practitioners can ill afford to ignore if they aim to obtain a fuller understanding of the American experience.

Michael S. Nassaney
Series Editor

Preface

This book concerns the process of racialization in historic America. My central concern is how modern-world archaeologists might investigate the subject of racialization as it pertains to immigrant groups, specifically the Irish and the Chinese on both sides of the American continent. Equally pertinent is the idea that race continues to shape archaeological practice, even though not all archaeologists might acknowledge that fact or appreciate its impact today.

American archaeology was founded to investigate race—that of the mysterious Moundbuilders of North America. However, race has not been a major focus even of historical archaeology. The lack of directed examination seems odd because historical archaeologists practice an archaeology that is especially well suited to studying race, a vector of social inequality that has garnered considerable and well-deserved attention in the United States. Even so, some historical archaeologists in America have confronted the archaeology of race, and this book is designed to build on and extend their efforts.

Numerous individuals have provided much-needed assistance during the preparation of this book. I wish to thank Paul Mullins, Stephen Brighton, Mary Praetzellis, James Delle, and Michael Nassaney for reading sections of this work and for helping me clarify and refine some of my concepts. I have been especially lucky over recent years to share an interest in the archeology of race with Paul Mullins, and I have greatly benefited from our discussions. Many people have provided assistance with the images, including Victoria Cranner of the R. S. Peabody Museum; the staff of the Chicago Historical Society; and Rebecca Yamin, Stephen Brighton, Paul Shackel, Christopher Fennell, Terrence Martin, David Gradwohl, and Mary Praetzellis.

I also wish to acknowledge the patience and support of the staff of the University Press of Florida, who have been gracious and helpful. I particularly wish to thank Michael Nassaney for asking me to think about an archaeology of race one more time. As always, this project would have been utterly impossible without Janice's assistance.

1

Race, Racialization, and
Why Archaeologists Should Care

In the earliest years of the twentieth century, thousands of immigrants flooded the shores of the United States. So concerned was the U.S. Immigration Commission, the federal agency charged with such matters, that they hired an anthropologist to prepare a *Dictionary of Races or Peoples*. In his brilliant *Working Toward Whiteness* (2005), historian David Roediger described how what concerned the members of the commission was not the "old" immigrants—Germans, British, Irish, Scottish, and even Chinese—but rather the "new" immigrants—Slavs, Hungarians, Greeks, and Italians. The racial place of the old immigrants had been fought over and largely resolved in the previous century. The Irish, who had entered the United States at a time when they were perceived as nonwhite, had either risen in the system—becoming entrepreneurs, political bosses, and city leaders—or had found their place firmly within the working class as police, firefighters, boardinghouse keepers, or in a thousand other professions. As I explore in Chapter 4, the racial position of the Irish in America was contested for many years before their place in America was established. Chapter 5 shows that the story of the Chinese was different from that of the Irish, because as men and women from "the Orient" they could not so easily be assigned to the "white race." Their outward appearance was a stigma that kept them apart from any claim of whiteness. At the same time, the racial history of Irish and Chinese as immigrants in the United States was strangely similar. Both Irish and Chinese, as old immigrants, had serious obstacles to overcome before they were accorded their place on the American racial ladder.

By 1900, the Irish and Chinese were no longer a major concern to men who worried about and watched over the rush of immigrants into America. The problem they envisioned came from Europe, which now referred to the southern and eastern fringes of the continent. Their concern was to identify and enforce the "proper" racial place of Slavs, Poles, Hungarians, Greeks, and other peoples whose points of origin were east and south of Western Europe. At the heart of the enforcers' problem and what they desperately felt they needed to know for certain was the true relationship between race and ethnicity. Though they did not put it into so many words, the subtext of their internal debate was to discern how the newest Americans should be racialized. Who was white, who was not, and just how white were the new arrivals? How much work would the American melting pot have to do to assimilate the newcomers, and should certain restrictions be placed on immigrants who might prove difficult to Americanize?

The first paragraph of the commission's dictionary, written by anthropologist Daniel Folkmar, best summarizes the commissioners' perceived dilemma:

Since eastern Europe became an important source of immigration many new ethnical factors have been added to the population of the United States. Early in the Commission's investigations among these newer immigrants it became apparent that the true racial status of many of them was imperfectly understood even in communities where they were most numerous, and the difficulties encountered in properly classifying the many ethnical names that were employed to designate various races or peoples suggested the preparation of a volume that would promote a better knowledge of the numerous elements included in the present immigration movement. (Folkmar 1911, 1)

Folkmar's language here is telling. He chose to characterize the recently arrived immigrants as groups that introduced new "ethnical factors" into the cultural and genetic mix of the United States, but what really mattered to him was their "true racial status."

The commissioners' concern about the racial status of the newcomers is especially interesting because they were not actually asked by Congress to investigate race or ethnicity. The federal legislation empowering the commission, dated February 20, 1907, only mandated a "full inquiry, examination, and investigation . . . into the subject of immigration" (ii). This charge is not inherently racial. The commissioners were not asked to racialize the immigrants, but that is precisely what they set out to accomplish.

The dictionary indicates the significance the commissioners attached to racial classification. But their task had not been easy. Folkmar noted that no one had yet been able to devise a common classification system for humanity (3). Linnaeus had identified four races, but Blumenbach had seen five. Others observed anywhere between three and sixty-three races. To clarify the issue and create a classification system census enumerators could use, Folkmar adopted what was at the time a common classification of five races—Caucasian, Mongolian, Malay, Ethiopian, and American (Indian)—further subdivided into stocks, groups, and peoples. In this scheme, a "people" called Finnish, for example, belonged to the Finnic "group" and to the Sibiric "stock." This system assigned the Finns the racial category of Mongolian (5).

This classification system, which was accepted by the Immigration Commission and ostensibly also by the U.S. Congress, was not benign. In fact, it appeared to provide government sanction for the treatment of people classified as non-Caucasian as inferior. Lawyers in Minnesota attempted, albeit unsuccessfully, to bar Finns from naturalization because they were considered to be Mongolian—that is, "nonwhite" (Roediger 2005, 61).

The racial controversies and debates that captured the attention of America at the beginning of the twentieth century had bedeviled the nation since before its founding. In Europe in the late eighteenth century, Enlightenment scholars seeking to distance themselves from the earlier Christian tradition of assuming the basic unity of humanity (Stocking 1987, 17–18) began to delve into the study of human diversity. Many scholars, political observers, and writers of popular nonfiction have analyzed, pondered, and written about race since then, and much of this literature has focused on the historical conditions within the United States. Though some have called race humanity's "most dangerous myth" (Montagu 1942), an "American obsession" (Terkel 1992), and a "persistent taint" (Muwakkil 2005), the practice of analyzing and attempting to understand race has had significant staying power in American life. Race continues to fascinate and to frustrate. Nobel Peace Prize recipient Ralph Bunche (1968, 69) noted as early as 1936 that a thousand anthropologists working on race could not dissuade people from holding the irrational belief that race is real.

The tenacity of racial classification in America (however the schemes themselves might change), and the perseverance of race-based action and hierarchy means that race, as a serious topic, should interest all social scientists. This attention is particularly warranted from historical archaeologists because the sociohistorical formations they examine, particularly in U.S. history, were all informed, to some degree and in various ways, by racial concerns. In various complex ways, racial concerns continue to shape archaeological practice.

Race in American Archaeology

The European preoccupation with race dawned in its modern form in the post-Columbian era, and as European travelers transported their views on race across the Atlantic, a frequently acrimonious debate began in American intellectual circles. In fact, it can reasonably be argued that the science of humanity in America was initially organized around arguments over race. The protracted obsession with race in America has diverse sources, but one of them relates to the dispossession of America's native cultures by Europeans. When Europeans first came to their "new" world and uttered Rousseau's (1984, 109) fateful words—"This is mine"—they did so with the understanding that the land was actually someone else's and that it had been so for generations. Since the early days of the republic, America's elite scientists and intelligentsia have expended an enormous amount of time and energy examining the history of native peoples in America. A substantial number of them attempted to disprove the longevity of native groups' occupation of the continent, but ultimately such claims proved baseless.

America's earliest dilettante physical anthropologists eagerly immersed themselves in the race debate. They began their labors with a painstaking investigation of the physical reality of human variation, basing many of their conclusions on their minute examinations of crania. Wilson Dickeson, Samuel G. Morton, and others voraciously examined every skull on which they could lay their hands in an effort to prove the skeletal reality of what they previously knew only as skin-deep variation (Bieder 1986, 55–103; Orser 2004b, 40–49). The project of physical anthropologists has not ceased today, but they have shifted their investigation from overt skeletal and physical morphology to microscopic biological variation. Yesterday's dolichocephalic/brachycephalic cranial distinctions are today's genetic subpopulations.

Highly educated scientists still labor to discover the true physical basis of human variation—what we might loosely call "race"—and their ideas remain controversial (Brace 2005; Sarich and Miele 2004). A solution to the scientific reality of race remains frustratingly elusive. The elasticity of race as a biological concept helps exacerbate and extend racial controversy. As W.E.B. Du Bois (1939/1973, 1) observed in the late 1930s: "No scientific definition of race is possible. . . . Race would seem to be a dynamic and not a static conception, and the typical races are continually changing and developing, amalgamating, and differentiating."

The dynamism and mutability of race as a category can be aptly demonstrated in the field of law, a milieu of modern-day life usually renowned for its standardization and rigidity. But race has stymied even legal professionals, particularly in settings long recognized for their diversity. In Louisiana, for example, the legal notion of race has provided at least two notable cases that demonstrate the problematics of race in the real world. In 1906, a man named Taylor Cousins petitioned the state to issue him and his sister birth certificates that changed their racial status from "creole" (nonwhite) to white; in a similar case, filed in 1973, Susie Phipps asked the court to change her official racial identification from "colored" to white (Domínguez 1986, 1–4, 93–95).

We might not be surprised by the Cousins case because it occurred during America's Jim Crow period, but the Phipps case encourages us to acknowledge that racial identification can be a matter of considerable debate even in the staid field of law. Such legal cases, and many more can be cited, enforce the notion that race is complex, highly nuanced, and often situational. The Cousins and Phipps cases reinforce the difficulty of attempting to define the biology of race with historical fixity (Omi and Winant 1986, 57).

The wisdom of Du Bois's insight was not known at the birth of American archaeology, and early excavators, possessing various degrees of technical skill, were rapidly enticed into the study of race by the third decade of the nineteenth century. The legal, though morally reprehensible, bondage of thousands of men, women, and children was fiercely enforced in at least half the nation at this time, but rather than confront the racial realities of such overt inequality, pioneering archaeologists turned their attention to the racial identification of a distant and mysterious people they called "the Moundbuilders." The challenge these excavators faced was to determine what race of men had built the often-majestic and impressive earthen mounds that dotted the fields and forests of the eastern United States.

The Moundbuilder debate began in 1838 with diggings into the Grave Creek Mound in today's West Virginia (Silverberg 1970, 75–78) (Figure 1.1). The sheer magnitude of many of the mounds—in dimension, height, and design—convinced many that their builders could not have been the ancestors of the indigenous peoples who had recently lived on the surrounding landscape. For example, in the early nineteenth century Caleb Atwater unabashedly announced that the Moundbuilders were Tartars from southern Asia or perhaps even "Hindoos" (Bieder 1986, 110; Williams 1991, 40–41). We appreciate today that Atwater's point was purely racialist and rooted in a tacit scale of racial hierarchy in which Tartars and "Hindoos"—also people of color—were considered biologically more advanced than Native Americans. Many of his contemporaries who pondered human diversity agreed with him, and the controversy over who built the mounds was not resolved for decades. Finally, in the final years of the nineteenth century, archaeologist Cyrus Thomas (1894, 17) explained the genealogy of the mounds in terms that few could deny: "The links connecting the Indians and mound-builders are so numerous and well established that archaeologists are justified in accepting the theory that they are one and the same people."

Thomas's findings eliminated the racial discourse among archaeologists delving into America's prehistoric past, and today we can characterize the cultural myth that the mounds were not built by Native Americans as a misguided detour in the collective archaeological project. Once this myth was

Figure 1.1. Great Mound at Grave Creek. Squier, E. G., and E. W. Davis, *Ancient Monuments of the Mississippi Valley Comprising the Results of Extensive Original Surveys and Explorations*. Smithsonian Institution, Washington, D.C., 1847, 169.

refuted, American archaeologists were free to perform the Boasian task of documenting the history of Native American prehistory. As their discipline matured, it appeared that they could forever reject the "science" of racial identification and the doctrines of superiority that accompanied it.

American archaeology's overwhelming preoccupation with Native American prehistory was tempered in the late 1960s with the development of historical archaeology. Before the recognition of historical archaeology's academic credentials—which came about as the result of myriad factors, some purely academic, others societal—American historical archaeologists, many of whom were sponsored by the federal government, largely devoted their time and energies to the excavation and interpretation of places that were prominent in the national ideology or were related to programs of physical reconstruction and tourism (Orser 2004a, 30–38; also see Linebaugh 2005). The intellectual justification for historical archaeology as a kind of historical anthropology meant that American archaeologists could justifiably investigate sites and properties associated with not-so-famous men and women. The pan-temporal approach, originally envisioned by Walter Taylor (1948) and intellectually confirmed by his processual and behavioral descendants, made serious historical archaeology possible.

Historical Archaeology and Diversity

Once the temporal restrictions on what constituted "real" archaeology were removed, American historical archaeologists were free to explore research topics of considerable importance to modern social history. The understanding grew among them that people who were traditionally ignored in the histories of the noteworthy—wealthy people and big events—could well become the subject of historical archaeology. This idea was initially formulated during the Civil Rights era, when women's and ethnic studies programs were forming. This was the period when historical archaeology was attaining anthropological respectability. The wider society's growing fascination with ethnic self-awareness and empowerment facilitated inclusiveness in archaeological research. As a focus of serious archaeological study, "common people" could thus mean *all* people: men and women held in bondage, immigrant laborers facing a lifetime on the factory floor, indigenous people forced from their homes and into poverty, seamstresses struggling to stitch in the dim light of a dingy tenement. With an overt focus on the poorly known and perhaps even undocumented inhabitants of the past, American archaeologists understandably gravitated to ethnicity as a topic for protracted study (McGuire 1982; Shennan 1989a). Archaeologists of this time period at first perceived the distinctions between the peoples of the historical United States as resting on ethnic diversity.

Historical archaeologists have made significant advances in connecting past ethnic groups with excavated material culture. Thus understood, ethnicity constitutes a collective understanding among people who find enough social commonality that they believe they constitute a group they can distinguish as "us." Their collectivity is distinct enough from others ("them") to constitute a sense of "peoplehood" (Gordon 1964, 24–29). The archaeological basis of ethnic study is the idea that material culture constitutes an important element of a people's commonality. The initial archaeological understanding was that a specifically identified, and thus unique, set of material things could be related to a distinct population of people who, through their commonality, used a roughly consonant range of objects in their daily lives. Because they were unable to identify entire assemblages of internally consistent artifacts that could be used to detect ethnic affiliation, historical archaeologists were sometimes willing to accept the appearance of one or two ethnic "markers." In this view, these ethnically charged objects could be viewed as cultural holdovers that had survived the American melting pot and could be used to display ethnic identity.

The prominent role of ethnic research in archaeology made sense. It reaffirmed the long-held archaeological tenet that culturally discrete peoples could be identified by their specific objects. The support for this view seemed unassailable because of its archaeological longevity. Early European archaeologists, for instance, had identified the "Celts" as people who used physical things classified as Hallstatt and La Tène (Wells 2001, 77). In fact, the basis for identifying archaeological cultures linked distinct peoples and their unique artifacts.

But just as Du Bois had observed about race, ethnicity is not necessarily as static as archaeologists might wish. A decade before Du Bois voiced his opinion, V. Gordon Childe (1926, 200) observed that "the path of the prehistorian who wishes to draw ethnographical conclusions from archaeological data is often beset with pitfalls."

Recent research demonstrates that ethnic affiliation is mutable. One's affiliation can depend upon a personal willingness to join the group, and a person's attitude about their ethnic commitment can change over time (e.g., Min and Kim 2000). Rebellious adolescents may choose to disaffiliate with their parents' ethnic group because they view it as too rooted in the traditions of the past. As they grow older, the same individuals who once eagerly adopted the mannerisms and material goods of another culture may decide to embrace their ethnic heritage. The generational component of ethnicity demonstrates that ethnic identity is not static.

The difference between ethnic identification and racial designation, however, is charged with social meaning. Defined in its simplest terms, "race" is an imposed label that agglomerates individuals based upon real or perceived physical differences. When viewed from this angle, the physical anthropologist's ability to identify races, clines, or other gradations of human variation as biological realities loses its relevance. Societal practice is of much greater import. What is central is that nonscientists who act within society think that biological races exist and that they know how to identify them. Their willingness to identify races and then to act on these identifications in concrete and often-discriminatory ways imbues race with social significance. This inclination is also what imbues race in America with archaeologically relevant meaning.

At its most basic, race is a label imposed from the outside by people who classify themselves as nonmembers of a racial group. In contrast, ethnic affiliation is self-imposed from the inside. A commonality—perceived or real—is the basis for ethnic association. Men, women, and children grouped together in a race are defined and compartmentalized; they are set apart. The grouping of people into races, however, need not be based solely (or at all) on physical appearance. Racial classifiers can use cultural practices, religious beliefs, traditions, and several combinations of physical and cultural attributes in their classificatory schemes. Race and ethnicity thus have different histories, and racial categorization has a distinct association with relations of power and control (Bonilla-Silva 1999, 902–903).

The controversy over whether microbiologists and physical anthropologists can link genetic characteristics with biological subpopulations whose individual members share enough traits to be considered a "race" is considerably less important for archaeologists than the outcomes of racial classification. Thus, while "race"—as an identifiable genetic characteristic—may not actually be "real," the outcomes of racial classification are most definitely real. Real individuals living in societies can be treated in specific ways based upon their perceived membership in a "race." Racial designations create distinctions that have social meaning (Smaje 1997).

The mutable nature of race and the ongoing effort to identify biologically distinct races suggests that historical archaeologists should distance themselves from the reification of races, whether or not physical anthropologists ever actually substantiate the somatic reality of race. A danger exists that archaeologists examining racial classification will leave themselves open to the charge of essentialism or presentism (Dawdy 2006). Because of these legitimate concerns, archaeologists of the modern world perhaps have a more substantial contribution to make to scholarship by concentrating their efforts on racialization by society rather than on classifying social groups by race.

Racialization

At its most basic, *racialization* is a process of signification "that consists of assigning men and women to essentialist groups, based upon physical appearance or some other readily identifiable characteristics, that allow them to be perceived as biologically inferior or socially unequal" (Miles 1989, 75). Racialization is an ongoing process that creates a racially meaningful social relationship where one previously did not exist (Omi and Winant 1986, 64–65). It permits individuals classified as "other" to be held in contempt by the collective members of the defining group (Fanon 1968, 212–213; Herzog 1998, 306–307; Omi and Winant 1983, 51).

Scholars who have investigated the history of racialization link its modern form to Europe's process of globalization in the nineteenth century (Hannaford 1996; Smedley 1998), when people in positions of authority forcibly racialized indigenous peoples as part of the colonial project (Bonilla-Silva 1999, 902). Even earlier, though, social thinkers had devised ranking systems based on perceived group attributes. In the seventh century, for example, Isidore of Seville used religion to classify the world's peoples into two groups: Christians and idol worshippers (Hodgen 1971, 58). Ancient Egyptians, Indians, Greeks, and Chinese took a different approach and created what we today would consider racialist classifications of human difference (Benedict 1942, 23; Gossett 1963, 3–4). These typologies, though important for understanding the antiquity of the human concern with cultural and physical difference, did not have the widespread impact of racialist classification in the post-Columbian era.

The expansion of European superpowers and the tenacity of their classification systems effectively linked diverse peoples together in a global network. This network was composed of a vast number of connections, many of which were intercontinental and long lasting. The European classification of East Indians, African Americans, and Australian aborigines as "colored" was a conscious attempt to supplant perdurable distinct cultural achievement with an invented commonality whose central feature was racial inferiority. In short, "race is one of the central conceptual inventions of modernity" (Goldberg 1993, 3).

The use of racialization in history constitutes a significant vector of social inequality. People have used racial designations to divide and segment, to identify and stigmatize. But at the same time, racial identifications can be used to empower. The Native American Red Power movement is just one example of the way in which a collectivizing designation can be used as a rallying point in the struggle for self-definition, dignity, and respect.

If the process of modern-era racialization is inexorably linked to the so-called age of European expansion, then it is reasonable to assert that racialization should constitute a subject of considerable interest for historical archaeologists. The monumental cognitive shift from differentiating peoples as Christians and pagans (in the Middle Ages) to defining human groups in terms of skin color and other observable physical features (since about 1500) suggests the importance of the topic. Given its significance, it seems obvious that archaeologists of the modern world should assume a central role in documenting the material aspects of racialization.

Racialization and Social Archaeology

The archaeological study of racialization falls within the purview of social archaeology. The term social archaeology, as currently used by archaeologists, has diverse meanings (Ashmore 2002, 1173, 1175; Hodder 2002; Meskell et al. 2001, 7–8). Put simply, social archaeology focuses on the social relations past individuals and groups created, enacted, and maintained over the course of their lives. The converse of this perspective is a more traditional archaeology that focuses on culture.

The connection between archaeology and the study of culture reaches back to the earliest days of archaeological research, when excavators, lacking written records, had to assume that a unique material culture assemblage represented a particular culture. By extension, then, a different material set represented another culture. The theoretical justification for this reasoning derived largely from ideas espoused by German geographers. Beginning in the late nineteenth century, these *Kulturkreis* ("culture circle") theoreticians attempted to draw boundaries around the territories the world's peoples occupied (Voget 1975, 348–355). These scholars used their geographical formulations to do historical reconstruction and help organize museum collections. With the roughly contemporaneous rise of serious professional archaeology, it was perhaps inevitable that archaeologists would adopt these methods as well and seek to organize ancient cultures in a *Kulturkries*-derived way.

The use of culture as an organizing principle was a constituent element of American anthropology from its beginning, but the role of culture was given its most cogent archaeological relevance by A. L. Kroeber, who is renowned in anthropology for his belief in the significance of broad cultural patterns. He defined patterns as "those arrangements or systems of internal relationship which give to any culture its coherence or plan, and keep it from being a mere accumulation of random bits" (Kroeber 1948, 311). Kroeber identified four patterns, the broadest of which was the whole-cultural. In Kroeber's view, peoples across the world created whole-cultures by their distinctive customs and traditions. In archaeology, the use of Kroeber's whole-culture model tended to reify and make inert otherwise dynamic social environments (Orser 2004b, 14–23). In other words, a unique material culture was thought to constitute the reflection of a wholly distinct past culture. This conclusion was not totally unwarranted (because it does have a commonsensical element), but for our purposes, it became too easy to designate a whole-culture—with its accompanying unique material culture—as a "race." The use of such labeling also entailed at least two additional implications: that archaeologists could identify "races" throughout the history of the world and through this process could effectively ignore the dynamic, ongoing process of racialization. Some insightful archaeologists, however, recognized the futility of such a program of research and argued instead for a distinctly social perspective in archaeology.

Archaeologists have long been interested in social subjects (Chippendale 1989). The modern era of examining past societies using archaeological materials was begun in the 1930s, with the work of British-trained archaeologists Graham Clark and V. Gordon Childe. Clark's *Archaeology and Society*, first published in 1939, outlined how archaeologists could use a societal perspective to interpret prehistory (Fagan 2001, 98). Clark offered insights on all aspects of human life—economic, social, intellectual, and spiritual—and promoted the understanding of past society as "social history" (Clark 1939/1964, 169–170). Childe was impressed by Clark's focus and became perhaps the most well-known proponent of social archaeology (Orser and Patterson 2004, 11–17). During his 1947 inaugural lecture as the director of the University of London's Institute of Archaeology, Childe agreed that archaeologists should study the dynamics of social change and seek to understand the lives of societies over the long term (Childe 2004, 82).

Archaeologists have devised numerous ways to investigate past society since the days of Clark and Childe. Archaeologists examining the modern world have the advantage in this project because of their access to written, oral, and often even pictorial sources. These diverse sources can help archaeologists understand the complexities of past social hierarchies and model them in ways that can include historically discrete systems of racial identification. Of the many ways to think about racialization and the creation of racial hierarchies, an overtly structural model has the most potential to create productive frameworks for archaeological research. We can understand the structural model by comparing it with the more common cognitive understanding of racialization.

The cognitive perspective of racialization maintains that individuals use a doctrine of racial superiority both to maintain the racial design of society and to perpetrate various acts of discrimination on men and women they designate as belonging to a subordinate race. Acts of prejudice can be subtle or overt, discretely passive or immeasurably cruel. In this view, racism and its racist acts—conducted within the constructed racial hierarchy—are perceived by nonracists as aberrant behavior. Nonracists argue that there must be something wrong with someone who uses racialization in this manner. The cognitive view of racism is that it is deviant psychological behavior (Bonilla-Silva 1997, 466). In this view, racism exists within the society, but is at odds with its governing mores.

The cognitive model, though perhaps useful for investigating the psychology of racism in living groups, has little archaeological applicability. Racialization viewed in this manner is effectively eliminated from the social organization because its implications are practiced idiosyncratically by social misfits. Class oppression based on racial identification is thus invisible when race is perceived as a personality trait. In the cognitive model, the source of racialization is individuals, not social organizations, and thus, individuals, not social institutions, are racist. But archaeologists investigating defunct or drastically transmogrified social organizations have little ability to amass information on personal attitudes toward race. Even the most complete set of written records would tend to reveal information about the attitudes and perceptions of specific individuals, not social groups. As a result, the cognitive model of racial perception has little archaeological relevance.

The structural model of racialization holds significantly more promise for archaeologists who want to investigate the historical roots and manifestations of racial classification. In this view, racialization and racism are not merely ideological; they create action and encourage practice within a carefully constructed system of power relations. Racialization creates a racial hierarchy in which some "races" are judged to be superior to others. The invented hierarchy is structurally designed to define and maintain prescribed social relations between the variously identified races. Racism is not aberrant within the system; it is a mechanism either specifically designed or cynically appropriated to maintain the social hierarchy. The structural understanding of racialization allows us to see the central controversy over the Cousins and Phipps legal cases: both of them threatened the racial hierarchy by promoting the idea that it was mutable, that some flexibility in the hierarchy was possible. These cases do not negate the structure of the racial hierarchy, though, because some individuals can pass from one racial designation to another (Cox 1948/1970, 430–431).

The construction of a racial hierarchy through the process of racialization has material outcomes that are amenable to archaeological investigation. In fact, some of the most discrete evidence of the racialization process may be retrievable only through archaeological methods. The racial hierarchy is structured in such a way that those at the top—who provide, enforce, and maintain the racial labels—have greater life chances and thus greater access to goods and services. Research shows that hierarchical societies are sites of constant struggle for material objects. The struggle creates substantive social distance between haves and have-nots and effectively creates "structures of consumption" (Bourdieu 1984, 183–184). The consumption structures can have a racial dimension in racially structured societies.

The connection between race and material culture in the modern world thus rests upon a foundation of consumption. At the root of consumption theory is the idea that people consume what is meaningful to them within the universe of what they can afford. The central issue for archaeologists viewing the remains of consumption practices is how to interpret the mundane world of personal possessions in ways that provide insights into "quite significant social issues, including racial ideology, nationalism, and affluence" (Mullins 2001, 159; also see Mullins 2004).

The purpose of this book, then, is to explore some of the connections between material consumption and racialization in a manner that has distinct archaeological relevance. My temporal focus is post-Columbian history, and my regional interest is the United States. As a social science dedicated to illuminating the conditions of daily life in the modern world, historical archaeology is especially well situated to provide information that may be available in no other source. Archaeologists of the modern world can use a collection of diverse sources—excavated, archival, oral, spatial—to provide special insights into the process of racialization. The serious archaeological examination of racialization will also strive to demonstrate the relevance of archaeological research to present-day history.

Racial experience—expressed in myriad ways at different times and places—has been an integral part of American life. Given the nation's history with immigration, slavery, and the dispossession of native peoples, it appears imperative that American historical archaeologists confront and engage racialization in both their research and their daily lives. Historical archaeologists have a special contribution to make to our understanding of the American experience because of our ability to unearth information that is not usually present in other sources. This contribution will not be made easily or without controversy. Some people find the very mention of race to be troublesome and its study to be decidedly unscientific and political. American historical archaeologists, however, cannot escape their responsibility to explicate the historical dimensions and expressions of racialization.

I make no effort here to be inclusive about U.S. history or to provide an examination of racialization throughout human history. Rather, I explore issues and raise questions that modern-world archaeologists may be able to answer with their diverse and often-rich sources of information.

2

Racialization and
American Historical Archaeologists

Today, some of the racial terms nineteenth-century archaeologists used may seem relatively harmless and simply habitual, mere reflections of the clumsy use of the language of the time. We may wish to excuse pioneering mound investigators Ephraim Squier and Edwin Davis for their use of the term "American race" (Meltzer 1998; Squier and Davis 1848/1998, xxxiii–xxxiv). When we look closer, however, we realize that even at the time their usage was not objective and innocuous. Their efforts to prove that Native Americans had not built the earthen mounds of the eastern United States were an integral element of the rationale supporting the U.S. government's push into the Midwest. By denigrating the ability of Native Americans to construct earthen mounds, Squier and Davis helped provide a scientific, and racialist, justification for removing indigenous peoples from sought-after lands (Patterson 2001, 24).

Later in the nineteenth century, the goal of racial identification was overtly designed to reinforce a racial hierarchy. Daniel G. Brinton (1890) and William Z. Ripley (1899), two major racial theorists, justified the existing racial hierarchy with scientific racism. Their widely read books promoted the idea that physical racial differences were tangible and real, and each consciously promoted the idea that late-nineteenth-century racial beliefs originated in antiquity. Brinton and Ripley used archaeological research to substantiate their claim that the concept of race extended to the most distant eras of human history. When Brinton (1890, 18, 28) wrote about the "white race" and said that "to our eyes all Chinamen look alike," he was adhering to the conventions of the racial scholarship of his time. That mid-twentieth-century physical anthropologist Carleton Coon (1939) continued to give the ideas of Brinton and Ripley serious consideration indicates the tenacity of scientific racism.

The ideas of these once-prominent scientific racists had long been rejected by most people by the time historical archaeology was instituted in the academy in the late 1960s. Yet few archaeologists addressed the issues of race and racialization before 1990, even at the African American sites they so carefully studied. Only a few archaeologists offered important statements about the archaeology of racialization before 1990. These works provide the archaeological foundation for the analyses that followed, although archaeologists' approaches and interpretations have become more sophisticated and nuanced over time.

The Early Years

In an innovative article published in 1971, pioneering visual anthropologist Robert Ascher and pioneering historical and plantation archaeologist Charles H. Fairbanks approached the subject of race, but only tacitly. Ascher and Fairbanks's goal in their innovative article (actually an early and largely unrecognized foray into interpretive archaeology) was to present multivocal information about a slave cabin ruin on Cumberland Island, Georgia. Using what was then a highly unusual presentation, they juxtaposed the archaeological findings with "soundtracks," personal memories taken from various sources. The archaeological presentation itself is traditional and devoid of obvious racial analysis, but the soundtracks are loaded with racial commentary. One speaker mentions that African Americans were "stolen from Africa" and another says that the first Africans brought to America were "stripped of everything" (Ascher and Fairbanks 1971, 8, 14). These comments provide an infrastructure for their more traditional (and seemingly unracialized) archaeological findings, but they quietly suggest the impact of racialization on both African American history and its archaeological interpretation.

American historical archaeologists did not respond to Ascher and Fairbanks's hints about the importance of an overt racial analysis in archaeology, and archaeologists usually have cited this article only as an early example of plantation archaeology (e.g., Orser 1988b, 10). An important exception to the silence from the archaeological community about race, however, was provided by John Otto, a doctoral student working under Fairbanks's direction.

Historical archaeologists today associate Otto either with Cannon's Point Plantation in coastal Georgia (Otto 1975, 1984) or with his examination of the relationships between social position and artifact possession on plantations (Otto 1977). Archaeologists working in diverse sociohistorical contexts occasionally cite Otto's artifact study, but most overlook his work that explicitly engages race as an archaeological topic (Otto 1980).

In the article published in 1980, Otto argues that on a plantation like Cannon's Point, and by extension hundreds of others throughout the slave-holding New World, individuals occupied a number of distinct, albeit interlinked, statuses. The intertwined nature of these statuses complicates a social analysis that relies on archaeological evidence as a primary source. But Otto argued that if archaeologists were to develop meaningful analyses of plantation society, they needed to devise ways to associate excavated material assemblages

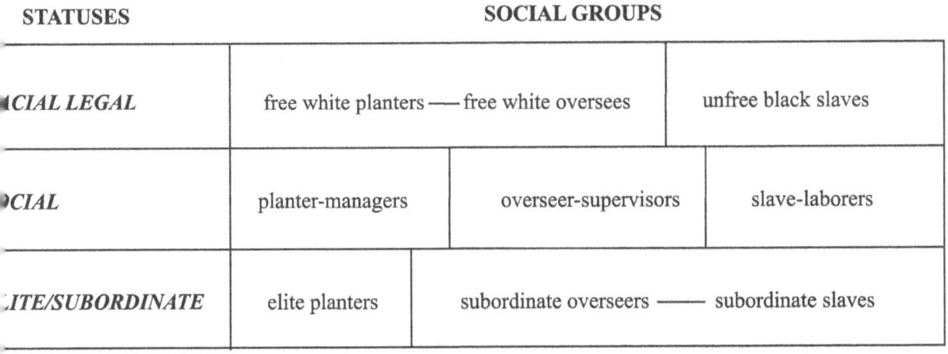

STATUSES   SOCIAL GROUPS

CIAL LEGAL	free white planters —— free white oversees		unfree black slaves
)CIAL	planter-managers	overseer-supervisors	slave-laborers
ITE/SUBORDINATE	elite planters	subordinate overseers —— subordinate slaves	

Figure 2.1. Otto's caste/class model. Drawing by author.

with past social positions. Otto believed that this task might be relatively straightforward at an antebellum plantation—such as Cannon's Point—because of the apparent rigidity of its prescribed social positions.

To unravel the complex nature of plantation society, Otto used the caste-class model rural sociologists devised in the early twentieth century (see Orser 2004b, 144–146). He identified three "statuses" that were apparent at a slave-holding plantation: racial/legal, social, and elite/subordinate (Figure 2.1). Each status (which perhaps might be more accurately termed a vector of inequality) divided the plantation's residents into at least three groups: upper-caste upper-class planters; upper-caste middle-class overseers, and lower-caste lower-class slaves. The social status—which was essentially occupational and separated people based upon the work they did—created managers, supervisors, and laborers. The elite/subordinate status divided the population based on their access to power and created two groups: elite planters and subordinate overseers and slaves. For our purposes, however, Otto's racial/legal status is the most interesting because it describes a distinctly racial milieu. The color castes of the Jim Crow era were created, maintained, and reproduced under the rubric of this status.

Otto's formulation has many problems that today's archaeologists both acknowledge and appreciate. But the point here is not that his final analysis was inadequate; rather, the interesting thing is that his use of a racial/legal status performed two significant functions at the time. First, it foregrounded the idea that racial identification was used in American history to segment the population into at least two distinct groups. And, second, though America was never divided into only two racial groups, the concept of social segmentation by race held great potential for the further archaeological analysis of racialization. That most American historical archaeologists failed to follow

Figure 2.2. Buxton, Iowa. Courtesy of the Iowa State University Archaeological Laboratory via David M. Gradwohl.

Otto's initial steps right away, however, may represent the immaturity of their field rather than personal attitudes that were overtly antithetical to research on racialization. On the other hand, perhaps most historical archaeologists did not perceive race as having archaeological relevance.

At the same time that Otto was exploring the social nature of racial identification at Cannon's Point Plantation, David Gradwohl and Nancy Osborn (1984) were beginning excavations at Buxton, a small town in southern Iowa (Figure 2.2). Buxton, which by then was deserted, had been established in 1900 as a coal-mining town inhabited mostly by African Americans. Gradwohl and Osborn, using information provided by former residents of the town, presented Buxton as a well-integrated and harmonious community with no racially motivated strife. Former residents remembered the town as a "black utopia" free of discrimination and racial hatred. Whether this perception was more nostalgia than reality is largely beside the point for our purpose. What is pertinent here is that Gradwohl and Osborn discovered an obvious locale for gaining archaeological entry into the material dimensions of racialization as it was practiced at the beginning of the twentieth century. In keeping with the archaeological scholarship of the time, however, Gradwohl and Osborn (1984, 190–191) explored diversity in Buxton in terms of ethnicity and national origin. I will return to ethnicity in Chapter 3, but suffice it to say here that their approach was consistent with the archaeological thinking of the time.

Race was not a topic of serious archaeological consideration in the 1980s, even at plantation sites that had been operated by enslaved men and women. Racialization tended to run under the surface of my own research at the time rather than constituting a major line of inquiry. I often downplayed the significance of racialization as a socially significant element of plantation society in favor of other vectors of inequality, such as class (Orser and Nekola 1985, 86; Orser 1988a).

The failure of American historical archaeologists to make racialization a serious topic of study until almost twenty-five years after the establishment of the discipline in the academy (but about forty years after American historical archaeology was first practiced) seems especially odd, since historians have long argued that no analysis of American history is complete without considering race (e.g., Fields 1982, 143–144). It took historical archaeologists as much as a decade longer than historians to "discover" racialization as a topic of inquiry. Based on this lag, we may well ask what happened between 1980 and 1990 that caused archaeologists to start investigating racialization?

The answer to this question is undoubtedly multifaceted, but the birth of the World Archaeological Congress (WAC) may have played a role in forcing archaeologists to realize the importance of racialization in their research. The WAC, along with the rise of post-processual and critical archaeologies—with their practitioners' cynicism toward the processualists' claims of scientific objectivity—helped push archaeologists toward research topics that have contemporary importance. Archaeologists' collective hesitancy to engage race as a topic may have been a facet of their propensity to stay safely on the sidelines of controversial political issues (Patterson 1995, 138–139). Many archaeologists considered contemporary politics to be outside the purview of their profession and did not wish to get involved.

The WAC was founded in 1986 as an explicit response to contemporary political controversies. The central issues of concern—apartheid in South Africa and the rise of indigenous rights movements throughout the world—though intensely contested, had profound archaeological implications (Ucko 1987). The WAC's overt linkage of archaeology with the pernicious practice of apartheid meant that topics such as racialization could no longer be easily ignored. After all, apartheid did not simply appear completely formed; it had historical roots that could be archaeologically investigated. By the same token, archaeologists' general disregard of indigenous peoples' wishes and beliefs was not merely personal; it related to the often-imperialist history of archaeology. Whether individual archaeologists were actually imperialist and ethnocentric was perhaps less important than the perception that their discipline was a tool of oppression and control from the outside. The connection between investigating the past and confronting contemporary social problems forcibly thrust archaeology into the contemporary world.

A major feature of the WAC archaeologists' concern was the unequal way archaeologists traditionally handled skeletal remains. The first two volumes of the WAC's *World Archaeological Bulletin* considered the racial aspects of this unequal treatment (Hammil 1987) and explored the racial elements of general archaeological practice (Blakey 1988; McGuire 1988). Michael Blakey made the point that underpins the structural analysis of racialization: "Racism is institutionalized and its expression is independent of personal intent" (1988, 46). The next issue of the bulletin continued the archaeological debate about race (Morris 1989; Nurse 1989). This increased discourse may have inspired archaeologists who agreed with the principles of the World Archaeological Congress to enter the study of historical racialization. In any case, racialization had become a topic of considerable interest to some American historical archaeologists by 1990.

The Middle Years

As part of its intellectual program, the WAC has published a large number of collected essays delivered at its 1986 conference. Two of the volumes consider the relationship between material culture and human diversity. The volume published first, *Archaeological Approaches to Cultural Identity* (Shennan 1989b), deals with the knotty issue of how archaeologists designate archaeological "cultures" by referring solely to material culture. Most of the authors, who were prehistorians, saw ethnicity as their primary interest. Many authors in the second volume, published in 1990, dealt more directly with racialization. This volume's title, *Politics of the Past*, evoked the original impetus for the development of the WAC and promoted the conscious recognition among archaeologists of the link between present and past, particularly as it pertains to tenacious systems of racial classification (Gathercole and Lowenthal 1990). *Politics of the Past* focused on Eurocentrism and presented racism as the most extreme form of this mindset. Presented in this way, racialization is "Eurocentricity as evolutionary superiority" and as "The White Man's Burden." The tenacity of Eurocentrism is integral to examining ethnicity, and it properly remains a central aspect of much historical archaeology, albeit sometimes only tacitly (Orser 1996, 66–71).

Three of the chapters in *Politics of the Past* are especially pertinent here because their authors confront racialization through the lens of how race has been depicted. In the first essay, Michael Blakey (1990) explored how museums have tended to avoid African American history, particularly slave resistance and the fight for black independence. Robert Paynter (1990) examined stereotypic Anglophile New England history against the backdrop of his research at the Massachusetts home of W.E.B. Du Bois (also see Paynter 1992). Paynter's observation that African Americans in New England have been ignored—even individuals such as Du Bois who were financially secure and prominent American figures—illustrated Blakey's claims. Ronald Belgrave (1990) continued this theme of exclusion by noting that people of color have resided in Britain longer than many Anglo-Saxons, even though the museum visitor would never learn this historical reality.

These three essays are relevant to archaeology for two reasons. First, they demonstrate that history can be told in ways that ignore huge numbers of people; and second, they show that archaeological research, which often holds a central place in museum presentation, can illuminate the past in ways that empower otherwise disfranchised groups. Blakey and Belgrave substantiate Paynter's claim that "racism and its denial by whites make research on Afro-American sites unavoidably political" (1990, 60). The enactment of "heritage politics" (Lowenthal 1990) illustrates the social and pedagogical implications of the archaeological study of historic racialization.

Also in 1990, two articles appeared in *Historical Archaeology* that further helped promote the archaeological study of American racialization. The authors of both articles sought to make race a viable archaeological topic.

In the first article, David Babson argued that archaeological studies of ethnicity, taken by themselves, do not account for the harmful social effects of racial ideology. Babson centered his essay on the idea that ethnicity, though a reasonable and important archaeological topic, was not able to provide useful information about the ideology of racism enacted on southern plantations. He perceived racism as a variety of ethnic interaction and noted that peoples of European ancestry could also experience racism (27). Babson concluded by accurately noting that the archaeological analysis of race had barely begun.

Terrence W. Epperson, had, like Babson (1987) earlier, also begun his initial research on the archaeology of racialization, albeit independently, during the era of the founding of the WAC (Epperson 1987, 1988). Epperson was arguably the first American historical archaeologist to adopt race as a serious subject of study.

Epperson's central argument in his 1990 essay was that archaeologists seeking to study the "construction of race" (another term for racialization) in a plantation setting needed to wrestle with several complex issues. The first and most obvious, he argued, is the role that racial ideology played in creating and enforcing the labor regime at a working plantation. The second, less apparent, issue concerns the way in which the practitioners of the various academic fields deal with issues of "otherness, inferiority, and fragmentation" (Epperson 1990a, 29).

Epperson (1990a, 29–30) used Carter's Grove Plantation in Williamsburg, Virginia, to document the enactment of plantation discipline. Within the racialist environment created in early Virginia, a plantation owner could use a variety of means to enforce his wishes on the enslaved workforce (Epperson 1990b). At Carter's Grove, as at hundreds of other plantations, that control encroached on all aspects of the slaves' daily lives, from naming practices to the construction of dwellings. The power and authority of owners could leave irrefutable archaeological signatures. For example, the owners' control over every facet of housing—location, size, appearance, materials—offers obvious opportunities for archaeological research, especially since the study of slave housing has been a consistent topic in plantation archaeology (see, e. g., Orser 1990, 126–128; Singleton 1991, 162–170).

But Epperson's use of the Carter's Grove slave quarters is not merely historic. He uses it to gain entry into his second topic: the presentation of slavery to the public. In 1989, the Colonial Williamsburg Foundation reconstructed part of the plantation's original slave quarters at the precise spot where archaeologists had found it. This reconstruction and its many implications for today's perception of the reality of slavery caused Epperson (1990a, 33–35) to address the issues museum personnel must face when attempting to create exhibits about American racialization. The reconstructed houses and their physical arrangement seem consistent with many of the spatial realities of the daily lives of slaves, but subtle ideological issues embedded within the exhibit may not be clearly apparent. For example, when presenting the hidden storage pits beneath the slave cabin floors (as located by Williamsburg archaeologists), how does an exhibitor separate the slaves' ownership of private property from the Enlightenment idea of rationality? In other words, does the slaves' acquisition of and willingness to maintain their own possessions indicate that they were accepting the precepts of private property and capitalism? Or do the pits represent resistance to the power and otherwise all-seeing surveillance of the owners? How do archaeologists present something as complex as racialization without voicing their own perspectives? And in their efforts not to exhibit racialization, are they doing so unknowingly? Epperson (1990a) could not answer such formidable questions, and archaeologists exploring racialization still grapple with them in various ways and in different contexts.

The questions Epperson raised about the Carter's Grove slave quarters exhibit illustrates the growing realization that archaeology (and especially historical archaeology) cannot remain shielded from present-day politics. That racialization has continuously played such a large part in American political discourse, if sometimes only implicitly, demonstrates the importance of the process in American life, both historic and contemporary.

The watershed event in forcing racialization into archaeological visibility was undoubtedly the excavation of the African Burial Ground in Manhattan in 1991–1992. The exhumation of over 400 burials from the six-acre cemetery caused almost immediate controversy for numerous reasons, racial identity being prominent among them. African American members of the local community raised questions about why the federal government had to disturb the burials to construct a multistory office building. They also asked about who would be charged with removing the skeletons (Harrington 1993). These questions were heavily laden with issues of racialization. At the very least, the controversy provided an emotional linkage between African Americans and Native Americans, two historically oppressed peoples who seek respect for their dead and direct stewardship of their history. The controversy over the African Burial Ground forced historical archaeologists to confront a central fact of their research: that many members of descendant communities care deeply about their people's collective history and many believe that they should share in telling and disseminating that history. How the public perceives historical archaeology has since become a major feature of much present-day research (see Little 2002; Shackel and Chambers 2004; Zimmerman, Vitelli, and Hollowell-Zimmer 2003).

Some historical archaeologists independently struggled with racialization during the period of the African Burial Ground controversy, striving to find ways to contribute to the study of racial inequality using archaeological materials. For example, J. W. Joseph (1993) sought to expand Babson's perspective by reinforcing the idea that slave-plantation ideology was rooted in racialization. The racial organization of an economically productive plantation was geared toward a racial classification that was reified and reinforced by perceived physical differences between groups of people. Adopting what is essentially a structural model, Joseph proposed that the construction of the hierarchical classification system created a social structure that permitted plantations to operate as economically productive units. He further argued that the classificatory mindset in the Low Country of South Carolina and Georgia—his region of interest—was transformed in the mid-eighteenth century from one based on racial classification to one that concentrated on labor skill.

Understanding the process of racialization plays a significant role in Joseph's interpretation, but his conclusions tended to minimize the effects of racialization as an enduring fact of plantation life. His argument that "with the shift to tidal rice agriculture, European-American planters stopped emphasizing the differences between Africans and Europeans, to the point that the material evidences of such cultural variation disappeared" suggested that racialization, though once a major organizational scheme, disappeared in importance with the development of the purely capitalist plantation (Joseph 1993, 69). In addition, his proposition that the distinctions between European planters and slaves of African heritage were differences of "culture" promoted a whole-cultural interpretation that is largely untenable in serious studies of racialization (see Orser 2004b, 14–19). Reducing social distinctions on plantations to cultural differences foregrounds ethnicity at the expense of racialization and diminishes the structural significance of the practical enactment of racial perception and identification.

James Garman extended Paynter's research on African Americans in New England by examining grave markers in a Newport, Rhode Island, cemetery from the period 1720–1830. Garman (1994) showed how the iconography of the gravestones presents and preserves the period's racial hierarchy in the segregated cemetery. African Americans who buried their dead in the cemetery attempted to respond to the imposition of the color line in complex ways, including using gravestones to mask racial difference during the period 1800–1830. Garman interpreted efforts to minimize gravestone design as an attempt to legitimize African American identity. Citing Paynter's work at the Du Bois site, Garman (1994, 90) argued that historical archaeologists should turn away from an almost exclusive focus on social conditions on plantations and toward a more inclusive approach that concentrates on the historical creation and maintenance of the color line.

In 1995, archaeologists published the results of their excavation of the backyard of the Wayman African Methodist Episcopal (A.M.E.) Church in Bloomington, Illinois (Cabak, Groover, and Wagers 1995). This church, which was founded in 1831, has one of the oldest African American congregations in the Midwest, and the archaeology was done at the request of its officials. A.M.E. churches developed in resistance to the process of racialization and the discrimination that accompanied it. As a result, any study of an A.M.E. church must necessarily include the study of racialization. During excavation of the privy along the back fence of the church's property, the archaeologists discovered numerous medicine bottles. These bottles provide mute testimony to a process of discrimination that denied African Americans health care equal to that offered to European Americans. As a result, many African American communities turned to their churches to provide health care services. This process, which apparently occurred at the Wayman A.M.E. Church in central Illinois, indicates one way that African Americans could successfully struggle against the racially based strictures they regularly confronted.

Robert Fitts (1996) added archaeological information to our knowledge about African American life in New England. Focusing on the Narragansett Plantation in Rhode Island, his intent was to demonstrate that the housing of slaves within the owners' homes represented the imposition of tight social control rather than a milder form of slavery, as many historians of New England have suggested. The segregation he documented outside the owners' houses—during church services, in cemeteries, and during meals—was consciously ideological: its goal was to reinforce the slaves' social position as "other." Segregation was thus an integral, albeit not absolute, element of the racialization process.

The controversy ignited by the excavation of the African Burial Ground, the growing realization among archaeologists that their pursuit was not purely about the past, and the expanding research on African Americans outside the plantation South had numerous ramifications for historical archaeology. One of the most significant aspects of these developments was the entry of historical archaeology into the mainstream archaeological discourse. One measure of the growing understanding of the necessary linkage between past (historical reality) and present (the way historical reality can or will be presented) was the growing number of symposia at professional conferences that focus on topics with present-day political and thus perhaps controversial dimensions. Such sessions indicated that historical archaeologists would not be able to stay safely on the sidelines, as many may have wished. Even raising the subject of the study of race was potentially controversial. Some archaeologists, however, were willing to take the professional risk to explore the racialization process and address their interpretation of it in searching ways.

A number of historical archaeologists collaborated at an important session presented at the 1996 annual meeting of the Society for Historical Archaeology. They dedicated the symposium specifically to questions that surround the excavation of African American sites and the political dimensions this research often entails. Issues of racialization underlie almost every essay of the volume that grew out of the symposium (Babson 1997; McDavid 1997b). The session participants, all of whom worked with descendant African American communities, saw the engagement with racialization as not only unavoidable but necessary. For example, Maria Franklin (1997, 40) proposed that despite conservatives' claims to the contrary, "American society remains profoundly polarized by racism." She noted that given this reality, archaeologists must question whether and how their research helps reinforce institutional racism. She observed that when the Carter's Grove slave quarter reconstruction was first opened to visitors, interpreters threw watermelon rinds around the yard as part of the exhibit. When viewed from the perspective of racialization, whether or not the enslaved at Carter's Grove actually ate watermelons is less important than that the use of watermelons perpetuated a hurtful stereotype that affects how we understand the past and perceive the present. After all, the re-creations at the Williamsburg slave quarter took place in the present. Franklin further noted that while American history belongs to all Americans, only those who have access to the telling of history—as well as the education, money, and time to do so—have the power to disseminate historical interpretation (41). This authority carries significant responsibilities, both to the past and to the present.

Cheryl LaRoche and Michael Blakey explore the politics of the connection between the present and the past in the same volume in their exploration of the circumstances surrounding the excavation and study of the African Burial Ground. One of the most illustrative issues that arose from this controversial excavation (and a point that substantiates Franklin's point about institutional racism) centers on the racial identification of the skeletons by physical anthropologists. Forensic anthropologists regularly and routinely assign a race to skeletons, and because this method is purely analytical, they tend to think little about its ramifications. They tend to view the tripartite classificatory system of human diversity—composed of Negroid, Caucasoid, and Mongoloid—as objective and scientific. The physical anthropologists originally contracted to conduct the analysis of the skeletons from the African Burial Ground argued that they were well qualified to assign racial affiliation to the remains because of their knowledge of the techniques of osteological analysis (see Epperson 1996, 113; 1999, 91–92). Members of the African American descendant community, however, raised concerns about the use of the designation "Negroid" because they believed it detached the real humans represented by the skeletons from an identifiable cultural history. The designation of racial category "thus constructs an identity that is culture-less, history-less, and biologically shallow" (LaRoche and Blakey 1997, 89). The questions raised by identifying the race of skeletons are far from simple, but at a minimum they provide ample proof of the need of archaeologists to engage local communities as much as is practicable. The need to involve communities may be more acute in cases where the archaeological subject involves racialization.

In his commentary on the collection of essays, Michael Blakey (1997) provided significant insight into the problems European American archaeologists can face while exploring African American history. Part of the problem is undoubtedly that most American archaeologists have been socialized in a system that institutionalizes inequality based on racial identification. This is not meant to imply that individual archaeologists are racists or that they have evil intentions when they investigate African American history. The problem is that archaeologists may unwittingly perpetuate the racialization process through their research. Thus, as Blakey noted, to understand the relationship between historical archaeological research and racialization, "one must consider how Euroamerican racism is expressed by the behaviors of archaeologists" (142). To illustrate his point, Blakey developed a "racist power relations routine" to model the way American archaeologists have approached African American history. These relations govern how archaeologists interact with all those peoples now commonly termed "the other," members of descendant communities who are not traditionally engaged in archaeological research on their own or, before the 1980s, not generally included in the research at any stage.

The first phase of Blakey's scheme is avoidance, when archaeologists blithely disregard and in fact even ignore "the other's" involvement in designing research, making decisions, and building interpretation. Archaeologists during this phase do not even consider contacting members of descendant communities. When archaeologists actually do contact descendant individuals, they do so merely to collect information they can use to further their own research. The "others'" recognition of their role as subjects has often led to resistance to research and an unwillingness to provide information. In such cases, individuals refuse to become mere "informants." In situations where the archaeologist attempts to acquire personally held information, he or she effectively becomes "the other," the outsider seeking entrance (McDavid 1997a, 119). The archaeologist in the avoidance phase may believe that as an educated intellectual, he or she has the right to obtain information.

The second phase in Blakey's racist power relations routine is characterized by attempts to exclude "the other" from the process if they demand inclusion. Federal laws against discrimination and state and local ordinances mandating public meetings can force archaeologists to include community members, but in such cases, those in power will seek to include the "outsiders" only in ineffective, largely ceremonial roles. Authorities—however they are defined—will make the final decisions about accepting the suggestions and advice of "the other."

In the third phase, after "the other" has demanded and received recognition and some voice in the research process, the archaeologists might cry "reverse discrimination" and argue that they have been treated unfairly. This seems to be what happened when the skeletal material from the African Burial Ground was transferred to Howard University under Blakey's control. Based on his own experience, Blakey notes that those in power find it much more difficult to marginalize "other" scholars who are well trained and well qualified to conduct the research or provide their knowledge and advice as consultants.

With the convening of the session in 1996 and the follow-up publication of the papers one year later, race and racialization firmly entered American historical archaeology. It is now more difficult to provide an inclusive overview of every archaeological study in which the author has explored some aspect of racialization. As a result, the following section presents the main arguments and topics pursued in the decade between 1996 and 2006.

The Recent Years

In the late 1990s, historical archaeologists began to organize conference sessions that focused on the archaeology of racialization. Some of these papers have been collected for publication. For example, a session of the annual meeting of the American Anthropological Association in 1992 became *Lines That Divide: Historical Archaeologies of Race, Class, and Gender* (Delle, Mrozowski, and Paynter 2000), a session presented at the 1997 annual meeting of the Society of Historical Archaeology was published as a thematic issue of *Historical Archaeology* (Wurst and Fitts 1999), and a special conference organized in 1999 by the University of Utah Press was published as *Race and the Archaeology of Identity* (Orser 2001). Even the American Anthropological Association, generally not known for its interest in historical archaeology, solicited an article on the archaeology of race for a "contemporary issues forum" on race and racism (Orser 1998).

During this period of increasing archaeological interest in racialization, archaeologists began to consider the relationship between racial identity and material culture. Paul Mullins emerged early in the recent period as one of the most insightful archaeological thinkers on the materiality of race. His work continued the intricate in-depth analyses begun by Terrence Epperson, though he used a different sociohistorical setting. Mullins was interested in African American consumption between 1850 and 1930, a period of intense social change in the United States and a time that had a significant impact on the lives of African Americans. Mullins's research resulted in a dissertation and a book (Mullins 1996, 1999a) and a series of articles (Mullins 1999b, 1999c, 2001). His research focused on Annapolis, Maryland, but it has much wider implications because of his overt linkage between the consumption of material objects—a mainstay of historical archaeological research—and African Americans.

Mullins's central concern is to examine African American interactions with the burgeoning consumer culture that exploded in the United States after the Civil War. How racial identity was created and how its accompanying racial ideology permeated society played significant roles in African American consumption patterns. Expressions of racism meant that African American consumers were not free to choose from among the complete range of consumer goods available in the United States. And since the developing consumer culture was being presented as part of the "American way of life," those in control of the marketing system had to find a place for African American consumers that would be consistent with the dominant racial ideology. Racist authors wrote tracts that created a racially based material discourse in which African American consumers were carefully defined (Mullins 1996, 60–70). For their part, African American merchants created networks of alliance within their communities to define their place in the consumer culture.

Mullins documents that African American consumers were never free of racism and that they adopted a series of strategies to struggle against how they were defined as consumers. According to his research, elite African Americans spent their money on genteel social performance rather than on conspicuous display. Less-affluent African Americans sought to purchase objects—such as parlor furniture, knickknacks, and decorative glassware—they could recontextualize within their homes. African Americans in Annapolis adapted their food consumption as a means of attempting to distance themselves from the racist stereotypes of the time. For example, archaeological deposits indicate that in the 1850–1880 period, African Americans consumed a large number of fish species. Other deposits indicate that their consumption significantly decreased between the late 1880s and about 1905, just when the commercial seafood market was expanding throughout the region (Mullins 1999c, 29–32). The archaeological remains also suggest that some African Americans in Annapolis sold their surplus fish throughout the city. The decline in fish consumption suggests a resistance to racist caricature (33).

Mullins (2001, 176) argues that African American consumers purchased objects they could use symbolically to situate themselves in the dominant social order without appearing to endanger its racialist foundation. This process of self-designed incorporation was complicated, multifaceted, and situationally sensitive. As a result, the process Mullins documents is fertile territory for future archaeological research.

Mark Warner (1998) provides an in-depth analysis of the linkage between food and racial identity in Annapolis using the same data sets as Mullins. Warner provided a thorough analysis of how African Americans in Annapolis created different strategies to work their way into the consumer marketplace and at the same time set themselves apart from it. When they chose to opt out of the system, they could minimize their exposure to racism and enact their own economic networks in the process. African Americans could raise their own poultry and catch fish without having to rely on interactions with potentially racist European Americans. Fish remains were particularly expressive of one

African American strategy, because they show that African Americans in Annapolis consumed a wide variety of fish they caught in the local estuaries; the city fish market sold fewer species, many of which were caught in deep water or even outside the immediate region. Archaeological findings also indicate that African Americans cleaned their own fish at home, thereby completing procurement and processing activities outside the racialized public sphere.

The materiality of race extended beyond the realm of portable material objects. In fact, spatial segregation, what some might call "ghettoization," is one of the most visible and, in some locales, most lasting facets of structural racism. Archaeologists interested in racialization recognized the significance of spatiality early (e.g., Babson 1987), but the topic continues to have archaeological resonance because of the visibility of building remains and the important practical and symbolic functions of social space. Following the lead of geographers, most historical archaeologists now accept that space plays a major role in the socialization process (Lefebvre 1991, 190–191). Since the identification of race is essentially the enactment of a relation of power, it only makes sense that race and space are intertwined. The spatial practice of race represents a significant line of inquiry (Orser 2004b, 179–195). An expression of the spatiality of race and its representation can be perceived by a quick look at the physical separations expressed at the World's Columbian Exposition of 1893.

This exposition was a defining moment in American intellectual life and a worldwide showcase for the ingenuity and vivacity of the United States. What is pertinent here is that the ethnological exhibits presented along the Midway and in the Anthropological Building (which held the Anthropometrical Laboratory, wherein the "races" were identified; Figure 2.3) shaped and perpetuated the concept of racial inferiority as mandated by an evolutionary hierarchy (Baker 1998, 57). People of dark skin were arranged at the bottom of the Midway, whereas those of lighter skin tone were at the top. The height of civilization was represented by statues of a boy from Harvard and a girl from Radcliffe. The use of space, and its relation to racialization, was unmistakable for those who wished to consider it, but its real power was subtle and unstated.

Historical archaeologists interested in the spatial dimension of racial practice have made examinations into all periods of American history and have conducted their research at different kinds of sites. Not surprisingly, plantations operated by enslaved men and women have provided an obvious arena in which to examine spatial separations based on racial identification.

Examining seventeenth-century plantations in Virginia, for example, Terrence Epperson (2001) discovered variations in slave housing. Whereas one

Figure 2.3. The Anthropometrical Laboratory, World's Columbian Exposition, Chicago, 1893. Courtesy of the Chicago Historical Society, neg. no. 35425.

planter may have housed his slaves according to their religious beliefs (Christians versus non-Christians), his neighbor may have housed his enslaved laborers in an attic over his living rooms. Each owner's decision had a great deal to do with his or her individual perception of race as well as the societal presentation of race at the time. Thus, the construction of race and its accompanying spatial dimensions were mutable and developed over time. Epperson demonstrates that the invention of race in America—which, as he says, was intimately concerned with the construction of whiteness—was operationalized in different ways by different people. The free exercise of unfreedom on the part of slaveowners provided the foundation for the structural institution of American racism that following the Dred Scott decision of 1857 (Fredrickson 2002, 80–81). What is perhaps most significant for archaeologists is that racialization had clear, albeit transforming, spatial elements that in many cases can be illuminated using archaeological methods.

In an investigation of racialization conducted outside the United States that has obvious relevance for all New World plantation studies, James Delle (1998) studied the manipulation of space at coffee plantations in Jamaica. He shows that at the end of the eighteenth century, Jamaica's elite planters sought to redefine social space, by altering the spatial dimensions of coffee production. During slavery, plantation owners constructed a built environment that gave precedence to lines of sight and surveillance. Slaves, for their part, sought to find places, like the plantation hospital, to resist the constant oversight. After emancipation in 1834, plantation owners developed a greater interest in mapping their estates. They tended to view the surveyed plats as mechanisms to permit them to divide their property into individual plots that could be cultivated by wage laborers. Estate maps, objects that otherwise might be perceived merely as two-dimensional representations of property, thus can constitute an important measure of changing attitudes toward racialization and the operationalization of its parameters.

Racial space, of course, was not restricted to plantations. In a study of Harpers Ferry in West Virginia, Paul Shackel and David Larson (2000) demonstrated the complex interplay of racial identification and labor. Harpers Ferry was one of the first industrial cities in America as well as a longtime manufacturer of the government's weapons. Free and enslaved African Americans worked alongside European Americans in the arms factories, and many of the residential buildings in town were integrated. Even so, labor assignment based on race was practiced in the armory; African Americans were excluded from the highest-paying positions. They were not excluded from the grounds of the weapons factory, but they were generally relegated to the more menial tasks of driving, carting, and handiwork. African Americans also were excluded from jobs with potential upward mobility. As the nineteenth century progressed, the presence of African Americans in the Harpers Ferry Armory decreased.

In addition to examining the historic dimension of the racialization process in plantation and nonplantation settings, some historical archaeologists have explored how racial perception can be represented in monuments, memorials, and other commemorative sites. The interest in how archaeological information is presented to the public largely grew out of the development of an explicit critical archaeology. This archaeological perspective was used extensively at Annapolis, Maryland (e.g., Leone, Potter, and Shackel 1987), and in critiques of the reconstructed slave quarters at Colonial Williamsburg (e.g., Epperson 1990a). Numerous historians have also examined how history is constructed, but the special role of historical archaeology is to explore and interpret how history—as specifically represented in standing structures and material culture—is created, manipulated, and presented. The creation of history obviously includes the topic of race (see, e.g., Shermer and Grobman 2000; Trouillot 1995).

In his examination of how history has been presented in Annapolis, Maryland, Christopher Matthews (2002) explored six "moments of danger" in the city's history. These moments shaped how social experience was formulated in the urban landscape. Much of Matthews's discussion focused on issues of class, but an examination of the intersection of race with class is unavoidable. Annapolis is well known in the annals of American historic preservation because many of its prominent residents were quick to recognize the potential of heritage tourism. But as much research has demonstrated, the telling of history is never entirely neutral; some elements of the past are invariably ignored, while others are highlighted and even embellished. In Annapolis, residents marginalized its African Americans and recent immigrants as they capitalized on the city's colonial and early republic history. People pushed out of the city's history were also relegated to spaces deemed undesirable by the city's elites. In their quest to create a memorialized "Ancient City," the elites of Annapolis were willing to make decisions about who "belonged" where. The spatial separation of poorer African Americans from wealthier European Americans created and reinforced differences that clearly contained a strong element of racial identification (Matthews 2002, 126).

Harpers Ferry represents another intriguing site for illustrating the relationship between the construction of race and material culture. In two studies, Paul Shackel (2000, 2003) has critically examined the archaeological dimensions of heritage creation. A large part of the story of Harpers Ferry derives from the way in which its history has been molded and transformed in the 150 years of the town's existence. A central feature of the town as a historical attraction is John Brown's Fort, the infamous site of resistance to human bondage. Research shows that various individuals in control of the telling of the town's history have presented disparate views to different constituencies. John Brown's Fort constitutes one of the few Civil War monuments African Americans embrace (Shackel 2003, 73), though its interpretation by European Americans has historically varied. Today the fort, though smaller in size than it originally was and slightly moved from its original location, is under the control of the National Park Service.

One of the most lasting examples of the significance of racialization in heritage management at Harpers Ferry is the Heyward Shepherd Memorial (77–112). Heyward Shepherd was an African American employee of the Baltimore & Ohio Railroad who was the first person killed by John Brown's men during the famous rebellion. White supremacists and southern boosters have incorporated Shepherd's death into their demonization of Brown's raid and have used Shepherd's lack of involvement with the raid to promote an ideology of the faithful slave. The tenets of this ideology were later memorialized and actually chiseled in stone in a granite monument unveiled in Harpers Ferry in 1931. As the monument became increasingly contested in the 1990s as a physical testament to American racialization, the National Park Service covered it with plywood. They later uncovered it and accompanied it with a plaque designed to contextualize the original monument.

Racialization in Summary

Understanding racialization and using it in archaeological interpretation is a complex process because race has had so many meanings since the time it was invented by Linnaeus and other modern-era classifiers of humankind. At certain times and in some places, individuals promoting a particular under-standing of race can base the concept on such complicated notions as lineage, subspecies, physical type, social position, and class (Banton 1987). Analysis of the process of racialization is fraught with difficulty because of the intercon-nection and interaction of various social vectors over time. Miscegenation may be acceptable in one decade and outlawed the next; freedom to settle any-where one pleases may be legal one year and severely restricted the next. Any thorough understanding of racialization thus must be intensively contextual-ized in time and place. The overriding importance of historical context thus makes a universal exegesis of racialization impossible except in the broadest of terms. Promotors of racialization can present their ideas in national dis-course using sensitive meanings that have cultural significance for that time and place; racialization thus becomes one element of a broader political proj-ect (Fredrickson 2002, 75; Omi and Winant 1994, 71). Racialization continues to interest scholars from many disciplines, including archaeology, though it confounds facile interpretation.

Archaeologists can contribute to the study of racial construction by linking historically charged meanings of racialization with material culture. Archaeo-logical studies conducted to date indicate that distinct material manifestations of racialization can appear in patterns of settlement, the acquisition of mate-rial possessions, and the way in which archaeological information is presented to nonarchaeologists.

Even this brief and incomplete overview illustrates that American his-torical archaeologists have become increasingly sophisticated in their under-standing of and analytical approaches to racialization over time. The collective research program has moved from a rather facile understanding of race as a simple status like any other to a nuanced conceptualization that includes associations with class and poverty. Perhaps the most important realization archaeologists have made about race, as well as about archaeological practice in general, has revolved around the concept of reflexivity. The archaeologists' acknowledgment of the analytical need for reflexivity, which has been given an institutionalized voice in the World Archaeological Congress and has been explored most fully in the modern world by critical historical archaeologists, has helped promote the archaeological investigation of racialization.

Reflexivity constitutes a key tool of the archaeology of the modern world (see Orser 1999, 2004c). Comprehending reflexivity is pertinent to the archaeology of recent history because racialization—a structural feature of industrial and postindustrial hierarchical society—is a modern project (Fredrickson 2002, 100). Reflexivity incorporates the idea that archaeologists can provide information that can have significant meaning and value to men and women who in fact may know little about archaeology (Shanks and Tilley 1987, 66). The ability to communicate the importance of archaeological findings outside the field of archaeology begins with the archaeologist's self-reflection. Self-reflection forces archaeologists to think about what they are doing, why they are doing it, who will ultimately benefit, and what might be the unintended consequences of their findings. Sometimes sincere interpretations can be used in ways that are abhorrent to their original proposers. A famous example is the Nazis' use of Childe's (1926, 209–212) conclusion that the Aryans were Nordic founders of western civilization. Childe, a lifelong committed Marxist deeply opposed to fascism, was never able to accept their appropriation of his research (Green 1981, 55).

Since the 1990s, American historical archaeologists have increasingly accepted the need for self-reflection. An important facet of reflexivity concerns community involvement. Community involvement, and especially descendant community involvement, represents an ongoing conundrum for archaeologists as they attempt to produce an archaeology that has social meaning. The central problem is how archaeologists can incorporate nonarchaeologists into their research. The archaeology of African American history has exploded in the United States since the 1970s (Franklin 2001), and, as shown in this chapter, a large number of archaeologists examining racialization in some capacity have researched slave-operated plantations. A huge amount of this research, perhaps even most of it, has been conducted within cultural resource management programs. The correlation between plantation study and nonacademic excavation is truly double-edged. On the one hand, the development of contract archaeology in the United States, in order to meet the requirements of federal legislation, has permitted historical archaeologist to investigate a number of sites that otherwise probably would have been ignored or even destroyed with no examination at all. The importance of the archaeology of cultural resources to the study of African American sites has long been appreciated (e.g., Orser 1984). But on the other hand, a more critical assessment is also possible. From this perspective, the high incidence of the examination of sites associated with African American history foregrounds the process of racialization in modern-day American life. The dramatic increase in the archaeology of African American life through contract archaeology projects reflects the racialized structure of the United States (Epperson 2004, 105). Simply put, African Americans are more likely to live in places that are slated for urban renewal, gentrification, or some other project involving land modification and federal funding—hence their study under the auspices of America's cultural resource protection laws. The inequality of life chances, which was effectuated through racialization, thus provides opportunities for archaeologists at the same time that it disrupts the daily lives of those in which archaeologists profess an interest.

Where racialization is concerned, the line between past and present is often difficult to draw. Numerous studies, many of them mentioned above, have documented the myriad ways in which this can happen. One incident from my own experience, however, will serve further to illustrate the linkage between present and past in situations where racialization may be at issue.

In 1984, I had the opportunity to participate in a salvage excavation at the first cemetery in New Orleans, Louisiana. This first official cemetery in the city was located at the outer edge of the Vieux Carré, or French Quarter, in a part of the city that was uninhabited in the early eighteenth century. The interments in this initial cemetery were all placed below ground (unlike the later above-ground cemeteries that today attract so much attention). The cemetery, which did not have an actual name but was usually referred to later as the "ancient cemetery," was opened in 1725 and closed sometime in the 1790s (Figure 2.4). The site was deconsecrated in 1800, when the lot was subdivided. By 1820, all of the lots were in private hands and had been built upon. By then, most people had forgotten the old cemetery, and the city simply grew over it.

The archaeological salvage excavation was occasioned when an investigative reporter from the main city newspaper discovered that contractors constructing townhouses on the property were unearthing, and disregarding, a large amount of skeletal material. When this desecration came to light, the city attorney, the police department, and the city's department of safety all became concerned about the wanton destruction of the cemetery, and they issued a stop work order on the construction company. After a considerable amount of legal maneuvering, the authorities permitted the recovery of some of the skeletal remains, but only as a strictly salvage project conducted during the construction (Orser, Owsley, and Shenkel 1986). The excavations recovered the remains of twenty-nine individuals.

The excavation of a cemetery is understandably a controversial activity. Besides the legal and ethical ramifications, issues related to racialization also can

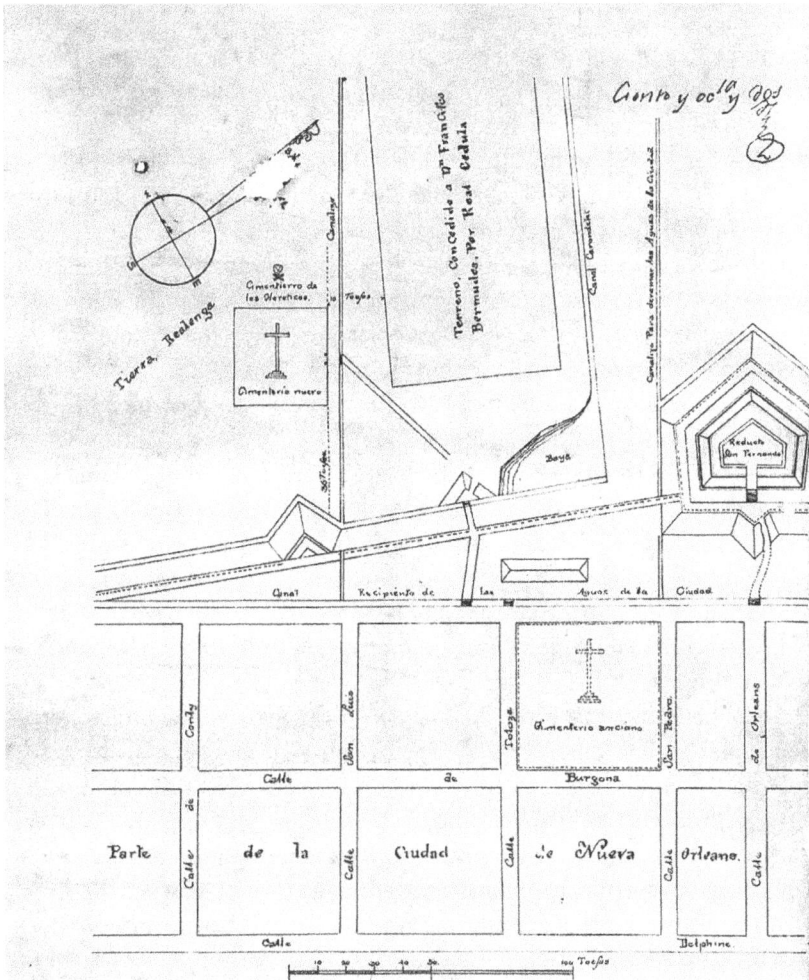

Figure 2.4. Carlos Trudeau's *Plano de los Cimentieros, Nuevo y anciano* (1801), showing the St. Peter Street cemetery, New Orleans. Courtesy of The Historic New Orleans Collection, accession no. 1950.32.2.

arise. The excavation of the African Burial Ground clearly demonstrated this. The discovery of human skeletal material is especially noteworthy in a city such as New Orleans that has a venerable and even much-mythicized history. In this particular case, however, what is especially intriguing is the reaction of the local community to the exhumations.

The only public outcry about the destruction of the gravesites came from members of the community who self-identified with French heritage. They were concerned that the graves of the city's original founders were being un- necessarily disturbed and terribly mishandled. Their complaints, however, were short lived. They dropped their objections when the osteological ex- amination, which included assigning racial affiliations to the remains, indi- cated that the skeletons were most likely urban slaves. Furthermore, contin- ued analysis indicated that the individuals represented in the cemetery were heavy-labor dock workers. Given the racial identification of the skeletons in the cemetery, the likelihood is strong that when the cemetery was slated for removal—as the city was encroaching—those descendants who could afford to remove their ancestors probably had them exhumed and reinterred in the new cemetery outside the city's limits. The enslaved did not have this luxury, so their ancestors remained buried in the ground beneath the new buildings of New Orleans.

This brief example further illustrates, as do so many of the projects men- tioned above, that the process of racialization is ongoing. Not only is it an important topic for American historical archaeologists, it is also a process that can affect the practice of archaeology and the telling of history. Racialization transcends time, and archaeologists who want to examine its myriad expres- sions must be prepared to embrace the reflexivity that its study entails.

A couple of interesting truths are revealed by this brief overview of the archaeological examination of racialization. First, almost all archaeologists who have examined racialization have done so through the lens of African American history. On one level, the correlation between African Americans and racialization seems natural. After all, African Americans have been most visibly affected by legislated and informal discrimination as well as by state-mandated unequal opportunities. The attempt to expand racialization beyond African American history is in no way intended to diminish their consistent and racially motivated unjust treatment. But on the other hand, the assign- ment of racialization only to African Americans implies that other groups who have not been racialized as "Negroid" have not faced similar inequalities. Historians make a strong case, for example, for racism against European Jews (e.g., Fredrickson 2002), and, as Epperson (2001) has noted, echoing several historians, racially based inequality cannot be fully comprehended without

Figure 2.5. New Philadelphia, Illinois. Courtesy of Paul Shackel, University of Maryland.

some notion of whiteness. In other words, racialization does not simply create "others"; it also must create an "us" category that is distinct enough to be readily discernable and different.

A second unrealistic image that may be discerned in this overview is the idea that racialization was a process that was mostly enacted along the eastern coast of the United States. This region was, of course, one of the first areas inhabited by slave-holding (or at least slave-accepting) Europeans, and it was the area where agricultural plantations were created. It was accordingly the site of the importation of thousands of enslaved men and women of African ancestry. The demographic dynamic created was thus quite different, though no less harsh in its particulars, from the enslavement of scores of native peoples by Spanish colonists.

But racialization was not simply an eastern phenomenon. To believe so would require a selective disregard of much of American history. As research in Buxton, Iowa, had the potential to show and the archaeology in Bloomington, Illinois, actually showed, the racialization process extended outside the American East. Archaeologists engaged in current research at New Philadelphia, Illinois, a town with a sizable African American citizenry during the early nineteenth century, are explicitly exploring the role of racialization in the settlement and maintenance of the town (Shackel, Martin, Beasley, and Gwaltney 2004; Figure 2.5). African Americans were racialized in America, to be sure, but they were not alone. I will demonstrate later in this book that the process of racialization extended to the Pacific Ocean and included people who were not African Americans.

Racialization, though infinitely complex on its own terms and mutable in time and variable in space, cannot really be addressed as if it were a distinct topic. In this chapter, I have treated this process as a stand-alone vector of social inequality. However, the construction of race can never be disentangled from issues of class. At the same time, racialization, reified as "race," is frequently conflated with ethnicity. The linkage of race and ethnicity has been a significant obstacle for the social archaeology of the modern world. Archaeologists using material culture as their guide have traditionally had difficulty distinguishing between ethnic commonality and racial designation. The reasons for the confusion are obvious and understandable. Nonetheless, any serious effort to examine racialization must be able to disentangle ethnicity from reified race. Accordingly, we must now turn our attention to the differences between race and ethnicity and outline a perspective for combining racialization with class in a manner that has archaeological relevance. It is no accident that those peoples designated as "other" also have been relegated to the lowest and poorest classes.

Race, Class, and the Archaeology
of the Modern World

The information presented in Chapter 2 indicates that a number of archaeologists in the history of modern-world archaeology have been interested in exploring race and racialization as serious topics. But no clear way to conduct such investigations has emerged. In this chapter I outline one way for archaeologists to pursue an analysis of historic racialization that has obvious links to the present. Much of this discussion follows on my earlier attempt to provide an archaeologically relevant way to examine the racialization process and its effects (Orser 2004b). My goal here is to explain my thinking and approach in a more abbreviated way, and by so doing, perhaps make it more accessible. I define a number of terms and concepts, explain my reasons for adopting them, and explore how they can be used in the archaeological examination of racialization.

A Question of Scale

The first issue for an archaeologist setting out to understand the material dimensions of historic racialization is the frame of reference, or scale. The decision of whether or not to adopt a particular scale will depend upon the framework the archaeologist initially believes will yield the most interpretive insight. I say "initially" because a multiscalar approach is needed to understand the racialization process properly.

At a bare minimum, an archaeologist may have to decide between two scales of analysis: a household, or individualized, scale and a societal, or structural, scale. The distinction between these two scales is central because which scale the archaeologist chooses relates to how he or she perceives the operationalization of race as a vector of social inequality. As an aside, I must make explicit my belief that it is unlikely today that any American archaeologist openly harbors any of the attitudes that prevailed during the days of Jim Crow racism. We have no reason to suspect that archaeologists are any different from most Americans who, surveys show, have given up the racial beliefs of the pre–Civil Rights era (see Bonilla-Silva 2003, 1–8). In fact, because they are trained as anthropologists, usually in the strong cultural relativist tradition of Boasianism, most American archaeologists probably learned early in their academic careers about the fallacy of biological race. Although anthropological activists working in the late twentieth century to promote racial equality were likely to find their life histories detailed in FBI files (see Price 2004), this kind of harassment did not prevent the message of racial reality from getting through among anthropologists (though the theory of racial superiority unfortunately persists in some quarters, albeit carefully masked).

The issue of scale is more than simply analytical because it incorporates one's personal understanding of racism. The term "racism" entered common usage only in the 1930s as a result of the public's growing knowledge of the Nazis' murderous racial genocide in occupied Europe (Fredrickson 2002, 5). As a concept, racism can be understandable as despicable but frustratingly difficult to conceptualize intellectually. Scholars who have closely examined racism generally agree that it can be perceived in two ways: as a cognitive construct internalized by individual people (as part of a personal belief system) or as a structural feature inherent within a social system. These two scales, of course, are not mutually exclusive because individuals who inculcate racist beliefs can live in systems that are designed as nonracist and, conversely, nonracists can live in racist systems. The relationship between one's understanding of racism and which analytical scale one selects deserves further exploration. The way a scholar, in this case an archaeologist, chooses to understand racism may have implications for how he or she may decide to interpret the past. So what is the difference between a cognitive and a structural understanding of racism and how does this understanding relate to archaeological analysis?

The cognitive interpretation of racism maintains that racist beliefs are internalized as wholly personal. A doctrine of racial superiority is included as part of this understanding. Certain individuals, for whatever reason, view themselves as racially superior to others, and their actions and words may or may not overtly signal their racist beliefs. What is arguably most significant about this perspective of racism is the view that because the person's racist beliefs are personal, mainstream society condemns their behavior and actions as aberrant and irrational. Men and women who express or act on their racist beliefs are thought to reside outside the parameters of acceptable society. These deviant individuals occupy social spaces that are at variance with most "normal" (i.e., nonracist) people in society (Bonilla-Silva 1997).

Even a brief reading of history shows that individuals can perpetrate overt acts of racial oppression that truly do appear deviant. Acts of racial violence can extend from subtle to homicidal and in their most vicious forms are correctly judged by most people as abhorrent and criminal. In fact, we should have it no other way. But what is important to realize, for analytical reasons, is that at its core the racism-as-thought perspective maintains that racism is attributable to a person's ideology, even when it is turned into despicable action. Mainstream science upholds this view. In this view, since race has no biological basis, some recent physical anthropological research notwithstanding, racism is irrational and baseless. As a result, a true understanding of racist thinking may lie within the realm of social psychology. Only mental health professionals are properly trained to deal with racists. The argument is thus that historical archaeologists, even though they have access to written sources of information that document racism, cannot be expected to study racism because its basis is purely psychological (even though this psychological attribute can be given observable manifestations).

Since holding and acting on racist beliefs are deemed illogical and wrong by most Americans, we thus have reason to expect that racially motivated social action would have been eliminated a long time ago (Bonilla-Silva 2003, 9). If this were true, the Voting Rights Act of 1965 would not have required extension in 1970 for five years, in 1975 for seven years, and in 1982 for another twenty-five years. As I write, federal legislators once again are discussing extending the act. If the Voting Rights Act had been written, proposed, and passed in 1965 as a permanent law, there would be no need to keep revisiting it; racist obstacles to voting would have been eliminated as all Americans came to accept that racism was illogical and wrong. But this clearly did not happen. Why not? That racist action has not disappeared must mean that it is located somewhere else than within the minds of a few misguided individuals. So what is the source of racism, and how does its location affect archaeological analysis?

To understand fully the weakness of the social-psychological perception of race for the purposes of archaeological analysis, we must return to the notion that racial identification constructs categories. The reality of racial identification—the process of racialization—rests not in biology but in elite society's perception of biology and its categorization of some individuals as biologically inferior. The goal of racial categorization is to create levels of society—to produce a hierarchy of men, women, and children based on criteria selected by a few elite individuals. The racial structure that has been created in post-Columbian history relies on white supremacy, a structure that designates some people as white (and dominant) and others as nonwhite (and subordinate). The creation of this racially based social hierarchy thus also invents social relationships. Individuals engaged in racial labeling tend to believe in the biological reality of their invented categories, and to supplement their decisions based on phenotype, they frequently also use physical and cultural markers as racial identifiers (Smedley 1993, 32). Members of the race deemed dominant seek to defend their superior place in the social order, so they create and promote various rationalizations to naturalize their superiority. In this way, a racially based social hierarchy is maintained over time by becoming the dominant ideology (Bonilla-Silva 2003, 9–10). Though not everyone in the dominant class may accept the racial basis of the structure—and in fact many may struggle against it and thus are sometimes castigated as "race traitors" (see Ignatiev and Garvey 1996)—the racialist system is nonetheless perpetuated over time by institutionalized social action.

The construction of the racial structure, though based on fallacious biological reasoning, nonetheless incorporates numerous all-too-real consequences. The design of the social structure creates opportunities for some and quashes those of others. People designated as part of the dominant race have greater life chances than those judged to be racially inferior. The idea that racial categorization has concrete material dimensions—that it relates to access to goods and services—raises the issue of social class. The issue of class may seem to move the discussion away from race and toward economics, but class is an entangled vector of inequality that must be confronted in any consideration of racialization in the United States.

A Question of Class

Class, like race, is an infinitely complex subject that remains contested in both academic and practical environments. William Wilson's *The Declining Significance of Race* (1980) was an important catalyst for reconsideration, and scholars have disagreed on whether race, taken by itself, really affects a person's chances in life. In a fully capitalist system in which class position may appear to determine almost everything, is race really even an issue?

Archaeologists can never be expected to answer this question, and we have no reason to think that they should. The color-caste theorists of the 1930s were the first American scholars to assert the irreducible nature of race and class (see Orser 2004b, 144–145), and research into the connection between the two has been constant, and contested, ever since. A protracted, often rancorous politicized debate has ensued around the race/class conundrum, and the question probably will never be answered to everyone's satisfaction. If, however, we can agree that racial classification and class standing have material dimensions, we can expect archaeologists of the modern world to be able to offer some special insights based on the unique nature of their research.

Without delving too deeply into the epistemological nature of class, it is pertinent here to acknowledge the economics of racial discrimination. If we can envision a racialized social system with two races—white and nonwhite—and accept the historical reality of the doctrine of white superiority in modern-era systems of racial classification, then we can understand that assigning people to the nonwhite race may include certain practical implications. In a capitalist system, we may expect that many of the implications will be economic in form. Scholars who have examined the way racial assignment has affected the acquisition of material goods—something that ideally we might suppose as purely class oriented—have termed race-based class distinctions "color-blind racism" (Bonilla-Silva 2003; Shanklin 1998).

We must note, however, that the link between race and class, no matter how clear it may seem to be, has not gone unchallenged. Some scholars have argued that the two vectors of inequality should be delinked. Among the many who have made this suggestion, Yehudi Webster's ideas are illustrative. Webster's (1992, 207–209) central argument is that race and class cannot be linked in social analysis because racial and class theories have been created separately to account for different kinds of social relations. Webster makes the interesting assertion that when attempting to conduct a race-class analysis, theorists tend to perceive the racial structure as real, whereas they envision class as a construct. As he notes, "What race-class analyses then become is a discovery of class elements in racially motivated policies and decisions" (213). But, he says, if you turn this idea on its head and adopt class as the social reality, then race is tautologically recognized as the search for attributes that identify it. Either way, to his way of thinking, nothing is resolved. Arguing further against materialist interpretations, Webster proposes that in most theories based on materialism, politico-economic variables take precedence over racial categorization by definition.

Webster's comments are engrossing but overstated. Histories of nations located on the Atlantic, which includes the United States at least during its formative years, is replete with examples of "racial supremacy combined with class superiority" (Linebaugh and Rediker 2000, 271). As archaeologists, we have no reason to overthrow our commitment to materialist interpretations in the study of racialization. Archaeological research is inherently material, even in its most straightforward sense. Though a significant thread of post-modern idealism runs through much contemporary historical archaeology, few archaeologists who seek to interpret the physical remains of the past could seriously argue against the core materiality of the discipline, no matter how they might frame their interpretations. I have argued elsewhere that modern-world archaeologists must be willing to confront and interpret the capitalist basis of commodification, commercialism, and material globalization. This confrontation is nothing if not material. To think otherwise makes archaeology traverse a path it was never intended to follow and on which it can never be wholly successful.

The linkage of race and class is obvious in the United States. A huge body of data exists, for example, to demonstrate that African Americans lag behind European Americans in income. African Americans are disproportionately represented below the federal government's poverty line, and they generally experience greater rates of unemployment (Harris and Curtis 1998; Leiman 1993, 88–145). Simple measures of economic wealth, when computed by racial classification, show great disparity. Statistics compiled in 1992 demonstrate that for the poorest group of Americans (those whose annual per household income is $15,000 or less), whites have a mean net worth of $47,214, whereas blacks have a mean net worth of $15,959. In the middle income group, whites average about twice the net worth of blacks, and in the top group, whites have almost three times the net wealth of blacks (Conley 1999, 26–27). Among the many factors accounting for the disparities are discrimination in hiring, obstacles to job mobility and advancement, and difficulty in networking (Feagin 2000, 159–168). Numerous commentators, critics, and social scientists have illustrated the relationship between race and class, but among all the verbiage recorded, perhaps two comments succinctly summarize the situation: "The Negro is poor because he is black; that is obvious enough. But, perhaps more importantly, the Negro is black because he is poor" (Harrington 1963, 73); and "To be a poor man is hard, but to be a poor race in a land of dollars is the very bottom of hardship" (Du Bois 1903/1999, 14). The historical association between racial assignment and economic potential is clear, though nuanced and mutable. As Bonilla-Silva (2003) says, if racially motivated injustice were not structural, these statistics would not be reproduced every time someone compiles them.

The realities of unequal material distribution are thus patently obvious, though perhaps debatable on theoretical grounds. The question for historical archaeologists to consider is how race and class determine, structure, and impact the distribution of the material objects they find at sites associated with people who have belonged to racialized groups.

Several archaeologists have confronted race and class in their efforts to interpret the meaning of the archaeological materials at the sites they have investigated. In a project completed in 1978, for example, Leslie Drucker (1981) investigated the race-class problem. In her work on a salvage project in south-central South Carolina, she was called upon to investigate and interpret an historically undocumented habitation called the Spiers Landing site. Excavation revealed that the site had minimal archaeological visibility; it consisted of a single small building—whose remains consisted of post holes, a dripline,

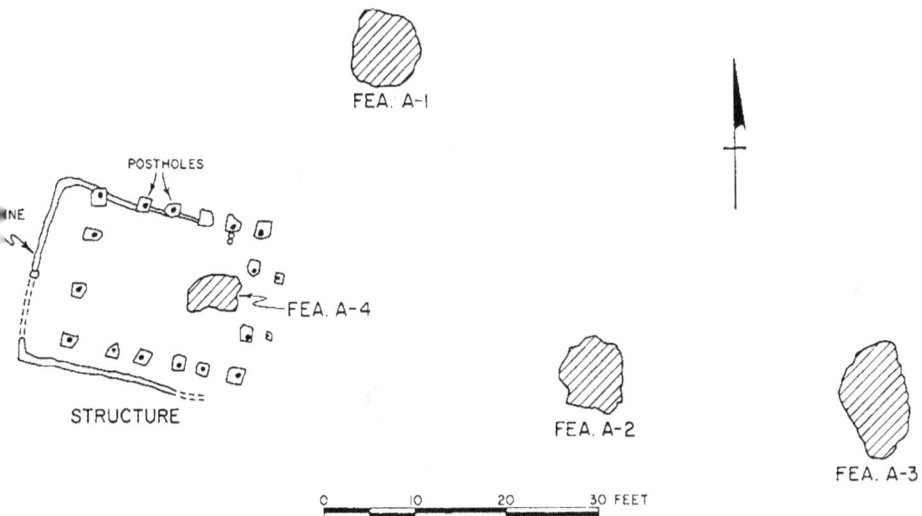

Figure 3.1. Spiers Landing site, South Carolina. Courtesy of the Society for Historical Archaeology.

and one small pit—and three larger pits in the yard (Figure 3.1). The analysis of the artifacts yielded a date range of 1780–1830, but the interpretative problem was compounded because historical records could not illuminate what sort of person had lived in the house during the years associated with the artifacts. Given the state of archaeological analysis at the time, Drucker understandably decided to compare the findings from Spiers Landing with the remains found at Cannon's Point Plantation to look for similarities (see Chapter 2). The Cannon's Point material provided a good comparative collection because its analyst, John Otto, was able to separate the archaeological deposits into planter, overseer, and slave components. Thus, following Otto's lead, Drucker analyzed ceramic shape and type, and, in comparison with Otto's slave and overseer samples, tentatively decided that "the Spiers Landing site reflects a low-status plantation worker occupation" (Drucker 1981, 65) Her verbiage, however, portrayed her central problem. The phrase "low-status plantation worker" can refer to unfree slaves (black) or free overseers (not black). The ceramics do not allow an unambiguous interpretation, so Drucker understandably had to rely on a class designation. Her use of this designation, however, does not mean that racial classification was unimportant. Quite the contrary, in a plantation setting it was central to work assignment. Her problem was strictly archaeological: how to decide.

The presence of a large percentage of colonoware pottery at the site (almost

40 percent of the total collection) appeared to offer Drucker a way through the interpretative maze. Archaeologists in the late 1970s were increasingly recognizing—though it still remains something of a contested issue—that at least some colonoware pottery was made by African Americans. Drucker realized, though, that the association of the Spiers Landing colonoware with enslaved Africans could not be absolute because slaves, free African Americans, and poor whites all could have used colonoware pottery "due to their low cost"; again, an economic conclusion (66). In the end, Drucker concluded that archaeologists had to find concrete ways to recognize the material manifestations associated with slaves, free workers, and rent-paying tenant farmers. The issue was never merely theoretical or trivial, because its resolution would determine just how American historical archaeologists would interpret their nation's history, much of which has been written as racial.

Drucker was not alone at the time in wrestling with the archaeological tangibility of race and class as intertwined vectors of social inequality. Using a collection of ceramics from an excavation completed in the 1940s, Vernon Baker was engaged in the same intellectual process. The important difference of Baker's situation (most would say advantage) was that he had historical documentation to substantiate the name of the occupant of the site in question. The resident was Lucy Foster, an African American woman who had died in 1845 at age 88. Lucy was given the racial label "Black Lucy," and she is so known by archaeologists today. The records indicate that she was probably an enslaved domestic in the Foster home. Because he had access to this personal information, Baker, unlike Drucker, was able to confront directly the issue of the "patterns of material culture distinctive of Afro-American behavior" (Baker 1980, 29); he did not have to guess about the racial identity of the site's occupant.

The linkage between social position and material culture (and here we may even interpret the word "culture" with a capital C to suggest its whole-culture nature; see Orser 2004b, 15–23) was significantly complicated, however, because Lucy Foster probably spent a sizable portion of her life in abject poverty (Baker 1978, 5). The appendix in Baker's report shows that the Andover overseers of the poor occasionally gave Foster wood and other supplies from January 1827 to January 1843. Given this historically substantiated practice, the artifact collection from the Foster site seems to offer an opportunity for an insightful comparison between the material possessions of free and unfree African Americans when compared with collections like those from Cannon's Point Plantation. Even so, Baker discovered, like Drucker, that he still could not unravel the precise vector that affected Foster's ability to obtain artifacts. Did poverty or racial identity affect her collection of material things? We

Figure 3.2. Willow ware plate from the Lucy Foster site. Copyright Robert S. Peabody Museum of Archaeology, Phillips Academy, Andover, Massachusetts. All Rights Reserved, B/W image 107.7616.

know that her poverty, though chronic, had infrequent relief because of the occasional support she received from local elites.

But what about those periods of huge gaps in the records? Foster received $4 worth of wood on December 1, 1828, but only another $4 of supplies on February 18, 1830, fourteen months later (115). What opportunities and limitations did she face in obtaining the plates, cups, mugs, and pitchers Baker studied (Figure 3.2)? He was forced to admit that the determination of what reflects poverty and what reflects racial categorization are central issues in the archaeology of social inequality. His conclusion was that only archaeological research at sites inhabited by poor whites might resolve the problem he faced.

The problems Drucker and Baker confronted were not unique. Their inability to solve the race-class problem is understandable. I have used their studies simply as examples of archaeologists who addressed one of the most tenacious issues of social archaeology relatively early in the history of social analysis: what personal or group characteristics affect access to material possessions? We still do not have concrete answers that will satisfy everyone, and part of the rationale for writing this book is to offer one possible path through an obvious minefield of analytical pitfalls and interpretive misunderstandings.

In surveying the history of archaeological analysis, the most significant advances in the understanding of the connection between race, class, and consumption have been presented by Paul Mullins (1999a, 2001). Focusing on African American sites in Annapolis, Maryland, Mullins has revolutionized our thinking about the role of racialization in controlling and creating access to material things.

Mullins shows how consumption in the United States between the years 1850 and 1930 was organized within a distinct sociopolitical environment. Despite the frequent platitudes of ideologues about the openness of the free marketplace in the United States, African American consumers did not have perfect access to everything that was available. Consumption, because of the structural nature of the racialized system, had also been racialized. White advertisers cleverly appealed to racist sympathies as they created and reinforced racial stereotypes, and African Americans were regularly denied the right to window shop, as this activity had been racialized as a whites-only privilege. African American aspirations were caricatured and commodified in minstrel shows and elsewhere in popular culture, and access to material things was organized around the color line.

Mullins's study demonstrates that the consumption of material things offered in the capitalist market was manipulated in racialist terms so that racial categorization affected acquisition. African Americans created various ways to accommodate and resist the stereotypes they confronted by constructing their own commercial networks. By so doing, they found a range of "tactical mediations" that helped them negotiate a sociohistorical structure that was replete with contradiction. But they were free to navigate the dominant marketplace only up to a point. As Mullins (1999a, 153) observes, the issues African American consumers faced were "structural dilemmas" of the sociohistorical environment in which they lived.

Archaeologists can focus their attention on the structural nature of race and class and on their crosscutting impacts on consumption. Some archaeologists today seek to retreat into a new kind of particularism that they generally define as interpretive archaeology, but this approach includes a danger that their highly personalized studies will push historical archaeology back into a trivial position within the social sciences. Such studies may have the highly contextualized appeal of in-depth microhistorical analysis, but by adopting a single-scale vision, they will miss the broader significance—a problem of missing the forest for the trees. The potential trivialization will reveal itself in racialization studies that promote (we hope unknowingly) the racism-as-thought perspective. In such studies, historical racism—the accounts of which might be enumerated in microhistorical detail or merely imagined and dramatized by the interpreter—will be something unfortunate that just happened to some people because of their historical circumstances. In this view, because it is not structural in nature, racialization is not inherent in the social system. Rather, although it is terrible, it is piecemeal, intermittent, and personal.

The archaeological problem here is that the personal trauma of racist treatment should never be downplayed. As anthropologists, modern-world archaeologists have a responsibility to demonstrate the fallacy of racialist thinking and condemn racist action. But the central issue for *archaeologists* is whether we can provide serious insights into the structural nature—and hence the continuance—of the effects of racialization by overcontextualizing racism as personal and circumstantial. This issue may appear to be purely philosophical, relating only to how each individual archaeologist perceives the goals of the discipline. I believe that one significant feature of Mullins's research is to show that racialization is not simply psychological. Instead, it is irrevocably connected to the hierarchical structure of capitalist society as one of its inherent features.

Studies like Mullins's demonstrate the importance of a structural analysis of racialization. Such an approach—which must incorporate class by definition—affords archaeologists the opportunity to understand the racial-material dimensions of American history in substantive and insightful ways. A piecemeal, highly individualized approach to interpretation—though perhaps interesting and enlightening on its own—will unfortunately downplay the structural, and hence historically contingent, process of racialization as a social vector of inequality that is incorporated into the deep structure of the social organization.

The approach advocated here rests on a number of key concepts. I have attempted to compile various anthropological and sociological sources into a concrete approach designed to yield interpretive insight. I believe that when collated into a conceptual whole, the approach I outline represents a perceptive way to examine the historical manifestations of the racialization process. The concepts I use are epochal structures, networks, the sociospatial dialectic, habitus, field, and capital.

Epochal Structures

My notion of the form and analytical importance of epochal structures derives from several sources. The term comes from Donald Donham's (1999) use of the concept in his study of power and ideology among the Maale of southern Ethiopia. Donham developed his understanding of epochal structures in reference to Marx's base-superstructure model but with some alteration because the Maale are a nonstate people, unlike those Marx examined. Like Marx, Donham's ultimate goal is to use social theory to understand history as it is lived every day. This understanding involves the recognition that understanding societal structures of inequality enhances our interpretations; such broad-scale analyses allow us to acknowledge the perpetuation of inequality over time.

Donham's model includes structural determination—the reproduction over time of social, economic, and politico-legal limitations and potentialities—and human agency. The form of the structures can change over time, but they are top-down structures: they are created by the power elite, who naturalize them simply as the way things are (Ollman 2003, 31). J. M. Blaut perfectly summarizes the effects of such naturalization by noting that the dominant group has a "fairly definite set of concrete worldly interests" and that "because of its power to reward, punish, and control, this group succeeds in convincing most people, including most scholars, that its interests are the interests of everyone" (1993, 39).

Donham was able to work out the epochal structures among the Maale using participant observation. This course of action is not open to most archaeologists, who must find other ways to tease out temporally sensitive structures. Historical archaeologists can discover the nature and form of the dominant structures through written records, including laws and statutes written and passed by dominant elites that are designed to maintain the structure during times of social stress. Laws enacted in the United States in the late nineteenth and early twentieth centuries to control immigration—which were occasionally modified to target the latest tide of immigrants—constitute one politico-legal epochal structure in U.S. history.

Donham's bipartite concept of agency constitutes another important element of his perspective. Archaeologists are aware of the concept of agency, even though the idea is now largely meaningless, having become "universalized and decontextualized" (Gero 2000, 37–38). Donham (1999, 52) does not rely on a trivial meaning of the concept but instead employs the concepts of "historical agency" and "epochal agency." Historical agency that is temporally and spatially relevant involves the struggles of various social groups defined along different vectors of inequality. Historical agency questions the historical continuity of inequality. Epochal agency, on the other hand, refers to the patterns of individual action that reproduce the broad structures of inequality. It is motivated by culturally mediated meanings and practices. They are relatively stable over time and are characteristic of the sociohistorical formation within which they occur. As we shall see shortly, both meanings of agency work in tandem to create and maintain the structural features of racialization. Both concepts of agency incorporate the notion of struggle within the structures of inequality. Used in this manner, agency is not simply the ability of a person to accomplish something or have complete freedom of action; it implies that people struggle for freedom of action within systems of inequality not of their making.

My second inspiration for the concept of epochal structures derives from the work of Fernand Braudel. In *The Structures of Everyday Life* (1985), the first volume of his far-ranging *Civilization and Capitalism*—originally published as *Capitalism and Material Life, 1400–1800* (1967)—Braudel explores the large-scale structures that were enacted in Europe as part of quotidian life. He was first and foremost an economic historian, so his interests are understandably geared toward market exchanges in the past, in this case the period 1400–1800. One example from his work will illustrate his concept of structure and at the same time show the relevance of Donham's notion of agency within it.

Braudel (1977, 19–20) writes of an artisan who travels between different market towns offering his services to all who are interested. The man, though only a modest consumer in his own right, still "belongs to the world of the market." This is, after all, the world within which he moves. Among the more active participants of the market is a peddler who sells a few goods on the street corner. This man is also "part of the world of exchanges, of calculations, of debit and credit, no matter how modest his exchanges and his calculations may be." If we can consider these two highly individualized cases in a broader way and think in more general terms, we can understand Braudel's concept of structure. The artisan and the peddler make decisions and travel within certain social structures they did not design or approve. Both are enmeshed in the structure even as their actions help define and recreate it.

Even the most highly contextualized historical study must include some notion of structure. Take, for example, the classic work in microhistory, Carlo Ginzburg's (1980) study of the miller Domenico Scandella. Ginzburg delved deeply into Scandella's life and trials and in the process invented microhistory. By reading Ginzburg, we almost come to know the miller personally; we sympathize with him during his trial in 1584 and we understand his passion for knowledge and open-minded reading. We also learn from Ginzburg, in intimate detail, that people like Scandella were not mere tools of society's elites. We come to understand and appreciate that the creation of ideas is not the sole purview of the rich and powerful but that everyone, even a miller, can have original thoughts that sometimes defy ideas advanced by elites. Using Donham's terms, then, we could say that Scandella was using historical agency within a framework of epochal agency.

Ginzburg's account of the life of Domenico Scandella set the standard for a highly contextualized, deeply personal history. But Scandella's life was not chaotic and his actions were not random; he was born, lived, and died within epochal structures. Ginzburg recognized these structures and worked within them. A class structure separates the high-born from the low-born, just as a cultural structure distinguishes between popular culture produced by the masses and culture made popular by the elites and imposed on the masses. The information printed in books was different from information circulated orally within the town square. The Inquisition before which Scandella appeared was founded as a politico-religious body mandated to keep the overarching structure sound. Without the structures that framed sixteenth-century life, the details of Scandella's life would have had little meaning. Even the authors of a widely regarded defense and extension of microhistorical theory argue that the minute intersects with the large-scale, a process they term "morphology": "the major theoretical question posed by the combination of microhistory and morphology . . . [is] what the connection is between morphological chains, sometimes spanning millennia, and the notion of a chronological sequence within a specific historical context" (Egmond and Mason 1997, 103). We may also call the "morphological chains" epochal structures within which people operate.

Ginzburg's portrayal of Scandella provides one more insight that forms an essential element of the approach I promote here—the idea that the miller and everyone he knew and with whom he would come in contact interacted within a series of complex social networks. Whereas the structures may endure for millennia, the interactions of members of the network are historically and socially situated.

Network Relations

Donham's use of a structural model is consistent with Bonilla-Silva's perspective on how racialization can be understood as a feature of hierarchical societies.

Accordingly, racism is built into the structure rather than merely representing the personal failing of racist individuals; racism is thus institutional. Donham's two kinds of agency throw into relief the idea that individual members of a social system are not mere automatons, unlikely to express themselves as they march to the mandates of an unrelenting system. We learn from the work of both microhistorians and global historians that individuals have what we can loosely term "agency," but we must nonetheless acknowledge that this agency is enacted within the structural parameters of the social system.

The anthropological and sociological concept that men and women (both individually and in social groups) interact through networks has a long history. Network thinking extends through the work of numerous prominent social theoreticians, many of whom are the intellectual forebearers of contemporary thought. When viewed in simple schematic terms, we can think of networks of interaction as individuals or groups—the nodes of the network—connected through their relationships—the lines connecting the nodes. The nodes and the lines together create a web, or network, of relations. Many scholars have used a network perspective in various ways, but A. R. Radcliffe-Brown succinctly summarized the way network theorists see social relations: "A particular social relation between two persons (unless they be Adam and Eve in the Garden of Eden) exists only as part of a wide network of social relations, involving many other persons" (1940, 3). Alexander Lesser (1961, 42) used the memorable phrase "weblike, netlike connections" to stress the interrelations between men and women living in an interlinked sociohistorical formation.

Social networks are mutable and tenacious at the same time that they are temporal and spatial. Conceptualizing them does not require the reification or totalization so many postmodern archaeologists condemn. But the networks are structural; individuals and social groups enmeshed in them have the ability to enact agency, but only within certain limits.

Social scientists who incorporate network models in their research generally use the term in two ways. A loose use is metaphorical and is usually intended to promote the idea that people and groups interact and are interconnected. An ethnographer, for example, may write about a network of fishermen who share boats and collaborate in dividing the catch. This use of the network concept does not require an empirical analysis of the network connections. In a more rigorous use of the concept, scholars may empirically measure the relational cohesion of the fishermen's network, the flow of authoritative power within it, the expression and strength of family connections, and a number of other social factors.

Regardless of how one wishes to conduct network research, almost all network theorists agree that analysis of social networks include at least four basic understandings. The first understanding is that social processes involving relations constitute a fundamental unit of analysis. In thinking about the schematic model of nodes and links, network researchers find the links as important as the nodes themselves. To put this in simple racial terms, the network theorist would find the relationships between whites and nonwhites as important as the social realities of life for both groups. Studies of race relations thus easily can be formulated as network analyses. Second, network analysts agree that social actors are interdependent rather than autonomous. In other words, in expressing their agency, social actors will act in relation to others. Network theorists see them as completely contextualized within the web of network relations. Third, network theorists acknowledge that the connections between people and groups are channels through which resources flow. Importantly for archaeologists, the resources can be material as well as nonmaterial. And finally, scholars who openly use network concepts agree that structure is represented as the patterns of relations between the actors (Wasserman and Faust 1994, 4). This last point means that the sociohistorical structure that is created and within which people act constitutes a pattern of relations, an idea that is similar to Marx's notion of the inner workings of the mode of production.

These four fundamental features of social network theory help frame the theory and practice of network analysis. Network analysis, though used by ethnographers and sociologists, does not require informants. As I show elsewhere (Orser 2004b, 120–125), several historians have successfully demonstrated how network analyses can be conducted using historical records alone. Such studies provide excellent guides for historical archaeologists wishing to undertake serious network analysis.

Ethnologists, social psychologists, and sociologists may observe the operation of a social network without paying too much attention to the physicality of its operation. In other words, the anthropologist observing a network of interacting fishermen may not be interested in the size and design of their boats or the distance between their houses; his or her overriding concern is to observe and analyze the operation of the network. Archaeologists, however, because of the nature of their research, must acknowledge that a social network is not just verbal, active, and proxemic. Archaeologists must consider the tangible, on-the-ground spatial elements that help frame the network interactions. They must focus on both the social situation and the locus of interaction. They must also take into account the tangible places—the walls, rooms, courtyards, roadways, and empty spaces—that help define and confine the social interaction. The practical implication of acknowledging the spatial reality of social networks means that the physicality of the network is not taken for granted and minimalized. On the contrary, the social network must be understood in spatial terms using the socio-spatial dialectic.

The Socio-Spatial Dialectic

Social theorists with backgrounds in geographical thinking have recognized that the interaction of social and physical networks cannot easily be separated in the real world. People do not simply interact socially; they interact in concrete places. They sit in chairs across tables from one another, they lean over counters, and they gossip in courtyards. This understanding, though commonsense, does not mean that social analysts have always acknowledged the connection between space and interaction. Rather, social theorists interested in space suggest that both temporal and spatial concerns must be incorporated at the beginning of all social theory construction (Thrift 2002, 114). The empirical connection between social enactment and physical space has led to the concept of the socio-spatial dialectic, a view of social interaction and its tangible spaces as truly inseparable (Soja 1980, 1989).

The basis of the concept of the socio-spatial dialectic is that space is as socially constituted as social relations and that people produce space as part of these social relations (Lefebvre 1979, 1991; see also Orser 2004b, 182–183). Space and place are thus social products, but unlike enacted social interactions, they may leave lasting tangible remains. Archaeologists actually may not be able to see the relations that existed between a slave master and his slaves, but they can certainly observe the physical distance between the slave quarters and the big house. This distance can be a surrogate measure for the social relations enacted in that place. The acceptance of the socio-spatial dialectic means, then, that anyone who adopts a network perspective must also accept the spatial dimensions within which the social interactions were played out. Failure to do so would deflate the importance of the research findings and, for archaeologists, might actually make them irrelevant.

Structures, networks, and the socio-spatial dialectic work together to provide a framework for analysis. They help us conceptualize some of the larger-scale issues we must confront when attempting to use archaeology to investigate past social relationships, including those concerning race. But these concepts cannot be used alone because they would provide no way to conceptualize the ways real human beings living in social groups—like those who have been historically defined in racialized terms—negotiated the conditions of their social inequality. To obtain this level of understanding, we can turn to the ideas of sociologist Pierre Bourdieu—habitus, capital, and field.

Habitus

The notion of the habitus derives from Bourdieu's practice theory, an insightful way to examine history because it provides a theoretically consistent locus for structural thinking, network analysis, and the socio-spatial dialectic. These overarching perspectives are not deterministic frameworks to which the analysis must conform. Rather, the concepts they contain help us understand and analyze the structural nature of social vectors of inequality, such as racial categorization. The usefulness of Bourdieu's view of social linkages as rooted in relationships of power is especially relevant to the study of racialization.

Numerous archaeologists have relied on the concept of habitus in their research, even though in many cases their understanding is partial and sometimes even misguided. Bourdieu's (1977, 88; 1990, 53) explanations of habitus, though difficult, consist of three central propositions (also see Orser 2004b, 129–133). First is the idea that the habitus, as a product of history, produces individual and collective action (including historical and epochal agency) in accordance with historically generated frameworks. Individual moments of daily practice make history, but in a nonteleological manner. Second, Bourdieu's practice theory incorporates the idea that the habitus is durable through time. Individuals develop their "dispositions"—a complex set of perceptions, uncertainties, and actions—as part of their socialization process, which includes the individual's internalization of the epochal structures within which he or she lives. The habitus, however, is not an immutable whole. Instead, it exists as a structured set of bits and pieces, a complex array of dispositions, many of which are situationally framed and relevant. The habitus, though largely created during childhood—Bourdieu says often in public schools—is never complete. The process of socialization continues throughout a person's lifetime. Without this concept of constant reappraisal and rethinking, it would be impossible to speak of habitus in cases of cultural change and individuals would have to be modeled as robots, incapable of personal action.

The second feature of Bourdieu's habitus is further complicated by the fact that it does not necessary govern all human action. For example, some highly ritualized activities may decrease the role of the habitus as individuals submerge their perceptions and understandings beneath rule-governed expectation. A role for individual action may present itself in such cases, but it need not do so.

The final feature of Bourdieu's habitus is the idea of "structured structures predisposed to function as structuring structures" (Bourdieu 1990, 53). What he means by this circular phrase is that the socialization process creates understandings of what is possible within the person's social position. The habitus tends to "reproduce those actions, perceptions, and attitudes consistent with the conditions under which it was produced" (Swartz 1997, 103). The habitus is thus both structured and structuring.

The concept of the habitus, as Bourdieu explains it, seems overly complicated. But in essence, we may think of it as a feature of human society that incorporates the rules, perceptions, expectations, ideas, and attitudes that are learned during the process of socialization. Because it is internalized, the habitus sets the parameters of social action within the social hierarchy for each class fraction. It sets limits within the social structure but at the same time generates perceptions and practices and allows for the creation of aspirations. These attitudinal features determine what is considered reasonable and possible and, conversely, what is unreasonable and out of the realm of possibility. All of these concepts have consequences for the study of racial categorization and its practical outcomes. The habitus structures how members of different racial categories may interact over time within the imposed epochal structures. A huge portion of a person's life chances, however, will be based on the accumulation and use of capital.

Capital

Bourdieu's use of the concept of capital is straightforward for people who have been socialized in a fully capitalist society. The concept of economic capital is the easiest to understand because we accept that some people in a hierarchical society can command more respect, authority, and power because of their access to money—capital in its purest form. Bourdieu's other forms of capital—social, cultural, and symbolic—work on the same basic principle as economic capital. Readers will recognize Bourdieu's use of capital because political pundits today commonly refer to "political capital." The idea is straightforward: a politician who attends the annual meeting of the National Rifle Association can garner political capital with his gun-toting constituents simply by his appearance at the convention. The question for the politician is whether this kind of capital is beneficial to his campaign, not whether political capital can be gained or lost.

Social capital is acquired in several ways. It can be ascribed—by being born in the right brahmin family—or achieved—by attending the "correct" boarding school or graduating from a prestigious university. A person's total volume of social capital is affected by the amassed capital of the social network in which he or she operates. A successful hunter in a small hunting and foraging band may have great social capital, but only in that sociohistorical formation. The computation of social capital is necessarily contextual. It would be absurd, for example, to compare the hunter's social capital with that of a Yale Law School graduate working for a major law firm in New York City. Individuals in large capitalist societies have abundant opportunities to acquire and accumulate social capital and capital of all sorts because of the complex variety of networks that operate within late capitalism. In a modern postindustrial setting, such as those studied by modern-world archaeologists where racial categorization is most important, individuals can "invest" in amassing social capital. Given the social hierarchy, however, the playing field is never truly level. A working-class student seeking enrollment in an Ivy League university, for instance, will not command the same volume of social capital as a student who has graduated from Andover Academy. In such a situation, habitus helps individuals understand and accept what they can reasonably expect within the social hierarchy.

Bourdieu's (1986) concept of cultural capital is more complex than the concept of social capital because it exists in three states. Cultural capital can be embodied as long-lasting dispositions of the mind and body and it can be objectified in objects—paintings, books, antiques, and prized objects. Educational qualifications can also be objectified as cultural capital. Individuals can purchase objectified and institutionalized cultural capital, but they must acquire embodied cultural capital or simply have it as an element of their humanity. Cultural capital can be incorporated as part of the habitus, but only over time, and within a hierarchical social structure, any attempt to force the recognition of one's cultural capital may be met with disdain and rejection. A nouveau riche investor may have the economic capital and the objectified cultural capital of the most respected old-money mogul, but without embodied cultural capital, he will never be on the same social level as the mogul. The epochal structures simply do not allow it.

Objectified cultural capital is especially pertinent for archaeologists because it can exist for centuries and can be recontextualized in ways that increases its social meaning. Places such as Colonial Williamsburg, Mount Vernon, Monticello, and other properties associated with famous, wealthy Americans have been venerated for decades in the United States. Such properties have been imbued with cultural capital by thousands of visitors as well as by the archaeologists and historians who have lavished attention on them. Much of early historical archaeology, in fact, involved attempts to provide respectability to the discipline through the objectified cultural capital of the sites examined. The cultural capital bestowed on Jamestown today—as the founding site of America—far exceeds that bestowed on it in the early seventeenth century by the transients who were moving into the New World but were not conscious that they were doing anything remarkable (Rutman 1971, 34).

Symbolic capital is the most difficult kind of capital to comprehend because of its subtle nature; it can be easily misrecognized as something else. According to Bourdieu, symbolic capital is a form of domination because those in positions of power use it to manipulate and convince. They have shifted their

attempt to dominate from overt action to management using symbols, slo-
gans, ads, and patriotic images. We can consider ideology, here defined in its
classic sense, as a form of symbolic capital because its goal is to manipulate
people's thoughts and actions and mask the unpleasant. Symbolic capital can
even be enacted materially in various concrete ways, including the construction and presentation of manicured landscapes that are intended to project
power, authority, and historical longevity (see Orser 2005, 2006a).

Fields

A key feature of Bourdieu's practice theory that archaeologists often overlook
is the concept of field. Bourdieu's understanding of field meshes well with a
network perspective because field thinking is at its core relational thinking
(Bourdieu 1984, 107; Bourdieu and Wacquant 1992, 96–97). To think of fields
is to envision networks. Fields can be perceived as multidimensional spaces,
such as networks, in which individuals and social groups are variously arranged. The fields are arenas of self-actualization and struggle within which
relations of power are played out. The habitus provides the underlying principles of practice enacted within each field, and the various kinds of capital
distribute power within a field.

One central feature of Bourdieu's concepts of capital and field is that in
any field, the kinds of capital interlink and crosscut. As a heuristic device,
the relationship between the various forms of capital can be represented as
a box, with the total volume of capital running from bottom (-) to top (+)
(Figure 3.3). The box represents the social space within which individuals and
social groups interact. The higher the position in the box, the greater the total
volume of capital. For Bourdieu, the most important field in a social system
is the field of power. Conflict within the field of power is the most important
dynamic as social groups struggle for material and symbolic resources (Swartz
1997, 136–137). In modern industrial societies—those that also incorporate a
racially based hierarchy—the struggle for power is usually played out in terms
of economic and cultural capital. Thus, in the box model, we can envision
cultural capital as extending from left (+) to right (-), and economic capital
extending from right (+) to left (-). A person in the exact middle of the box, at
the intersection of the vertical and horizontal lines of economic and cultural
capital, would have equal amounts of economic and cultural capital.

We can learn more about Bourdieu's use of the field concept by taking
a closer look at two of his empirical studies. In *Homo Academicus* (1988),
Bourdieu examined the field of academia, where he was primarily occupied
as a professional living in modern-day France. As a sociologist, Bourdieu was

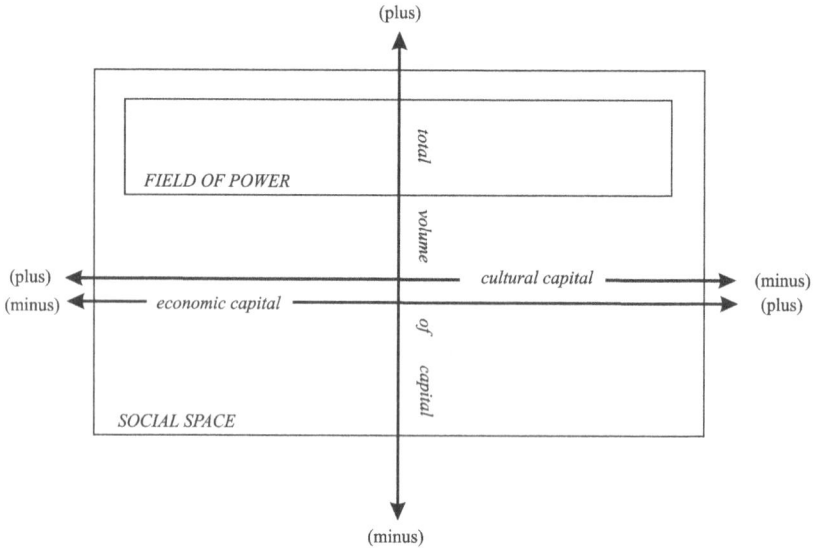

Figure 3.3. Bourdieu's social model. Drawing by author.

interested in how scholars from diverse disciplines with different intellectual traditions construct a social world using various kinds of capital and forms of power. Much of his discussion is difficult for Americans to understand because of the peculiarities of the French academic world, and much of its subtlety is lost without an understanding of the habitus of the system. What we do learn from Bourdieu, however, makes abundant sense within a capitalist society. The social groups with the highest volume of economic capital are professors of law and medicine, while those who teach and study literature have the lowest volume of economic capital. Why this is so relates to the epochal structures reproduced over time and how the practitioners of the various disciplines use capital. A scientist with a huge government grant has more cultural capital within a university setting than a literary scholar examining the role of racism in children's literature. Outside the field of the university, however, the literary scholar's research may have greater social value to human rights activists, especially if the scientist is engaged in military weapons research. But within the power structure, the system is constructed to ensure that the scientist has greater economic capital than the literary scholar. The reason relates to the nature of the epochal structures.

We also learn from Bourdieu another reality: one's father's profession affects a person's total volume of capital. The scale Bourdieu presents, from lowest to highest, ranges from a working-class father to a craftsman father to a white-collar father to a father who holds a prominent position in industry. Bourdieu focuses on a system that is inherently open only to certain social classes—universities—and he does not consider the issue of race. In fact, he does not engage racial categorization at all. Even so, we learn from him about hierarchical social space, here academic space, and the ways the actors marshal and use capital to promote and sustain their institutional power within the reproduced epochal structure.

The field of artistic production is another realm that captured Bourdieu's attention. In *The Field of Cultural Production* (1993) he examined how cultural and economic capital combine to create the structure of the artistic (art and literature) field. How does an unknown artist break into a structure when he or she has no capital, cultural or otherwise? We have all heard of the starving artist or unpublished author, individuals who may have considerable talent but who are not recognized and thus are not compensated. The field of artistic and literary production, like all fields in a capitalist society, is enmeshed within a field of power. It has relative autonomy within the field of power because it structures its own economic and political principles. If the field of artistic production ever lost this autonomy, it would cease to exist. Cultural capital would lose its meaning if the "worth" (that is, the total volume of capital) of a writer or artist was measured solely by book sales or auction prices. Writers of the tackiest romance novels would become the world's greatest authors and producers of the most trite pictures would be history's greatest artists. That great writers and gifted artists are not recognized by sales alone means that a struggle occurs in the field of cultural production (art and literature) within the dominant class (men and women with the greatest economic capital to bestow). In other words, authors seeking to write the Great American Novel who do not wish to compromise their plot for commercial reasons may have great cultural capital but low economic capital. While they toil without recognition, they do not acquire cultural capital until some elite reader or collector bestows it on them. The act of bestowing cultural capital on the writer, however, may constitute an act of symbolic violence because of the way the writer has been manipulated and used to increase the cultural capital of the bestower. The tardy "acceptance" among elites of Outsider Art provides an excellent example.

What is for us most important about Bourdieu's work is his explanation of the way power and capital is intertwined within fields. We can use this understanding to construct a useful approach for analyzing racialization with archaeological remains. At the same time, Bourdieu's interpretation of capital and power means that we need not abandon class, clearly the analytical mainstay of any capitalist society.

Modern-World Archaeology and Racialization

Why overcomplicate the archaeological study of racialization with such complex terms as field, habitus, and the socio-spatial dialectic? Would it not be
better, if not much easier, to provide a narrative of the workings of racialization in a particular social setting and let it go at that? Would not the narrative
tell the story of how racialization was both enacted and reacted against? As
archaeologists, could we not examine race at an individual household in the
absence of such confusing terms and concepts? We cannot doubt that using
a particularistic and highly contextualized narrative would provide an intimate understanding of how racialization affected the lives and livelihoods of
a household's residents. This approach would permit us to learn something
about the way the particular men, women, and children who lived in the
house were categorized either as racially inferior or superior. There is nothing
inherently incorrect in investigating race in this minimalist manner. In fact,
given the site-specific nature of archaeological excavation, deep contextual-
ization offers a good opportunity for historical insight. When finished, we
would certainly have an understanding of how racial categorization affected
the particular household of our focus. But would this approach ultimately be
satisfying? In the long run, perhaps. After archaeologists had completed many
similar studies in the same area, a compiler of the information could develop a
broad understanding of how racialization was enacted, enforced, and resisted
in one particular area. Such compilation may be possible in the future, but this
approach is not feasible at present.

On a deeper level, the main failing of any particularistic approach is that it
would tend to personalize racialization. It would reduce it to something that
happened to some people at discrete places and times in history. This perspective adopts the view of race as psychology. Using this approach, it might
be difficult to sustain the view that racialization is a historical process created and used to define a social hierarchy that is systemic within the capitalist
project. Historians who have adopted a broad-scale transnational perspective
have fully documented the epochal structures in which real men and women
struggled within the system (i.e., Breen 2004; Linebaugh and Rediker 2000).
At least one prominent historian of race in the United States argues that identity in America always has been about race and that ethnicity has served only
as a clever way to avoid the harsh realities of racialization (Roediger 2005,
21–34).

The central problem with using Bourdieu's terms and concepts stems from
his failure to consider race in any substantive way. This failure was not simply
an oversight, however. In fact, Bourdieu considered some vectors of inequal-

ity, such as race, to be "subsidiary characteristics" of society that were not the "real underlying principles" of class formation (Bourdieu 1984, 102; 1987, 7). Bourdieu was firmly convinced that class and power were the dominant determinants in the distribution of capital. As a result, we cannot use his perspectives by rote to understand the material dimensions of historical racialization. To transform Bourdieu's analytical framework, we must turn to still another source, one that concentrates on the analysis of gender relations.

We can find a way to use the best of Bourdieu's analytical approach with the archaeological investigation of racialization by studying its application by sociologist Leslie McCall (1992). McCall was interested in determining whether she could find a way to use Bourdieu's concepts in the study of gender. Bourdieu had perceived gender, like race, as only a secondary dimension of inequality, merely a subsidiary of class. His focus on the middle class as the site of contemporary struggle meant that he missed other vectors of social inequality, such as gender (and race).

McCall rejected the primacy Bourdieu attached to occupation and education as significant aspects of class position and proposed instead that the intersection of class and gender is the most important social feature to consider. She relied on Bourdieu's concept of embodied cultural capital to make this claim. When Bourdieu defined embodied cultural capital, he said that it appears in the form of tenacious dispositions of the mind and *the body*. It is this inclusion of "the body" that was significant to McCall because it means that one's very person—and, by extension, its outward characteristics—can constitute a form of cultural capital. This rereading of Bourdieu means that personal characteristics such as gender assignment can be analyzed as cultural capital. Accordingly, McCall proposed that women who obtain the highest economic capital because of their occupations really embody a form of symbolic cultural capital rather than just economic capital (through an increased salary, though perhaps one that is lower than that of a male counterpart). The same case can be made for racialized categorization.

We can adopt McCall's insights to the study of racialization by considering racial category as a kind of embodied cultural capital. Race is an especially ambiguous form of cultural capital because it initially results from an exterior—and usually unfriendly—classification. This means, of course, that the original designations of white and nonwhite, which were historically changeable, were intended to set parameters on the life chances of individuals within the hierarchical social order. The establishment of the racially based hierarchy means, by extension, that the idea of being racialized becomes part of the habitus. One accepts his or her expectations and aspirations during the socialization process. Acceptance provides, as Bourdieu (1984, 471) says, a "sense of place." Returning to McCall (1992, 849–850), this understanding as it pertains to gender means that women entering previously all-male professions discover several obstacles, not the least of which may mean being labeled with derogatory terms (which, by the way, may approximate racial slurs). The struggle in the workplace is duplicated in the racialized society as members of the dominant race complain that some members of the subordinate races do not "know their place." The not-knowing-of-place upsets the tranquility of the habitus and may lead to overt acts of violence and terrorism.

Seeing Race in Things

The problem that remains, of course, is the basic one that confronts all social archaeologists, including those concerned with the examination of race: how does one actually "see" the affects of racialization in the deposits of the past? How can archaeologists relate the artifacts they excavate and the features they uncover with the racial categorizations created and enforced in history?

We can see in Mullins's (1996, 1999a, 1999b, 1999c) careful research a case study of how racial position and artifact consumption are related. As Mullins (2004) points out, however, competing theories exist to explain consumption behavior that range from the theory that people consume merely to emulate others to the theory that people consume signs that evoke nonexistent realities. Psychiatrists even argue that the acquisition of artifacts is hard-wired into the human brain as an innate survival mechanism (e.g., Whybrow 2005).

Clearly, the relationship between racial category and consumption is nuanced and infinitely labyrinthine. The reasons individual men and women choose to consume are admittedly complicated and situationally sensitive. Despite the apparent complexities that surround consumption, historical archaeologists must engage this subject because of the huge role consumer behavior and social inequality played in the acquisition of modern-era material culture. Because they are cognizant of this historical reality, it would appear that archaeologists might best adopt an overt social approach, one consistent with the principles enumerated above. A conscious recognition of the social inequalities constructed within the system of capitalist production and distribution has the potential to allow archaeologists to see the relationships between racial categorization and artifact consumption. (Of course, this overarching perspective does not diminish the need for the minutely contextualized investigations at which historical archaeologists excel, and the next two chapters provide this sort of analysis at two discrete places in the United States.)

Accordingly, I adopt a social-relations view of consumption. I envision the consumption of material things as "part of the cultural production of social relations, a rather concrete process carried out through social practices in mundane life" (Slater 1997, 148). The social-relations perspective owes much to insights provided by Mary Douglas and Baron Isherwood (1979), which were reinforced by numerous researchers who followed their lead. A network model is inherent in this approach. Material consumed is viewed as flowing within an intricate network of social relations. Rather than being purely mechanical, however, individual people (or for historical archaeologists, individual households) skillfully manipulate the consumption network within the boundaries of their habitus. They reinterpret and modify their needs and desires in ways that can both reproduce and challenge the existing social order.

Non-native people (and increasingly even native peoples) living in the United States were enmeshed in a capitalist system in which commodities circulated widely and openly. Marx, who understood commodities as well as anyone, described the flow of commodities with his famous C-M-C model. A commodity (C) is exchanged for money (M) and in the process undergoes a metamorphosis (Marx 1967, 103–124). The change in the commodity (the second C) is effectuated in the transition from exchange value (for the seller) to use value (for the purchaser).

The imposition of money in the exchange and transformation process is deceptive. At first consideration, money can act, as Georg Simmel (1978) believed, as an equalizer of human relations. Thus conceived, the amount of money a person controls may outweigh other vectors of social inequality. As Daniel Miller notes, money "tends to extend a concept of equality, in so far as the perception of inequality becomes based upon differences in the possession of money, rather than on an essentialist notion of intrinsic differences in persons" (1987, 73). Since money is a potential equalizing force, it appears to follow logically that it has the power to level social distinctions. The medium of money, because it is qualitatively equal from one person to the next, can only be used to distinguish between individuals quantitatively. Social value is increasingly equated with personal wealth, even to the point of using what someone is "worth" to mean their financial holdings. Modern Americans can easily recognize this reality by the way wealthy celebrities, regardless of their actual talent, are constantly presented as role models strictly because of their control of economic capital. Newspapers are filled with accounts of wealthy athletic superstars who seem to be exempt from many of society's norms and sometimes even from legal strictures.

The belief that money is a social equalizer, however, is thrown into sharp relief when we consider the various vectors of social inequality that run through the inherently hierarchical, capitalist social formations of modern history. One of the great insights Mullins (1999c) offers in his close examinations of African American consumption in Annapolis, Maryland, is that material objects figure into the class struggles of individuals relegated to the lowest rungs of the racial ladder. These men, women, and children encounter consumption paradoxically. Their material possessions can be homogenizing as they extend across the color line, effectively making artifact assemblages undiagnostic across differently racialized groups. At the same time, the same artifacts can be radicalizing because they may promote strategies of resistance to racialist ideology. Mullins's conclusion is worth citing in full: "Racism was essential to consumer culture's evasion of class structure and the increasing acceptability of race as a basis for dispensing social privilege. To truly understand class in emergent consumer culture, it is essential to acknowledge that labor, consumer space, and social and material privileges were—and in many ways still remain—fundamentally structured by race" (35). The racial structure is thus an epochal structure that individuals must confront every day of their lives.

Geographer Bobby Wilson (2005) has provided a cogent and insightful analysis of the relationship between racial categorization, the epochal structure of racial identification, and material consumption. Wilson's analysis centers on the social changes African Americans experienced in their transition from bondage to freedom. He charts the ways free blacks struggled for economic security in terms that are wholly consistent with Mullins's reading of the times. With the development of mass marketing, it seemed that the potential leveling of society through material objects was a distinct possibility for the postbellum United States. Even though African Americans were relegated to the lower half of the social order, they were able to amass considerable earning and hence buying power. But because of the racialized structure of the social order, white Americans expected blacks not only to be inferior but also to look inferior. The problem for white America was that the material distinctions between whites and nonwhites were being eroded by the flood of material goods. In the 1930s, sociologist John Dollard (1957, 92) observed this leveling in "Southerntown." Whites and blacks throughout the apartheid South could own similar belongings, even though the racial rules of the day were definitely segregationist. Whites thus experienced a "shock of sameness" (Hale 1999, 195). For their part, blacks could resist the consumerist aspect of their imposed racial inferiority by purchasing and displaying consumer goods. The archaeological findings Mullins (1999c, 2001) presents—in the visual appearance of parlors and the acquisition of bric-a-brac—fully supports this interpretation.

As Wilson noted (2005, 595–596), the problem whites who were seeking to uphold the racialized social structure confronted arose because money did not provide the visual demonstration of white supremacy that was apparent during slavery. Mass production and the mass marketing that accompanied it sought to provide material things to whomever could afford them. That green was the main color of interest is a truism. But because of the racialized epochal structure of the United States, those individuals who were judged to be nonwhite had to be slotted into subordinate positions to reproduce the social order, even though the sphere of commodity circulation militated against it. The growing presence of a black middle class repudiated the racialist conception of humanity.

The way to resolve the apparent paradox of African American consumption came through the enactment of a conscious doctrine of separate but equal. Enforced segregation would not violate the commodity exchange system inherent in capitalism. Men and women relegated to the lower "races" could obtain material goods and services, but usually only after certain racialized rules were observed. In the American South, for instance, blacks could attend county fairs but on different days than whites, they could ride buses but only in the back, and they could be served at a diner but only after the needs of white customers had been met (Wilson 2005). As Mullins (1999a) substantiates, African Americans could adopt various strategies to obtain consumer goods, by using mail-order catalogs, by frequenting black-owned shops, and in some cases, even by "passing" as white.

The lesson inherent in the racial strategies of the United States vis-à-vis consumerism has clear archaeological implications. Where racialization exists alongside capitalist economics—and I would argue that this has been the case throughout the entire modern era—archaeologists may find it extremely difficult to separate the material assemblages of the various "races." In other words, excavated material assemblages may appear to have little if any identifiable differences when compared between historically defined "races." We can expect some homogenization in material culture because of the entrepreneurs' urge to sell as much as possible to as many people as possible. Without discernable differences, however, an archaeology of race would seem impossible. And it may very well be the case that the archaeological analysis of class may have greater analytical merit than the archaeological investigation of race. At present, historical archaeologists have yet to resolve this important issue. I do not believe, though, that we can abandon the archaeology of race before we have sufficiently pursued several avenues of inquiry. Prior archaeological research on race and racialization offers too many intriguing investigative directions to be dismissed. Our task, then, is to discover ways to observe racialized differences in the material culture generated during capitalism.

One possible answer to the conundrum lies in recalling the socio-spatial dialectic. One of the features of the separate but equal doctrine was the segmentation of space. Members of the dominant "race" in positions of power could impose spatial restrictions on those they had racialized as inferior (Wilson 2005, 602). Thus, "ghettoization," taken in tandem with material culture, may provide a distinctive way for historical archaeologists to research the relationships between racial identity and material culture. In this way, all of the elements noted above coalesce into a reasonable way to investigate race in historic America. Artifact assemblages taken alone may only reflect the shock of sameness that whites experienced when they saw nonwhites dressed in the same clothes they were wearing. When combined with segregation, however, artifact assemblages may indeed begin to appear distinctive as visual elements of racialization. Thus, when investigating the role of racialization in artifact distribution, rather than speaking of a socio-spatial dialectic, we may perhaps think in terms of a "spatial-material dialectic" that is socio-spatial in essence but "racio-spatial" in reality.

Racing the Past

The ideas and concepts presented in this chapter are not the only way to examine the historic process of racialization in the United States. Different analytical approaches presented in the future may provide greater interpretive power. At this time, however, the concepts outlined here, when used together, offer a rigorous and interesting way to investigate how race was used in the United States to structure society, to control the essence of the hierarchy, and to keep nonwhites in assigned places. As may well be imagined, the process of racialization in the United States was not only complicated and mutable over time, it is ongoing. The special purview of modern-world archaeology in the study of racialization is to investigate and interpret the assignment of race in the past. The frames of reference must necessarily be limited to those spheres in which archaeologists have particular expertise.

To show how the concepts explored above can be used to provide an archaeological analysis of racialization, I will examine two archaeological deposits in the next two chapters. Both of these sites are associated with "old immigrants" to America, people who came in the nineteenth century and who usually were racialized as nonwhite and were relegated to low-paying, often dangerous jobs. In the next chapter, I consider the Irish in New York City. Although today Irish are considered to be white, they were not so viewed when they first arrived. The nativist racism Irish encountered in the streets of New York, which was rooted in attitudes toward and fears about Irish religion and culture, caricatured their physical appearance as brutish. Only by depicting

Irish immigrants as ape-like could nativists rationalize racializing as inferior an immigrant group with light skin.

The second case study, presented in Chapter 5, comes from Stockton, California, and is associated with the Chinese. The Chinese were reviled like no other people in the nineteenth century, mostly because of their appearance and their culture. Nativist Americans, however, did not perceive that Chinese religious beliefs constituted the same threat as Irish Catholicism. Chinese religion, being non-Christian, was easy to denigrate as heathenish and thus inordinately silly.

Investigating these two apparent ethnic groups in racial terms has a number of distinct advantages. First, because they settled on opposite coasts of the continental United States, they demonstrate that racialization in the United States was not confined to one part of the nation or to one people. On the contrary, the transcontinental nature of racialization was built into the deep structure of the national discourse and was carried west in the toolkit of Manifest Destiny. Second, the study of racialization with two diverse peoples demonstrates how racialization was not simply constructed based on phenotype. Racialization in the United States could be based on cultural traditions, religious beliefs, and place of birth. Third, both of the archaeological deposits examined derive from the late nineteenth and early twentieth centuries. The temporal proximity of these deposits to our own time forces us to confront racialization and admit that it was not something that was perpetrated by a few misguided souls in early American history or that it existed only during the time of slavery. The examination of the Irish and the Chinese also forces us to admit that African Americans were not the only group to experience racialization, even though their experience is perhaps the most historically visible and tenacious.

The understanding that we must confront racialization in our own time is particularly important to me personally, because elsewhere (Orser 2004c, 284) I have argued that modern-world archaeology, however one wishes to conceive it, must have present-day relevance. I believe that our striving for relevance will demonstrate the power of historical archaeology as a tool for understanding the way the post-Columbian world works and will provide a unique vantage point for investigating the American experience.

4

The Irish in New York City

This book's first case study of racialization in the United States and its accompanying archaeological manifestation comes from New York City, specifically from a part of the city known as the Five Points. Archaeologists excavated the material used in this chapter from the backyard of an Irish tenement located at 472 Pearl Street. My reasons for using this site are twofold. First, archaeologists recovered the evidence from the tenement as part of a huge recovery effort that occurred within a cultural resource management framework. This project was thus done on a scale that far outstrips most academic projects. The large scale of the effort and the huge amount of material recovered during its progress has meant that a large, finely detailed, and exemplary site report (Yamin 2000a), one doctoral dissertation (Brighton 2005), and several published articles have already appeared. Given the breadth of the project, more publications will surely result, even though the artifacts were lost on September 11, 2001. In writing this chapter I have relied most heavily on the site report and the dissertation. All of my archaeological knowledge about 472 Pearl Street derives from these sources, as I did not participate in the fieldwork. The quality of the data is so good and the supporting information so detailed that my lack of direct experience with the site does not constitute a significant problem.

My goal in this chapter and the next is to illustrate one way historical archaeologists can investigate racialization in U.S. history using archaeologically recovered materials. Needless to say, such artifactual information must be supplemented with extensive documentary materials. I have chosen the two case studies because of their abundance of professionally collected archaeological materials and the detailed historical sources that support the archaeological findings.

Before any archaeological analysis can be pursued, several sociohistorical contexts must be established, beginning with background information on the site under investigation that includes the basic details of the property and its residents. This information, though only descriptive, becomes pertinent during the archaeological examination. Since we are dealing with immigrants in both this chapter and the next, we must develop some understanding of the habitus of their home countries. This information must be brief and somewhat superficial; a full ethnography is not possible here. It must be rather general because we cannot know the exact prior location of each immigrant family. In nineteenth-century Ireland, for example, the townland—the smallest administrative unit on the island—was the family's prime locational referent. American immigration officials and census takers did not record this level of detail because they were only interested in the immigrant's country of origin. Further locational detail is thus lost to history.

A central aspect of understanding the racialization process and being able to disentangle it from the mute archaeological remains is knowledge of the epochal structures immigrants encountered upon entering the United States. At a minimum, these structures were social and politico-legal. The social structures consist of the various networks of individuals and groups who were allied against the immigrants and those who worked for their benefit. The politico-legal structures are mostly expressed through laws and statutes designed to restrict the actions and conduct of immigrants—as part of the racialization process—on federal, state, and local levels.

The racialized immigrants—in my specific examples, Irish and Chinese—would have encountered the epochal structures in various ways and in different situations. Most of the personal or group actions they took, as examples of historical agency, lie beyond the scope of archaeological visibility and in fact may be lost to historical analysis as well. We nonetheless can develop some understanding of habitus transformation as those individuals who were racialized learned about the structure of race in America and their subsequent position within it. This learning process—which would have had a strong transnational character—may have had significant impact on their access to and acquisition of material culture. The way racialized households recontextualized their objects within the United States will help demonstrate how archaeologists can investigate the racialization process over time.

The final element of the analytical framework is the archaeological implications of the findings. This consideration will bring us full circle to the site under study.

Background of Excavation

The materials used in this chapter were collected by archaeologists from Historic Conservation and Interpretation, Inc. between May 1991 and January 1992. The project was designed to salvage information from the historic Five Points area of Manhattan before the construction of a new federal courthouse at Foley Square (Figure 4.1). The courthouse was situated on the eastern two-

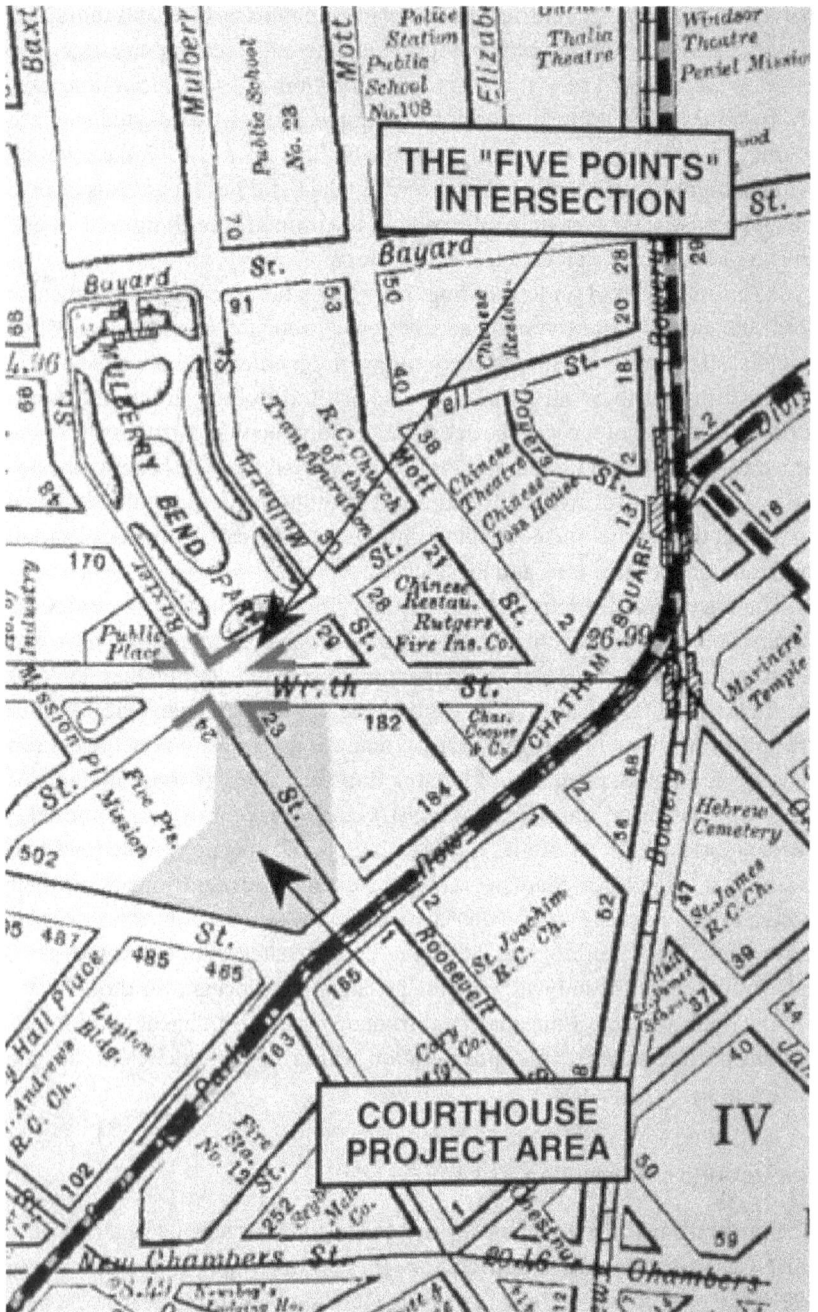

Figure 4.1. Location of the Five Points project, New York City. Courtesy of U.S. General Services Administration and John Milner Associates.

thirds of Block 160, so the archaeologists concentrated on this area. They excavated twenty-two of the fifty recognized archaeological features in the block
and recovered almost 1 million artifacts. Archaeologists with John Milner
Associates, directed by Rebecca Yamin, conducted the laboratory research,
devised the interpretations, and wrote the site report. Under Yamin's direction, the interpreters sought to tell the story of the forgotten men and women
who called the Five Points their home (Yamin 1997, 2000b). The huge data
set compiled as part of this project has tremendous potential to illuminate
the associations between material possessions and racialized position in nineteenth-century America.

The Irish at the 472 Pearl Street Tenement

Peter McLoughlin, a native of County Sligo in northwestern Ireland, bought
the lot at 472 Pearl Street in 1839 and ran a liquor store there until the 1840s.
In 1848, he had a five-story brick tenement built on the lot to house Irish
immigrants. Two years later, about twenty households—roughly 100 people,
the majority of whom were Irish-born—occupied his tenement, along with
McLoughlin's brother and sister-in-law. With the increase in residents (which
included boarders living with tenants), McLoughlin felt compelled to update
the building's sanitation facilities. He constructed a cesspool about fifteen feet
behind the tenement (Yamin 2000c, 1:98). My analysis in this chapter concentrates on the artifacts excavated from the privy (Feature J) associated with the
tenement from 1850 to 1870 (Figure 4.2).

The decennial census allows us to develop some understanding of the social setting at 472 Pearl Street during the 1850–1870 period. The census figures
reported by Stephen Brighton (2005, 284–293) show that the number of individuals living at the address was fairly consistent, fluctuating between 74 and
107. Census figures are suspect because of the vagaries involved in recording
the information, but they still afford the opportunity for an impressionistic
understanding of the social dynamics that may have operated at the tenement
during the period of interest. Table 4.1 shows the reported number of residents
at ten-year intervals. Even if the totals are not perfectly accurate, they indicate
the relative numbers of individuals crammed into the tenement during these
years. The number of males and females remained fairly constant during the
three decades even as the number of boarders declined from 36 to 1. The number of households fluctuated from 20 (1850) to 14 (1860) to 19 (1870). Calculations of the average age of the residents and the boarders indicates that the
boarders tended to be older than the residents (Table 4.2). All of the tenants,

Feature 2
brick wall

Feature J
stone wall

wood

bluestone
sewer pipe

posthole

Feature T

wood

Lot 5
foundation

7.08' below grade

Feature J
stone wall

wood

concrete

Analytical
Strata

0   1m

0   4ft

I
1 10YR 3/4 dark yellowish brown sandy loam; cat. no. 232
2 10YR 4/3 brown sandy loam; cat. no. 367
3 10YR 3/3 dark brown sandy loam

II
4 10YR 3/4 dark yellowish brown sandy loam with pockets
   of yellow clay; cat. nos. 324, 368, 392, 421, 468, 471, 472,
   473, 474, 491, 768, 769, 783

III
5 7.5 YR 3/4 dark brown sandy loam with layers of ash; cat.
   nos. 280, 295, 393, 470, 490, 551, 552, 553, 627, 644, 650,
   662, 785, 787, 788

IV
6 7.5YR 5/4 brown silty sandy sandy loam with ash; cat. nos.
   489, 784, 791, 794
7 10YR 3/1very dark gray ash lens; cat. no. 829

V
8 10YR 2/1 black silty sandy loam with ash; cat. nos. 708,
   738, 739, 752, 758, 762, 767, 780
9 10YR 4/1 dark gray silty sandy loam with ash; cat. nos. 795,
   812, 823, 825, 851
10 10YR 5/3 brown silty sandy loam; cat. nos. 764, 830

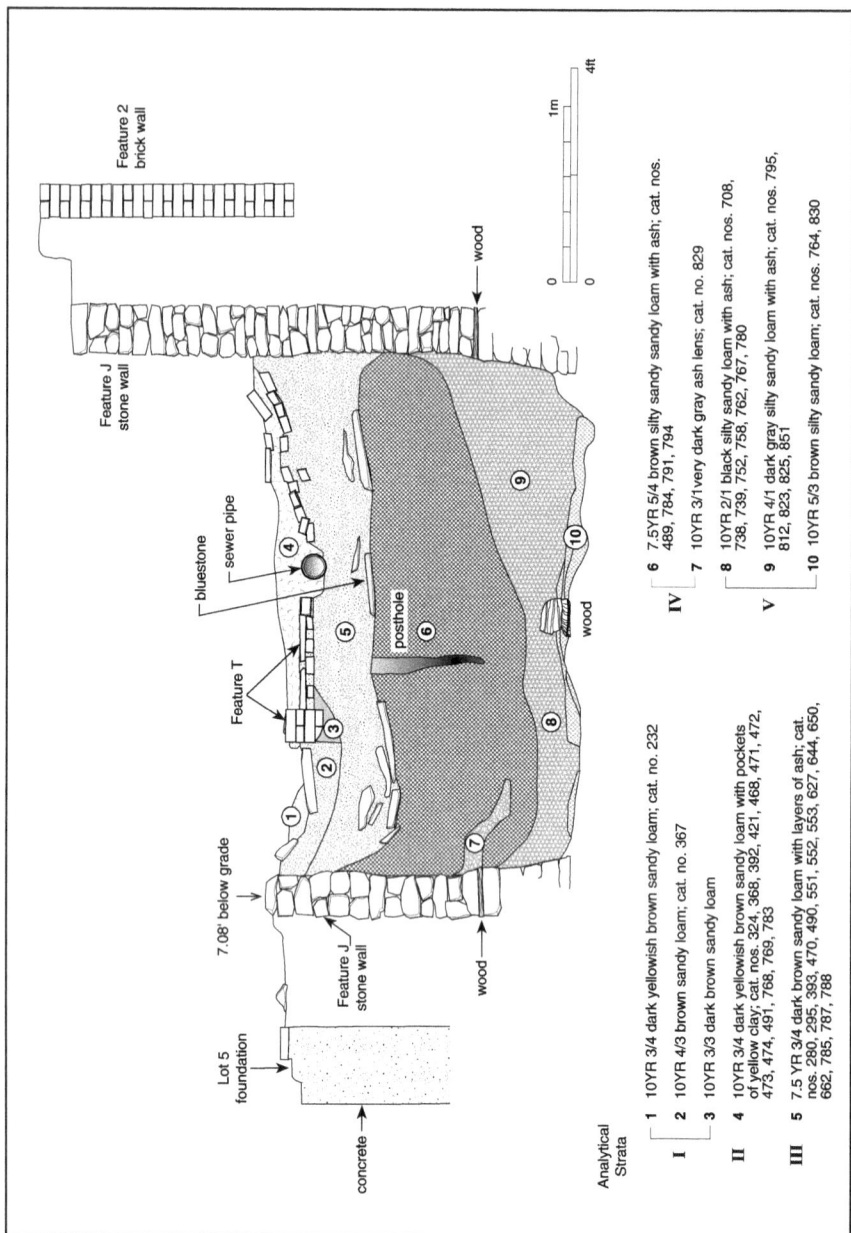

Figure 4.2. Feature J privy at 472 Pearl Street. Courtesy of U.S. General Services Administration and John Milner Associates.

Table 4.1. Occupants of 472 Pearl Street, New York City, 1850–1870

TOTAL NUMBER OF RESIDENTS, BY GENDER AND RESIDENTIAL STATUS

	Male	Female	Male Boarder	Female Boarder	Total
1850	37	34	19	17	107
1860	20	31	15	8	74
1870	47	48	1	0	96

NUMBER AND PERCENT OF MALE AND FEMALE RESIDENTS

	Males	Females	Total
1850	56 (52.3)	51 (47.7)	107 (100.0)
1860	35 (47.3)	39 (52.7)	74 (100.0)
1870	48 (50.0)	48 (50.0)	96 (100.0)

NUMBER AND PERCENT OF RESIDENTS AND BOARDERS

	Residents	Boarders	Total
1850	71 (66.4)	36 (33.6)	107 (100.0)
1860	51 (68.9)	23 (31.1)	74 (100.0)
1870	95 (99.0)	1 (1.0)	96 (100.0)

Source: Stephen A. Brighton, "A Historical Archaeology of the Irish Proletarian Diaspora: The Material Manifestations of Irish Identity in America, 1850–1910" (Ph.D. diss., Boston University, 2005), 284–293.

Table 4.2. Average Ages of Occupants at 472 Pearl Street, New York City, 1850–1870

	1850	1860	1870
Males, in family	21.9	20.8	18.9
Females, in family	24.1	23.5	21.3
Male Boarders	29.4	23.8	—
Female Boarders	27.6	37.8	—

including the women and children, were engaged in some kind of manual labor, either permanently or temporarily.

Census records also permit a glimpse of the transience of tenants at the property. Of the twenty households recorded in 1850, only three were in the tenement ten years later. Only three families continued to reside at the address between 1860 and 1870, and only one was noted in all three census counts. Even if we can agree that the census enumerators were probably not as diligent in the tenements as they might have been—given its narrow, dark, and frequently dangerous hallways and stairs—we can nonetheless use their information as evidence that tenants frequently moved in and out of the building. Conscious resettlement and unexpected necessity undoubtedly required frequent relocation.

Especially pertinent for this examination of racialization are the notations the census takers made of the residents' places of birth. The residents of the tenement at 472 Pearl Street were overwhelmingly Irish by birth or Irish American (the progeny of Irish-born parents). Census records reveal that most of the Irish immigrant families had children born in New York. The ages of the children suggest a minimum number of years each family had been in the United States. If an Irish-born husband and wife were reported as having a child six years of age born in New York, then we can conclude that the parents had lived in the United States for at least six years. Only the 1850 and 1860 censuses can be used for this purpose, because the even numbers of the ages recorded in 1870 suggests that the enumerator, or perhaps even the parents, merely guessed the ages of the tenements' residents. The ages reported for Daniel Callaghan provide an example. In 1850, he was listed as 6 years old, but in 1860, he was listed as 11 years old, a difference of only 5 years. In 1870, his age was recorded as 20. If he was indeed 6 in 1850, he should have been 26 in 1870.

Another important feature to note about the tenement is that not everybody who lived there was Irish-born or Irish American. Germans are recorded as residents in each of the censuses. In 1850, a 51-year-old tobacconist resided there with his 63-year-old wife, both of whom were born in Germany. The couple were gone in 1860, but another German, a 30-year-old cigar maker, was living in the tenement. Another German-born cigar maker, a 35-year-old, boarded with a German-born family. The father of this family worked as a trunk maker, and he and his wife had a 7-year-old son born in New York. In 1870, a different German family lived in the tenement. The father of this family was also a cigar maker, and he and his wife had two children, the oldest of which, at 10, had been born in New York. A 40-year-old clerk, also born in New York, boarded with them.

In summary, historical sources indicate that the residents of the crowded tenement at 472 Pearl Street were mostly, though not all, Irish and that as families they were fairly transient. Men, women, and children worked either inside or outside the home, and many of the family members were fairly new to the United States, though the number of newly arrived immigrants declined over time.

Having provided this brief description of the tenement dwellers, we must now investigate the world they left behind. The habitus they brought with them would have provided the worldview and the adaptive skills that would have helped them to survive in their strange new world.

Homegrown Habitus

The emigration of the Irish to the United States was of monumental proportion given the size of their island. Historians who have studied Irish immigration to America have generally spoken of three periods. Nearly 250,000 Irish
entered the country before 1776, and another 100,000 came between 1776 and
1815. The greatest number of immigrants came to the United States between
1815 and 1855, most notably during the mass evictions associated with the
Great Hunger of the late 1840s, when over 2 million Irish men, women, and
children are thought to have entered the United States (Whelan 1999, 195–196;
Figure 4.3). In 1841, 90 percent of the Irish at home lived in the countryside
(Kennedy, Ell, Crawford, and Clarkson 1999, 27), so "most Irish emigrants
were children of the soil—sons and daughters of tenant farmers, rural arti-
sans, or agricultural laborers" (Miller 1985, 9). For this reason, we must look

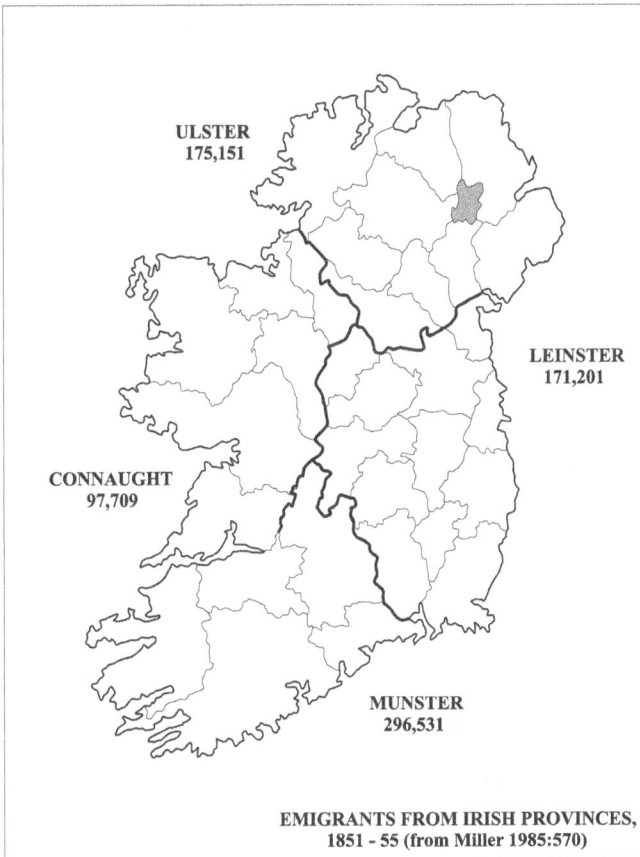

ULSTER
175,151

LEINSTER
171,201

CONNAUGHT
97,709

MUNSTER
296,531

EMIGRANTS FROM IRISH PROVINCES,
1851 - 55 (from Miller 1985:570)

Figure 4.3.
Ireland, show-
ing immigra-
tion from the
four provinces.
Drawing by
author.

to rural Ireland to understand the general habitus of the Irish who entered the United States as immigrants and those who lived for a time in the tenement on Pearl Street.

Long before the tenement Irish were born, Gaelic Ireland was organized as a mixed pastoral and farming culture with a seasonal cycle and settlement pattern that was influenced by the requirements of the cattle herds. Throughout the year, settlement was divided into the *baile* or bally (homeplace) and the *buaile* or booley, the milking place used during the summers (Evans 1957, 27). Wealth and social prestige was partly based on the number of cattle owned, and the society was structured as a complex hierarchy. Social ranks revolved around the family's control of the productive forces, but rank could also be found in personal ability and an individual's position in a multitiered system of clientship (Patterson 1994, 150). A complicated system of fosterage and honor-price also contributed to the acquisition of capital that was embedded within the interwoven network of social relations. Some members of the society would always have a high total value of capital because of their lineage, their personality, and the size of their cattle herd, but commoners could obtain high cultural capital—but not high economic capital—by being gifted storytellers or musicians. The image of the blind harper, such as Turlough O'Carolan, constitutes one highly emotive example of this path to cultural capital (see Edelstein 2001).

The Gaelic social system was also sociospatial. Its settlement network was composed of large ringforts inhabited by lords or other nobles surrounded by a series of smaller ringforts inhabited by individuals who controlled less capital of all kinds. Royal ringforts, the largest in Ireland, were usually sited near religious buildings or ritual sites (see Stout 1997).

The Gaelic world was unsettled when the Normans arrived in the late twelfth century. They established a manorial system in which former pastoralists became rent-paying tenants. Rent-based agriculture quickly became widespread throughout eastern Ireland, though people in the more remote west retained their Gaelic herding traditions far longer. The practice of tenant farming was largely cemented in Ireland with the beginning of the Tudor plantations in the mid-sixteenth century (Mitchell and Ryan 1998, 307–308). The agricultural system created by such landlord-tenant relations continued until the time the residents of 472 Pearl Street left the shores of Ireland for New York City.

Federal census information for the tenement indicates that the vast majority of the residents during the 1850–1870 period were born in Ireland in the first decades of the nineteenth century. Only one or two of the oldest residents had been born in the late eighteenth century. As a result, the Irish-born residents of the tenement were part of the population explosion that began in the late eighteenth century and only ended with the mass starvation and emigration of the late 1840s, during the Great Hunger (Kennedy, Ell, Crawford, and Clarkson 1999, 26). The world they left behind in Ireland was one of landlord-tenant relations and everything this system of social inequality entailed.

The Irish-born tenants of 472 Pearl Street would have learned their collective habitus around their cabin's hearth, the "focal point" of the Irish home (Danaher 1964, 15). Here, children would have listened to traditional stories, internalized gender roles, accepted the annual religious cycle—many of the observances of which represented a mixture of pagan Celtic and Roman Catholic ideas—and learned everything else that Irish custom entailed (see Danaher 1972). Many also would have spoken the Irish language, having acquired it through an extensive set of oral lessons and traditions.

The seasonal cycle for Irish farmers consisted of three different though obviously related sets of activities (Figure 4.4). Most Irish farmers in the early decades of the nineteenth century relied on potatoes for subsistence. The potato cycle consisted of planting in May—in the characteristic cultivation ridges, often referred to as "lazy beds"—and harvest in October. For the poorest farmers, this cycle resulted in the "hungry months" of June and July, just after the previous year's crop had been eaten. The millions of tenant farmers who lived in rural Ireland typically paid their rent in two parts; half was due on May 1, the other on November 1. Given the vagaries of the market, the weather, and other factors farmers could not control, they often found themselves in arrears for their rent. Arrears provided a convenient excuse for many landlords to evict their tenants. For example, at Ballykilcline, in County Roscommon, the landlord, the English Crown, evicted several hundred people for nonpayment of rent in the fall of 1847 and the spring of 1848 (Orser 2004b, 207; 2006b). Farmers typically paid their rent with money they acquired through bartering eggs or raising and selling a pig, duties that usually fell to the women of the family.

The religious cycle—which began with St. Brighid's Day on February 1 and ended on January 6 with Epiphany, which the Irish also called Little Christmas or Women's Christmas—provided the spiritual anchor rural people needed to sustain the often-harsh irregularities of the agricultural cycle and the annual need to pay rent. Numerous festivals and observances colored the year, and when farmers lived near a market town, they could also attend occasional fairs and weekly markets.

The farming people of Ireland—which undoubtedly includes some of the men and women who lived in the Pearl Street tenement—lived in cabins made of stone, turf, or mud and thatch. The cabins were often loosely arranged in a settlement termed a *clachan*, an irregular cluster of homes and fields that,

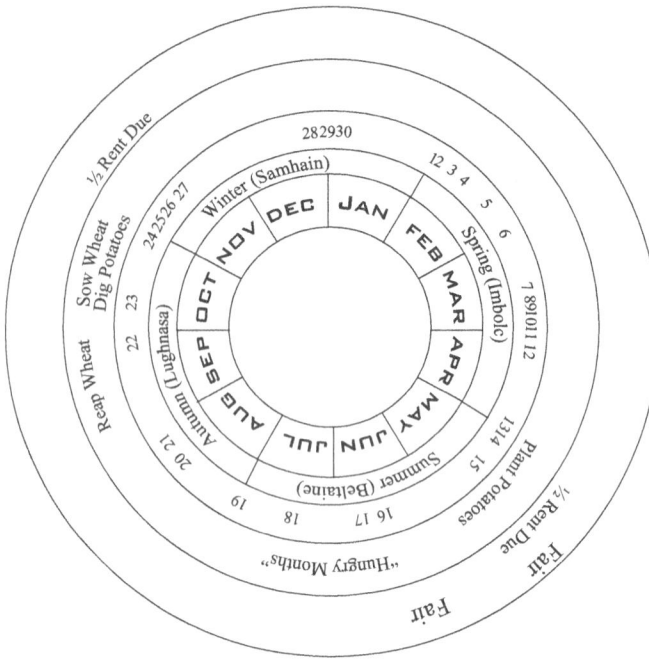

1. Feb. 1 - St. Bridhid's Day
2. Feb. 2 - Candlemas
3.   Shrove Tuesday
4.   Chalk Sunday
5.   Ash Wednesday
6.   Lent
7. Mar. 17 - St. Patrick's Day
8. Mar. 25 - Feast of the Annunciation
            (Lady Day)
9.   Palm Sunday
10.   Good Friday/Easter Sunda
            (The Dance of the Sun;
            The Cake Dance)
11. Apr. 1 - April Fool's Day
12. Apr. 1-9 - The Borrowed Days
13. May 1 - May Day
14. May 3 - Ascension Thursday
15.   Whitsuntide
16. Jun. 23 - St. John's Eve, Bonfire N
17. Jun. 29 - SS. Peter and Paul Day
18. Jul. 15 - St. Swithin's Day
19.   Lughnasa
20. Aug. 15 - The Assumption, The Fes
            of Our Lady in the Harve
21. Aug. 24 - St. Bartholomew's Day
22. Sep. 29 - Michaelmas, The Feast of
            Michael the Archangel
23.   The End of the Harvest
24. Oct. 31 - Hallow E'en
25. Nov. 1 - The Feast of All Saints
26. Nov. 2 - All Souls Day
27. Nov. 11 - Martinmas, St. Martin's I
28. Dec. 24 - Christmas Eve
            Dec. 25 - Christmas
            Dec. 26 - St. Stephen's Day,
            Hunting the Wren Day
29. Dec. 28 - The Festival of the Holy I
            Dec. 31 - New Year's Eve,
            The Night of the Big Por
            Jan. 1 - New Year's Day
            Handsel Monday
30. Jan. 6 - Epiphany, Little Christmas,
            Women's Christmas

Figure 4.4. Seasonal cycle of rural Ireland.
Drawing by author.

unlike towns, had no stores, churches, or public buildings. As the presence of the English grew in the countryside and Anglo-Irish Protestant Ascendency began, rural Irish were encouraged to build houses along roads in a linear fashion (Evans 1992, 60). Even though Ireland was regionally diverse in many cultural features, the main field of experience in nineteenth-century rural Ireland was thus composed of home, fields, and neighbors. The home and the yard was generally the women's domain, whereas the fields were under the men's control (Hull 2004, 254–257).

Considerable romanticism has been constructed around the image of the Irish cabin and its surrounding fields. Rural Ireland before the horrors of the Great Hunger appears to be an idyllic land shrouded in the mists of Celtic time. In truth, however, the rural Ireland of the Irish-born tenants of 472 Pearl Street was a place with a substantial hierarchy built around capitalist notions of power and personal enrichment. In the countryside in Ireland, as elsewhere, economic capital was embodied in the land.

One excellent way to gauge the divisions in rural Irish society during the early years of the nineteenth century is to examine the census of 1841. However, we must admit at the outset that the census was designed and used as a tool of English colonial overlordship. Ireland was part of the British kingdom, and its rulers—who were foreign to the Irish in custom and tradition (as English) and ecclesiastically distinct (as Protestants)—wanted to know just how many Irish people lived on the island. Knowledge was power, and knowledge of the number of the people and their level of "civilization" would help the British rule them in the short run and transform them in the long run. Although the census is imperfect as a tool of historical inquiry, it does provide some important insights into the world the tenement residents left behind.

Like all census takers, though, the commissioners of the Census of Ireland in 1841 had to devise a terminological system that all data collectors could use in the field. Consistency in collection would ensure that the information they gathered from one end of Ireland to the other would be comparable. But the process they undertook to create the "right" classificatory definitions was clearly not a simple one. The angst they felt over the seemingly straightforward concept of "family" provides a useful example of their efforts to divide the Irish population into meaningful units.

The commissioners of the 1841 census noted that the concept of the Irish family had to be carefully considered (Hamilton and Wilde 1843, xvi). They observed that earlier censuses in England had used a common definition of "family" (as defined in Samuel Johnson's famous dictionary) as everyone who lives in the same house. The takers of the 1821 Irish census used this definition but supplemented it with the idea that all the residents had to be supported by the same head of household. This definition thus included apprentices, laborers, and servants who lived with a family whose head of household provided them with room and board. Ten years later, the commissioners altered this definition to include all those people who lived together and who used the same kitchen. Under this definition, a lodger living under the same roof but not actually boarding with the family was deemed a separate family. Their decision to retain this definition in 1841 meant that a "family" was considered to be anyone living in a house or in part of a house with "his or her" (their

Table 4.3. Frequency of Houses by Class, Ireland, 1841

Class	Frequency	Percentage	Residents
1	43,000	3.3	landlords, gentry
2	265,000	20.0	large farmers
3	535,000	40.4	cottiers, small farmers
4	480,000	36.3	laborers
Total	1,323,000	100.0	

Source: John Keating, Irish Famine Facts (Dublin: Teagasc, 1996), 11.

language in 1843) own means of support. This family also included servants and even visitors if they all subsisted by a common means of support. A single male who lived under the roof of a family and paid rent but ate alone also constituted a family.

Without question, the conscious manipulation of the meaning of "family," to give but one example, muddies our ability to understand rural Irish social structure with certainty. Whether such imposed social divisions actually represented the situation on the ground is less important for our purposes than that the commissioners recognized that rural Ireland was not a homogeneous social body of individuals tied to the land in some idealized way. At the very least, they recognized that rural Ireland was a society composed of complicated groupings that crosscut one another and often conflicted.

The obvious consternation and likely debate that preceded the commissioners' final decision about what constituted a family carried over into their decisions about how to enumerate housing. The commissioners created a hierarchy of housing that consisted of four classes. They considered the fourth (and lowest) class of housing to be a one-room mud cabin. A mud cabin with two to four rooms and windows belonged to the third class. A cabin, which they termed a "farm house" (it could also be a house on a small street in a town), with between five and nine rooms and windows was a second-class dwelling. Any residence of better quality than any of the other classes was a first-class house. In 1841, the commissioners counted just over 1 million houses as third and fourth class and a small minority as first class (Table 4.3). And, as might be expected, members of different social classes (or in Bourdieu's terms, members of groups having different total volumes of capital) lived in the various houses. People with greater financial resources (albeit sometimes only on paper) lived in houses of the best quality and of the largest sizes.

The commissioners' division of Irish rural housing into four classes reveals something of the social divisions that existed within society at large. Economics was the most important vector of inequality because the dependent variable was land ownership. Ownership entailed the ability to collect rent from farmers farther down the agricultural ladder. The richest landlords lived in the most fashionable mansions surrounded by well-manicured demesnes, complete with expansive meadows, deer parks, ornamental gardens, ponds, and contemplative follies (see Barnard 2004, 188–225; Malins and the Knight of Glin 1976; Orser 2006a).

The process of dividing the rural population into classes based on economic capital thus seems rather commonsensical and straightforward. The reality, however, was obviously much different because the commissioners stated that they "felt a difficulty in laying down any rule as to what really should be considered a farmer" (Hamilton and Wilde 1843, xxiii). Was any rural landholder a farmer? What about a laborer hired by another farmer? Were such individuals true farmers? And what did the people themselves think? In one parish alone, the commissioners reported that of the 210 landholders, only 170 "returned themselves" as farmers. This rather surprising finding indicates the complexity of the social world the Pearl Street residents left behind.

What is important is the idea that rural Ireland was a place in which social divisions, though perhaps not easily determined, nonetheless were quite real. The simplest agricultural scale, noted by Arthur Young (1780, 14) in the late eighteenth century, consisted of three levels: head landlords (typically families living on demesnes); head tenants (heads of families who may have lived in second- or third-class houses, paid rents to the head landlords, and were listed in the rent books kept by the landlord's agents); and sub- or undertenants (heads of families who lived in third- or fourth-class housing, paid rent to a head tenant, and were most likely unknown to the head landlord and thus not listed in the rent rolls). Landless laborers (those at the bottom of the scale) inhabited the worst kind of fourth-class housing and subsisted on seasonal work and part-time employment at the whim of someone higher up the agricultural ladder. The disparity between head landlords and landless laborers was apparent in every possible way, often even in religious observance because most upper-class landlords were Protestants.

The apparent simplicity of the agricultural system is deceptive, however, because of regional variation. Elsewhere, I have presented the different systems analysts have created in the attempt to understand the epochal structure of Irish agriculture during the mid-nineteenth century (Orser 2004b, 214). This is the system the residents of 472 Pearl Street would have internalized and remembered. Scholars of Irish agriculture generally agree about the broad outline of the agricultural system, the one Young summarized in the late eighteenth century: at the top were landowning landlords and at the bottom were landless laborers. But analysts disagree about the levels in between these two poles. For our purposes, it does not matter whether a "small farmer" controlled nine acres and a "farmer" ten acres, only that distinctions existed between the farming households.

Another aspect of daily life in Ireland was the occurrence of protest, or what were then called "agrarian outrages." Irish farmers, embedded in networks of landlord-tenant relations, created and joined a number of secret societies with colorful names such as Ribbonmen, Whiteboys, and Molly Maguires. Historians disagree about the impetus and eventual goals of the various societies, but we know that Irish farmers occasionally collectivized to fight the overwhelming power of the landlord class. Because they lacked the capacity (economic and judicial) to engage the landlords in open class warfare, they used guerrilla tactics to get their messages heard (Beames 1983, 95). Members of secret societies attempted to resist eviction, decrease rents, and punish harsh landlords.

In a study of agrarian outrages in County Roscommon, Anne Coleman (1999, 38) notes that scholars wishing to judge the incidence of purely farming-related violent protest face difficulties because the people who recorded the crimes often did not separate "regular" crimes from those committed in the name of justice and fair play in the countryside. The records for 1845, however, make it possible to distinguish between agrarian violence and regular crime. Among the protest crimes the government's representatives recorded were committing aggravated assault, setting intentional fires, committing robbery, demanding arms, being armed, writing threatening letters or notices, threatening potential tenants for agreeing to pay too high a rent, vandalism, stealing wool or timber, administering oaths, and firing weapons into buildings. County Roscommon had 383 such offenses in 1845, the highest number in the country, followed by County Tipperary with 286. We may easily suppose that landless laborers at the bottom of the agricultural hierarchy committed agrarian crimes against the landlords at the top of the hierarchy, but some of the crimes were also committed by people inhabiting the middle range of the scale. In other words, undertenants were known to have committed crimes against the head tenants to whom they paid rent (Sigerson 1871, 332). The fact that these outrages were perpetrated in the countryside by people the big landholders probably did not know—because they were subtenants—helped perpetuate the myth that Irish farmers were lawless for no good reason.

This information about homegrown habitus, albeit brief, suggests that rural Ireland was a complex place where individuals and the social groups they occupied were interwoven into numerous webs of social interaction. Rural Ireland was not the idyllic place presented by today's tourist industry. The acquisition of capital in early-nineteenth-century Ireland (in both Marx's classic sense and in Bourdieu's expansion of it) was typically capitalist. Many farmers continued to practice ancient patterns and modified Gaelic customs in remote places such as County Donegal, but the modern practice of farmers paying rents to landlords existed throughout most of Ireland. These landlords could be absentees living in comfort in England (a frequent complaint of the secret societies), "rack-renting" landlords who lived locally but charged exorbitant rents, or owners of large farms who charged rent to the island's less capitalized agriculturalists, and social unrest often bubbled just beneath the surface of Ireland's daily activities. The propertied class worried about expressions of rural unease such as protests, boycotts (a term invented in rural Ireland), crimes against property and person, and even murder. These actions encouraged many landlords to adopt programs of "assisted emigration," whereby they would pay for their tenants' transportation costs out of Ireland. In the case of the Crown estates, such as Ballykilcline in County Roscommon, the British government paid the cost of transporting Irish emigrants to places such as New York City (see Ellis 1977; Orser 2006b).

The habitus of the individual immigrants was well formed when they stepped onto the wharfs of New York. Each person would have known his or her place in the rural hierarchy, they would have understood the limitations the system placed upon them, and they would undoubtedly have formulated expectations about what the future could hold for them and their kin. Prior to the horrors of the Great Hunger—with its mass sickness, disease, and starvation and the evictions that would occur in its wake—the typical Irish man or woman living in the countryside probably did not know too much about the United States or the conditions they would find there. But the rural Irish were not backward-looking ignorant "peasants." Quite the contrary; rural Irish families were conversant with elements of the wider world through the return of migrant laborers and letters sent home from emigrants who had preceded them. Temporary workers began to migrate to find seasonal work before the beginning of the nineteenth century; in some counties, as many as 27 people per 1,000 pursued this labor strategy in 1841 (O'Dowd 1991, 66–67). The experiences of the migrants would have provided at least some information about what others could expect when they left their familiar hearths. Letters from earlier emigrants would also have told families and communities about what to expect in the United States and elsewhere. Such letters could contain factual information and personal experiences that could alert emigrants to the futures they would face. And though historical evidence about how willing the emigrants were to leave their Irish homes is contradictory (see Miller 1985, 223), the fact is that millions of Irish men, women, and children did leave their homes. Some of them landed in New York City and ended up living at least for a time at 472 Pearl Street. But what kind of world did they enter, and, when they entered it, how were they racialized? To discover the various elements of Irish racialization in the United States, we must turn to the epochal structures of the American racial society at the midpoint of the nineteenth century.

Epochal Structures in Irish America

To say that the United States is a nation of immigrants is indeed trite. But gauging the number of Irish immigrants who lived in the country in the 1850–1870 period is a useful exercise because it provides an indication of the magnitude of in-migration from Ireland. This knowledge helps us contextualize the attitudes of nativist Americans toward the Irish. Federal censuses report that the number of Irish-born residents increased from 961,719 (1850) to 1,611,304 (1860) to 1,855,827 (1870) (DeBow 1853, xxxvi; Kennedy 1864, 621; Walker 1872, 340). In 1860, New York City, Boston, and Philadelphia alone had 345,279 Irish-born residents (Kennedy 1864, 608–610). The influx of hundreds of thousands of men, women, and children from purely rural backgrounds, many of whom undoubtedly continued to retain some components of pre-Christian customs in modern form, changed the cultural formula of the United States. One overriding issue that occupied nativist Americans was how to categorize the Irish so their place in the field of American power and authority would cause as little anomie as possible. Nativists used the strategy of marginalizing the Irish as racial inferiors in their attempts to accomplish this goal.

Most Irish entered the United States as unskilled laborers, a fact that suited nativists well. By mid-century, Irish immigrants constituted about 87 percent of the unskilled work force (Brighton 2005, 109). Irish men and women were consigned largely to menial jobs in America's expanding factory system, while Irish women entered sweatshops, did piecework in their tiny apartments, or hired themselves out as domestics. The image of "Bridget" or "Biddy," the bumbling, incurably stupid Irish servant girl, became a staple of nineteenth-century American humor in all forms of media, including on the stage and in song (Schlereth 1991, 72–73; also see Knobel 1986).

The work positions open to newly arrived Irish men and women indicate that one of the most significant epochal structures in the United States of the mid-nineteenth century was the conflict between nativists and immigrants. Although the United States was an independent nation that had fought two wars with Great Britain, it retained its English character, including its language and literature. The nation's strong link with Britain, if perhaps only emotional, meant that Americans maintained some of Britain's attitudes, including a perspective on the "wild Irish." One prominent politician of the early Republic expressed this attitude by stating that legal restrictions were needed to prevent "wild hordes of Irish" from upsetting the tranquility of the new United States (Wilson 1998, 48).

Opinions such as these intensified after the 1830s. The economic capital of the nineteenth-century immigrating Irish was generally lower than that of the Protestant Irish who had emigrated earlier. This was largely related to the lack of economic opportunity for the new immigrants, which declined precipitously as the new wave of immigration began. In 1820, only 21 percent of the immigrant Irish were classified as unskilled, whereas sixteen years later, almost 60 percent were so identified (Anbinder 1992, 5). During this period, some states enacted statutes intended to identify and monitor immigrants. The New York legislature, for example, passed An Act Concerning Passengers in Vessels Coming to the Port of New York in February 1824 that required each immigrant to file a "report of himself in writing, on oath or affirmation" with the mayor or city recorder within twenty-four hours of reaching the United States (Abbott 1924, 107). Failure to do so would result in a fine of $100.

Nativist perceptions of the incoming Irish—which focused on their perceived lack of skilled (i.e., urban) trades and on their religious beliefs—created an overriding epochal structure based on racialization. Historians examining American race, mostly through the lens of whiteness, have documented the racial treatment of the Irish in America. Much of their fascination with the Irish stems from the reality that when the so-called famine Irish entered the United States—most of whom were Catholic, poor, and skilled in agriculture rather than industry—nativists assigned them a nonwhite status.

In his study of whiteness and its role in creating the American working class, David Roediger (1991, 146–147) documents how Irish workers were slotted into the racial structure. In the American South, slaveowners and labor bosses often considered them to be more expendable than costly African American slaves. Roediger notes that people often referred to gangs of Irish workers as "Irish slaves," and commentators frequently compared free Irish and enslaved African men and women. An English member of Parliament traveling through the American South in the 1870s dryly observed that some of the tenant farmers' houses he saw were so bad that they were even "unfit for an Irishman" (Campbell 1879, 393). The transition Roediger charts over the nineteenth century details how Irish immigrants used various strategies to adapt to the U.S. context. A major feature of this adaptive process involved an Irish claim to coveted jobs because of what they perceived as their entitlement for being white.

Noel Ignatiev (1995) explores the process by which the Irish were racialized during the nineteenth century. He notes that nativist Americans used racially charged language founded on anti-black bigotry to identify the Irish as "niggers turned inside out." African Americans were similarly labeled "smoked Irish" (Ignatiev 1995, 41). In summarizing the situation facing the nineteenth-century Irish in America, Ignatiev concludes:

> In the course of my research I learned that no one gave a damn for the poor Irish. Even the downtrodden black people had Quakers and abolitionists to bring their plight to public attention (as well as the ability to tell their own stories effectively), but there is no Irish-American counterpart of the various Philadelphia studies of the condition of free colored people, let alone an autobiography to stand alongside the mighty work of Frederick Douglass. (178)

Concerted efforts to denigrate the Irish actually had a long history in the New World and an even longer history in Ireland. Though whether the Irish, as a group, were racialized remains controversial among historians, good evidence exists to indicate that the racialization of the Irish in the New World had its roots in mid-seventeenth-century Britain. During this period, Oliver Cromwell used mass murder and forced relocation in a conscious program of ethnic cleansing of the Irish in Britain. Historians have estimated that during the 1650s, over 50,000 Irish men, women, and children living in Ireland were transported to the tiny island of Barbados as indentured servants. The terms of their indenture mirrored aspects of bondage, and the Irish there were treated little better than slaves (O'Callaghan 2000, 75). This was not the only place in the New World that whites attempted forcibly to indenture or perhaps even enslave Irish people; in 1653, 400 Irish children were stolen from their beds and sent to New England and Virginia (Linebaugh and Rediker 2000, 59).

But the process of racialization actually began much earlier in Ireland. This line of investigation is as controversial as the study of the racialization of the Irish during the nineteenth century, but Theodore Allen's (1994) study of the racialization of Ireland by the colonizing English is compelling. He notes that Irish history provides an excellent example of "racial oppression without reference to alleged skin color or, as the jargon goes, 'phenotype'" (22). In other words, the power of the example of racialization of the Irish stems from the removal of skin color as a physical marker. This makes the process considerably more nuanced and complex than we might otherwise suppose.

Allen outlines how English colonizers in Ireland enacted racialization through a series of events that, when examined as a whole, assume the character of a long-range strategy. The first phase of the strategy began with the Anglo-Normans, who sought to establish themselves as lords over the agricultural Irish. The second strategy was enacted by English settlers and their descendants born in Ireland, and involved the destruction of recalcitrant Gaelic chiefs and the co-opting of the more compliant ones. Both strategies were messy affairs because they necessarily included intrigue, bribery, and double-dealing as numerous factions struggled for position, power, and control. The Protestant plantation—which took place in the provinces of Munster and Ulster and in the midlands before the mid-seventeenth century—constituted the third and most long-lasting aspect of the English colonial strategy. This scheme entailed replacing Irish natives with Scottish and English farmers with the goal of "civilizing" the landscape.

The Protestant Ascendancy, the rise in power of Anglo settlers in Ireland, was an important feature of the Anglification of Ireland. One historian of the Ascendancy summarized it as a historical period in which individuals considered Protestant and properly English excelled and those who were not did not: "For the Catholic Irish, the eighteenth century was a period in which they were legal unentities, bereft of elementary rights, punished for their religion, isolated from any say in the development of their own country. For the Anglo-Irish, it was the most constructive and fruitful period of their existence" (McConville 1986, 130). Allen (1994, 81–90) documented how the institution of the penal laws (or, as they were then called, "the popery laws") provided the legal basis for discrimination against the native Irish. These laws, which existed for most of the seventeenth century, were designed to stifle, if not end, Catholicism in Ireland. Parliament enacted the first two penal laws in 1695 and did not repeal the final act until 1829, a date that may have been personally remembered by some of the older residents of the Pearl Street tenement. Various penal laws were designed to repress Catholic worship services, exclude Catholics from public office, and sanction discrimination against the clergy. Historians consider one of the most important penal laws to be the Act to Prevent the Further Growth of Popery (enacted in 1704) which, in Bourdieu's terms, was designed to limit the ability of Catholics to acquire economic capital. Under this statute, a Catholic could not purchase land, inherit land from a Protestant, or take a lease longer than thirty-one years. For Allen, statutes like the 1704 law were designed to racialize the Catholic Irish legally by depriving them of their civil rights at the same time that British lawmakers were passing laws also disfranchising Africans in Virginia (Allen 1994, 84). Given what we now know about the overall plan of the British empire (e.g., Ferguson 2002), it is not difficult to view the two events as philosophically linked.

Centuries before the rise of the Protestant Ascendancy, English authorities in Dublin had become increasingly concerned about the Gaelicization of the English settlers. Outnumbered and away from home, fourteenth-century English settlers learned Irish ways, including the Irish language. To terminate this process, which we might term "colonialist acculturation," the authorities enacted a series of statutes designed to keep the English and the Irish apart in a general program that at least one Irish historian has labeled a medieval example of apartheid (Lydon 1994, 155). In an important cultural sense, the Protestant Ascendancy was the historical culmination of the process of Anglification, even though it took much longer to accomplish than English colonial officials would have wished.

The thesis Allen outlined is controversial because he claims in part that Irish men and women, and even their children, learned the theory of racialization through practical experience in Ireland, long before most even imagined that they would live and die in the United States. Allen's point is important because he stresses that the theory of racialization is inherent in the capitalist project. By racializing some people as inferior, it is easier—both practically and ethically—to confine them to the lowest-paying, dirtiest jobs available. In rural Ireland, during the era characterized by inherently unequal tenant-landlord relations, Irish tenant farmers were expected to work hard, pay their rent, and continue to provide the funds that supported the lifestyles of the wealthiest landowners. The process of learning race was most certainly continued in America, but there, unlike in Ireland, American nativists had large populations of "others"—people of African and Asian heritage—on whom they could turn their attention. In any case, the racialization of the Irish began in Ireland, but it was perfected in America.

In an earlier study of one townland in the Irish midlands, Ballykilcline in County Roscommon, I investigated the enactment of racialization in a small locality (Orser 2004b, 196–246). This examination, which was also meant to illustrate a multiscalar method that links epochal structures with localized archaeological sites, shows the practical characteristics of racialization in Ireland before the mass depopulation of the late 1840s. In this particular instance (which was played out in countless places throughout rural Ireland at the time), the basic structure of landlord-tenant relations was embedded within a social field that had been racialized by politico-legal enactments such as the penal laws. At the same time, the atmosphere created by the anti-popery laws provided a backdrop for the unease and paranoia of the landed class. They were acutely aware of the violent actions of the Molly Maguires, the Ribbonmen, and other clandestine organizations. The situation at Ballykilcline, a Crown estate, was somewhat unique because the tenants' landlord was Queen Victoria. In the final analysis, though, even given her exalted position on the world's stage, she was just another absentee landlord to her Irish tenants. The tenants still had to pay rents to someone they would never meet and who undoubtedly would not have met them even if she had had the chance.

One important element of the New World racialization of the Irish was the frequent conflation of them with Africans. Such comparisons were not strictly a New World phenomenon. Numerous visitors to rural Ireland—both English and American—compared the people of the Irish countryside with the "Hottentots" of southern Africa (Orser 2004b, 1–3). Charles Kingsley, while traveling through northwestern Ireland in 1860, made the egregious statement that the Irish were "white chimpanzees" and opined that if they were black, "one would not feel it so much" (Kingsley 1892, 236). By "it," I imagine that Kingsley meant disheartenment at the condition of the white "primates." The dilemma for Kingsley was not that the rural Irish were debased and oppressed, only that they were light skinned while they were experiencing such hardship.

Conflating the Irish and Africans was a common convention in popular literature. In 1848, the English magazine *Punch* published verses that included a line about "Six-foot Paddy" that said "You to Sambo I compare" (Curtis 1996, 45). Part of the racial mythology of the nineteenth century held that when Irish men and women were sent to the Caribbean as workers, they would actually turn black through long their association with Africans. Englishman Thomas Moore (1857, 562) published a poem entitled "Paddy's Metamorphosis" in which this transformation takes place. He observed that after only two years on "some West-India island," Paddy from Cork had turned black and had developed wooly hair (see Orser 2004b, 4).

The project of racializing the Irish in America thus has trans-Atlantic elements; we find evidence of it in both the United States and Great Britain. In this chapter, I explore only two of the expressions of how the Irish were racialized. Both represent pertinent aspects of the racial epochal structure of America during the time 472 Pearl Street was inhabited by Irish. The first expression appeared as pictorial images intended to create and reinforce Irish stereotypes, and the second appeared in anthropological science intended to provide a scientific basis for Irish inferiority.

Word images that were specifically designed to denigrate the Irish, such as Kingsley's, accompanied the colonization efforts of the English by the sixteenth century. The use of pictorial images to do the same were more widely accessible because they did not rely on literacy to be effective. In the early nineteenth century, the cartoonish image of the crude devious Irish character made the rounds in London. One image, dated May 4, 1804, entitled "Knavish Pat—A Tale," shows a crude-looking Irish man sitting at a table being waited on by a nicely dressed young lady who holds a plate of food in each hand (Figure 4.5). She looks as if she is going to place the food on the table for Pat.

Pat has the short-stemmed clay pipe—the ubiquitous dudeen—in his mouth as he tilts the chair forward. At his feet is a hungry dog, possibly his traveling companion, and at his side is a bindle. The tale appears thus:

An Irish man came late unto an Inn,
And ask'd the Maid what Meat there was within,
"Cow heels," she answer'd, "and a Breast of Mutton."
"Then," quoth the Irish man, "as I'm no glutton,
Either of these will serve; to night the Breast,
The Heels i' the morning, then light Meat is best."
At Night he took the Breast, and did not pay
I' the Morning took the Heels and ran away. (Curtis 1996, 35)

One interesting element of this portrayal is that Pat the Irishman is deemed deficient because of his character, not because of his genetic composition. Anti-Irish caricaturists typically depicted the Irish as oafish brutes until about the 1840s, when they started to "simianize" them. This process continued until about 1890; it reached its apogee in the 1860s (Curtis 1971, 29). Artists executed drawings of the Irish with wildly apish features in concert with the growing controversy over the African slave trade, which coincided with the Irish occupancy of 472 Pearl Street. As a result, the pictorial simianization of the Irish constituted part of the lived experience of the tenement residents during their stay in the building and, for the older residents, a possible feature of their memories of their homeland. The simianization project began only five years after the British outlawed slavery in its empire. Britain's official pronouncement on human bondage, however, did not put an end to anti-black racism. Quite the contrary, after emancipation white bigots could imagine that freedmen and -women—and those of African heritage who had never been placed in bondage—continued to represent a threat to white hegemony.

L. Perry Curtis (1971) has made an exhaustive survey of the process of visual simianization of the Irish. An examination of the images he reproduced in his study provides a quick primer on the aping of the Irish. As Curtis explains, the "pre-simian" phase of representing the Irish peasant focused mostly on rural political uprisings but also included the attempt of the Irish to repeal the Act of Union. Artists of the time depicted the Irish as brutish Celts, but their overall design was to imprint on the English and U.S. publics an image that depicted behavior of the Irish as uncultured and their appearance as primitive. Curtis demonstrates that artists did not make the transition to full simianization of the Irish until the 1860s. At that point, anti-Irish artists no longer illustrated their subjects as merely crude; they presented them as fully ape-like. The simian Irish in imagery of this period have the ape's unkempt hair, pug

Figure 4.5. "Knavish Pat." London, 1804.

nose, and extended jaw. Their wild poses, which often include jumping in the air, are also meant to telegraph the Irishman's similarly to orangutans and chimpanzees. Artists continued to promote the image of the Irish Celts as simian throughout the twentieth century, even as the conflict in Northern Ireland continued to express the colonial realities of daily life for those Irish who lived on the island but outside the Republic of Ireland (Curtis 1996, 82–83).

Numerous images illustrate how some American artists worked to link the Irish in Ireland with Africans and thus provide a visual lesson about the supposed genetic link between the two in America. One especially telling drawing is Frederick B. Opper's "The King of A-Shantee," which was sketched for the American humor magazine *Puck* (Curtis 1971, 63). The drawing, published on February 15, 1882, shows an Irish man and a women with exaggerated ape-like facial features (Figure 4.6). The man sits cross-legged on a wooden tub outside a wooden cabin. On his head he wears the three-legged iron kettle that was used in every Irish home in the nineteenth century. Every Irish person alive at

Figure 4.6. "The King of A-Shantee." *Puck*, vol. 10, no. 258, February 15, 1882, 378.

the time would have readily recognized this object. In his left hand he holds a tiny white clay smoking pipe (the dudeen). He has a short club (the shillelagh) tucked under his right arm. The women, who is partly in the shade, stands inside the door of the cabin, looking at the seated man. An apparently empty liquor bottle lies on the ground near the wooden tub, and a goat stands on a steep hill in the background.

At least two elements of this image are relevant here in addition to Opper's obvious attempt to provide a denigrating image of the Irish that would resonate with nativist Americans. First, his play on words for "A-Shantee" was intended to link Ireland and Africa in the psyche of his readers. With this clever word, Opper evoked both the Ashanti of West Africa and the shanty Irish, a term used in the United States to describe the working-class Irish who built the nation's canals and railroads. Of course, the vast majority of Americans who saw the image would have had no real knowledge of the Ashanti in Africa. Opper apparently intended to play on the concept that the idle Irish, like Africans, were a primitive people. Second, the drawing demonstrates that Opper had no knowledge of rural Ireland. The house style he depicted was unknown in Ireland; it bears a greater similarity to poor rural housing in the American South. Irish builders never used the clapboard sliding he depicted. Opper's mistakes are enlightening because they demonstrate that his drawings did not rely on ethnographic accuracy. His intent was purely ideological; he sought to depict the Irish in an unfavorable light and thus to appeal to individuals and groups who despised Irish immigrants.

The second drawing, entitled "American Gold," depicts Opper's view of the trans-Atlantic link between the Irish Celts and their American immigrant counterparts (Curtis 1971, 65). The drawing appeared on May 24, 1882, also in *Puck* (Figure 4.7). Opper's picture is divided into two panels. On the left side, stereotypical Irish laborers are involved in "city improvements," digging up the street and carrying bricks for building construction. In a small inset at the top, an apparently Irish woman bends over a large wooden washtub (the same kind of tub that Opper used in "The King of A-Shantee"). In the right panel, Opper shows an Irish family sitting on the edge of a cliff on the west coast of Ireland, waiting for a ship under both steam and wind power to make landfall. The boat is filled with huge sacks bearing dollar signs. The family consists of a husband, a wife, four small children, and three pigs. An empty liquor bottle lays at the family's feet, as it did in Figure 4.6, and behind them on a steep hill is a dilapidated house, identical in type to the house in Figure 4.6. A crudely built unstable flagpole stands in the background near the house with a pair of patched breeches waving from it. The inset in this panel shows two men who are presumed to be professional agitators standing on the coast looking through telescopes. Both are peering at the distant ship, and behind them is a stool holding a wooden ballot box. The side of the box reads "Agitation and Disturbance Fund." According to Curtis (1971, 65), Opper's intent in this image was political, to show that the hard-earned dollars Irish immigrants made in America and then sent back home really went to professional agitators rather than to the relatives who needed them, who were idling about.

Opper's images of the Irish at home and in the United States are highly racialized and do not draw from lived reality. They were central to the program of framing the epochal structures of American race as it pertained to people like those living at 472 Pearl Street. The presence of such images, and there are many more, in a widely distributed American magazine demonstrates the role of anti-Irish racialization as an element of habitus formation for non-Irish Americans. That the images were published in the 1880s demonstrates the

Figure 4.7. "American Gold." *Puck*, vol. 11, no. 272, May 24, 1882, 194.

tenacity of anti-Irish sentiment in America and expresses the desire of some citizens to demonize the Irish just as some Irish individuals were obtaining prominence in white America as politicians and business leaders.

The racialization of the Irish in Ireland and the United States was not conducted in a vacuum. Artists did not dream up their biased images from whole cloth. Even Curtis (1971, 90–91) acknowledged that some Irish men and women exhibited midfacial prognathism, a physical reality that anthropologists had proven with empirical measurement. The history of this research agenda, which reaches back to the earliest days of human physical analysis and forward into the mid-twentieth century, revolves around the identification of Irish men and women as Celts.

The word "Celt" or "Celtic" has at least three meanings. It can refer to a language family, a style of art, or a people who share distinct physical and cultural characteristics. The association of the word "Celt" with physical features is most pertinent for the present discussion because of the way various writers and analysts have used the concept to mean a distinct race of people.

Greek and Roman writers were the first to take note of people they termed "Celts." They perceived them to be a distinct race of people, by which they meant that the Celts were different from themselves. Chroniclers such as Herodotus largely invented the Celts as a people. Once they were so identified, others continued to promote their existence. For example, Caesar consciously constructed the Celts as a culture residing west of the Rhine to promote his own prowess as the conqueror of a strange, fierce race (Wells 2001, 114–118).

Commentators who wrote about the Celts sought from the beginning to identify them by their physical appearance. Their observations stressed that one could identify a Celt simply from the way he or she looked. Early writers such as Posidonius and Strabo identified the tall stature of the Celts as their most distinguishing characteristic. Polybius, in the first century BCE, linked the physicality of the Celts to their distinctive "Nordic" appearance: light eyes, hair, and skin (Holmes 1899, 283). Physical anthropologists long continued to associate Celtic heritage with Nordic physical characteristics. Having made this connection, it was easy for mainstream scientists to conclude that Celts represented part of the "white race."

The notion that Celts were white constitutes an element of the Teutonic Origins Theory (Gossett 1963, 84–122). Scholars throughout the world used writings from ancient authors such as Tacitus to promote the concept of a white race and then set out to identify its members. Several influential American writers promoted the concept of whiteness in the late nineteenth century, just when nativist hysteria about immigration was growing. Scholars such as Daniel G. Brinton (1890) penned highly influential works that provided a scientific basis for a concept of whiteness that included the Celts. His work, though seriously flawed, was at least an improvement over that of John Beddoe (1885, 11), who wrote that the Irish represented a strain of the "Africanoid" race.

It seems incongruous that Brinton could include the Celtic Irish under the rubric of whiteness at a time when strong anti-Irish sentiments pervaded the Anglo-American world. He was no Hibernophile; in fact, he was just the opposite. Brinton linked physical appearance with mental capacity and held a strongly romantic view of the Celtic past. To him, the great Celts of Ireland were the majestic Tuatha de Danann, mythic warriors of antiquity who gloriously fought all invaders and tenaciously held on to their homeland. In Brinton's mythology, immigrants to the shores of the United States and Great Britain were not part of this glorious past; they were part of the degenerate Irish. Brinton believed that the Irish were doomed to extinction because of their character. He stereotypically perceived them as "turbulent, boastful, alert, courageous, but deficient in caution, persistence, and self-control." He further noted that the Irish have "never succeeded in forming an independent state, and are a dangerous element in the body politic of a free country." As if this were not enough, he added that they were "fanatic and bigoted" in their religion (1890, 155).

Brinton's bias was probably based on his attitude toward the Irish men and women with whom he came in contact or, like so much racial bigotry, on messages he received from racialized caricatures and newspaper accounts and the comments of his acquaintances. His "lectures on ethnography" have the ring of science, but his efforts were nowhere near as rigorous as those of other scholars. A thorough understanding of the plan to promote the science of Irish physicality can be understood by looking at the work of William Z. Ripley (1899), Carleton Coon (1939), and Earnest Hooton and Wesley Dupertuis (1955).

William Ripley believed that human groups exhibited two types of characteristics: cultural and physical. He argued that two distinct cultures that came into direct face-to-face contact could commingle their cultural characteristics, just as they could combine their physical traits through marriage and procreation. Human groups could create political and national boundaries, but these divisions were artificial; they could not hide the true racial composition of the people. As Ripley put it: "Race denotes what man *is*, all these other details of social life represent what man *does* (Ripley 1899, 32, emphasis in original). Ripley understood the task of the racial investigator to be scientific discovery of the physical characteristics that identified the various human races. The inherent physicality of race was a given; the scientist's job was to discover its variations.

Ripley accepted the scientific wisdom of the late nineteenth century and postulated that scientists could identify human races by such characteristics as head form, the color of hair and eyes, and stature. He disputed that skin color distinguished the different races because he saw no correlation between it and anatomy. He believed that identifying the world's four races by skin color was misguided because the "real determinant" of race was the color of the hair and eyes.

Using such ideas as his framework, Ripley decided that no single white race existed. Instead, he favored the presence of three white races: Teutonic, Mediterranean, and Celtic. The Teutonic race was characterized by a long head, a long face, a narrow nose, light hair color, blue eyes, and a tall stature. Members of the Mediterranean race also had long heads and faces, but they had broad noses, dark brown or even black hair, and dark eyes. They were also of medium height. The Celts presented Ripley with special problems, however.

Ripley's "Celtic problem" resulted from his uncritical acceptance of the views of leading ethnologists that Celts had blonde hair and blue eyes. They were what most people today would imagine as "Aryans." But Ripley noted that some Celts were short in stature and had dark hair and eyes. He noted the presence of two kinds of Irish Celts in the United States: those with red hair and freckles and those with light-colored eyes and dark hair. Given what he perceived as the problem of identifying the "Celtic race," Ripley decided that only linguists could correctly use the term "Celtic." He thus decided to call his third European race "Alpine" rather than "Celtic." He used the term to refer to the prehistoric Hallstatt culture, which, according to archaeologists, had occupied a geographical area fairly consistent with the range of the Celtic language. Ripley's next task was to determine the racial characteristics of this Alpine race, which he identified as a round head and a broad face, a somewhat broad nose, light chestnut-colored hair, and hazel-gray eyes. Members of the Alpine race were usually of medium height and of stocky build.

When Ripley examined the racial classifications devised by other scholars, he chose to debate their schemes rather than question their overall research design. The question was not whether distinct human races existed, but how they were to be properly recognized in the real world. Within the structure of the three races, Ripley perceived the world's peoples as divided into "existing varieties." He believed that anthropologists' use of the term "race" was the same as zoologists' use of "type" (Ripley 1899, 598).

Years later, Harvard-trained physical anthropologist Carleton Coon continued Ripley's project. In fact, Coon (1939, v) was so enamored with Ripley that he glowingly dedicated his book *Races of Europe* to him. Coon's goal was to use Ripley's work as a starting point but to update it based on the findings of early-twentieth-century physical anthropologists. Coon agreed with Ripley that the word "race" presented inherent problems, but he nonetheless presented his *Races of Europe* as a full investigation of the "white race." He was intent on identifying the origins of whiteness and began his book with a thorough examination of "Pleistocene White Men."

Coon was a sophisticated researcher. He relied on a multidisciplinary approach to press his claims, which sought to chart the history of whiteness from the Pleistocene to the Middle Ages, which he referred to as the "threshold of the modern period" (Coon 1939, 241). Like his intellectual mentor, he too categorized the "Kelts" as members of the white race. Also like Ripley, Coon examined skulls from the Hallstatt region and, concluding that little homogeneity existed among the crania, decided that the "Kelts" were as mixed in "race" as in culture. But from this admixture, they had developed into a recognizable national "type."

The concept of the national type brought the modern-day Irish to the forefront of the analysis. Coon, in his effort to describe the Irish Celt, noted that the "composite Irishman" (in the 1930s) was about 35 years old, roughly 172 centimeters tall, and about 157 pounds in weight. Coon's Irishman was muscular and powerful with broad shoulders and long arms. His vision of the Celt is reminiscent of the image originally presented by Caesar and others in the ancient world who attempted to idealize the Celtic warrior as a fierce combatant, a member of a culture whom only the brave could overcome.

Coon's image of the perfect Celt was a departure from his otherwise staunchly scientific ethos. But his true perspective on the Irish, and perhaps by extension his perspective on all non-WASPs, is demonstrated by his argument that Irish Catholics were the descendants of European Cro-Magnons, whereas Anglican Protestants were "Nordic" in origin (Coon 1939, 378–379). These racialized opinions by a renowned physical anthropologist demonstrate many things, but perhaps most telling is the extent to which a racialized habitus can seep into all social classes. His usage shows how such views can trump scientific methods and empirical findings. Coon's view recalls Robert Knox's comment, printed long before the advent of scientific physical anthropology, that "civilized man" could not sink lower than the rural Irish (1850, 324–325).

One perhaps can forgive Coon's perspective on the Irish as a "national" type. After all, he did his research and wrote his book in the 1930s, a period in U.S. history when the future of the nation was very much in question. Huge numbers of unemployed men and women walked the streets as a result of the depression, and the accompanying labor unrest—much of it promoted by radical European immigrants—must have caused educated elites such as Coon considerable consternation. It also was not entirely clear at the time where people of Irish heritage would throw their allegiance after the rise of Hitler. In fact, after April 1933, the director of the National Museum of Ireland was a member of the Nazi Party (see O'Donoghue 1998). Coon, who was a member of the Office of Strategic Services, the precursor to the CIA, must have found this alarming.

At the same time that Harvard graduate Carleton Coon was writing his study of European race, professors at his alma mater were starting an extensive examination of the anthropometry of Ireland. In fact, Coon used the data the Harvard team had collected during its preliminary investigation into the Irish race (Hooton and Dupertuis 1955, 239). The directors of the project, Earnest Hooton and Wesley Dupertuis, called their project the Harvard Anthropological Survey of Ireland. They conducted their field research in January–May 1934 and December 1934–May 1936 but did not publish their findings until 1955. Their goal was to map the "racial" characteristics of Ireland with the intent of discovering discrete populations within the island. Part of their rationale stemmed from the fact that the Boston area in which they lived had such a strong Irish association: "Here in Massachusetts we live among Americans of recent Irish extraction; we work with them; we play with them; sometimes we dispute with them, and most of the time we are governed by them," they wrote (Hooton and Dupertuis 1955, v). In addition to the anthropometric fieldwork, the Harvard project involved ethnographic research conducted under the direction of Lloyd Warner. The publications that resulted from this work, dedicated to Warner and Hooton respectively, are classics in anthropological ethnography (Arensberg 1937; Arensberg and Kimball 1940).

Hooton and Dupertuis's methods are intriguing from our twenty-first-century vantage point. After conducting what archaeologists derisively term a "windshield survey"—driving through the countryside and looking for discrete physical types—the team discovered that their task would be formidable. They quickly concluded that they would need help acquiring willing subjects. They discovered that they could not simply approach country people and expect an affirmative reply after asking whether they could measure their physical features. Hooton and Dupertuis had to turn to the clergy for help. Most religious figures were sympathetic to the project, and several parish priests announced the need for volunteer subjects at Mass, embellishing their comments with the grand notion that the parishioners' could benefit "the glory of Ireland" by submitting "to being measured by the good doctor from America" (Hooton and Dupertuis 1955, 7). In some cases, the local priest was not persuasive enough and Hooton and Dupertuis had to hire "a local whipper-in . . . to round up a collection of men from the area" (7). Comments such as these suggest that these twentieth-century physical anthropologists retained some of the ideas of late-nineteenth-century classifiers such as Ripley; they appeared to view their subjects as zoological specimens. In any case, the Harvard team did take measurements throughout Ireland, north and south, and reported their findings under the heading "Catholics by County Subgroups." The identified groups are of interest here because they approximate the racial types accepted by most early twentieth-century physical anthropologists who had investigated human variability in Europe.

In keeping within the tradition set by their colleagues who sought to categorize the races of Europe, Hooton and Dupertuis identified eight races in Ireland: Pure Nordic, Predominantly Nordic, Keltic, East Baltic, Dinaric, Nordic Mediterranean, Pure Mediterranean, and Nordic Alpine. They presented detailed anthropometric information on the distribution and physical characteristics of each type (Figures 4.8 and 4.9). They based their conclusions on detailed empirical measurements, including calculations of head height, head circumference, size of forehead, thoracic index, stature, size of ear lobes, facial asymmetry, and so forth. They also used the classic qualitative measures of hair and eye color to define the races. Reporting these empirical data consti-

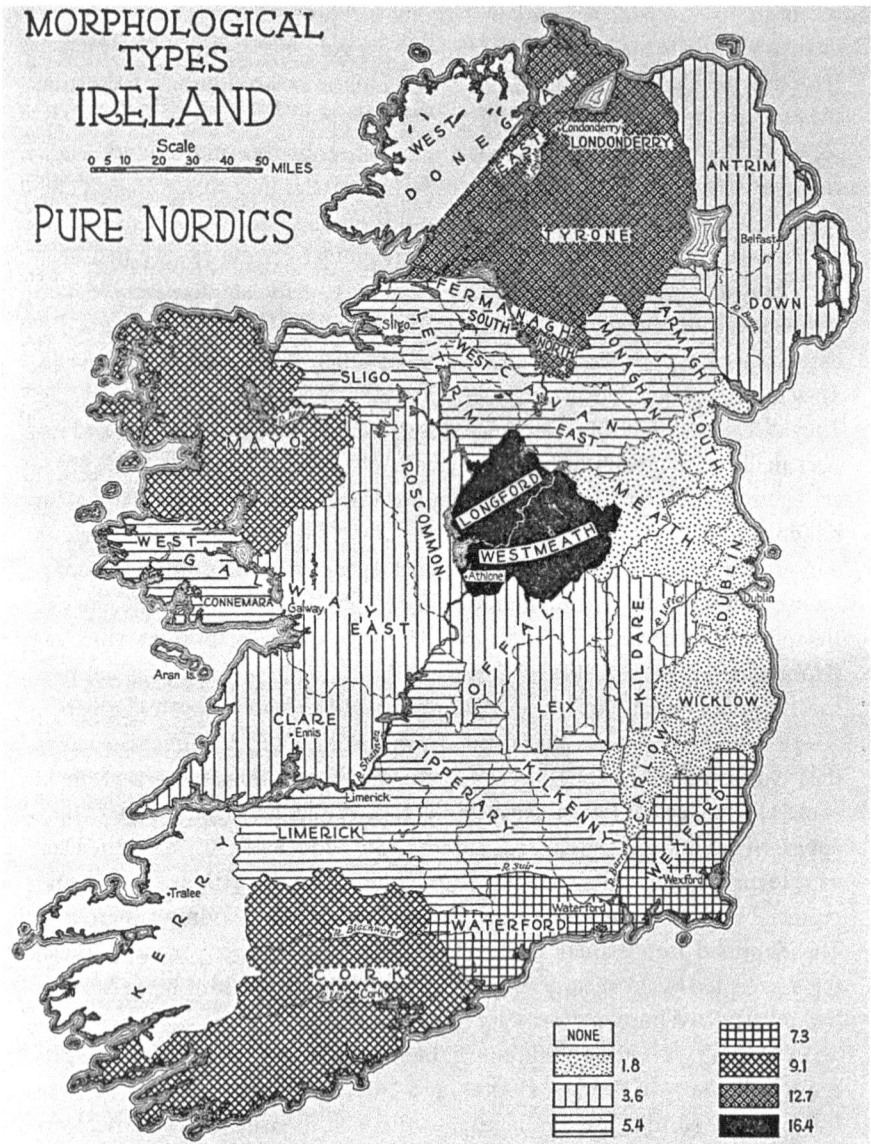

Figure 4.8. Hooton and Dupertuis' distribution of Pure Nordics in Ireland. Earnest A. Hooton and C. Wesley Dupertuis, *The Physical Anthropology of Ireland*, Papers of the Peabody Museum of Archaeology and Ethnology, vol. 30, no. 1–2, 1955. Reprinted courtesy of the Peabody Museum of Archaeology and Ethnology, Harvard University.

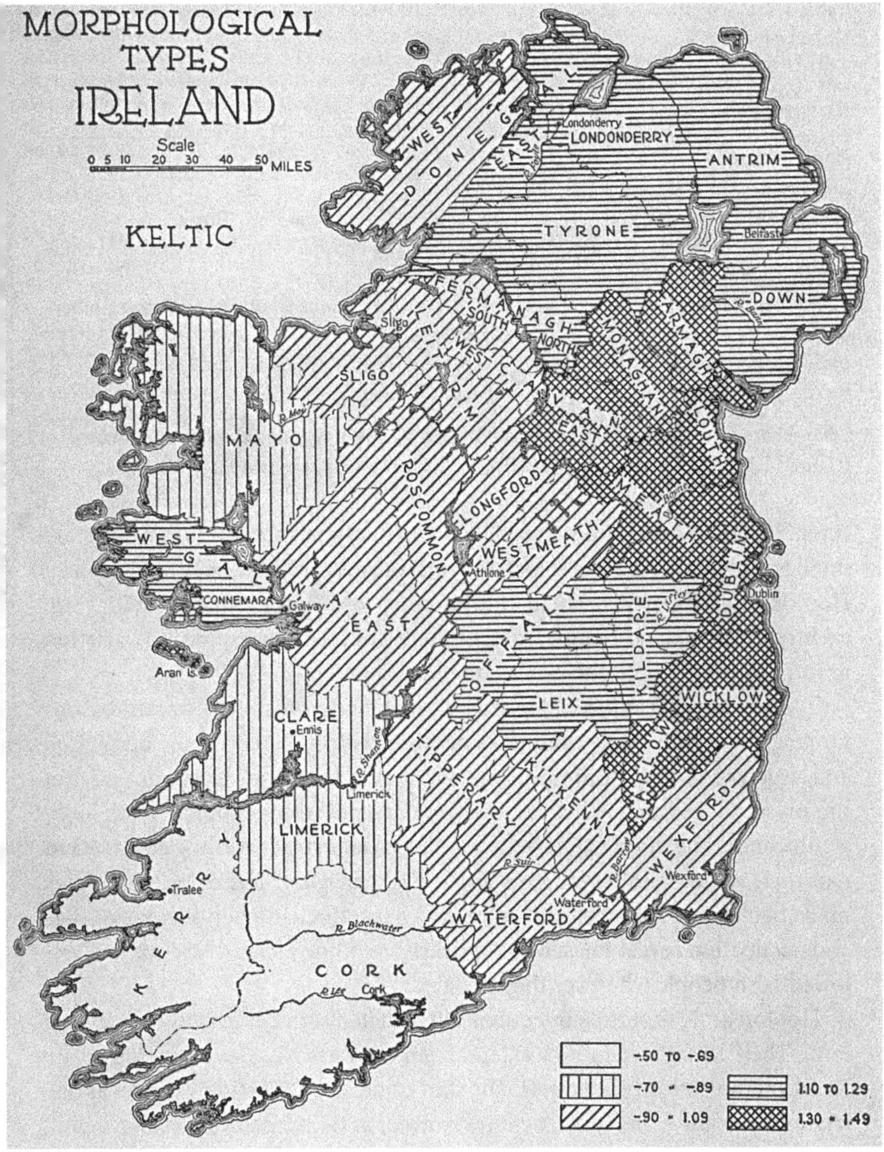

MORPHOLOGICAL
TYPES
IRELAND
Scale
0 5 10 20 30 40 50 MILES

KELTIC

-50 TO -.69
-.70 - -.89 | 1.10 TO 1.29
-.90 - 1.09 | 1.30 - 1.49

Figure 4.9. Hooton and Dupertuis' distribution of Keltics in Ireland. Earnest A. Hooton and
C. Wesley Dupertuis, *The Physical Anthropology of Ireland*, Papers of the Peabody Museum
of Archaeology and Ethnology, vol. 30, no. 1–2, 1955. Reprinted courtesy of the Peabody
Museum of Archaeology and Ethnology, Harvard University.

Table 4.4. Correlation of Hooton and Dupertuis' Irish Educational Rank and Skin Colors

Racial type	Educational Rank	Skin Color
Pure Nordic	1	pink skin
East Baltic	2	pink skin
Predominantly Nordic	3	almost as pink-skinned as Pure Nordic
Dinaric	4	lighter than Nordic Alpine, far darker than East Baltic
Nordic Alpine	5	10.0 percent dark skinned
Nordic Mediterranean	6	86.2 percent pink skinned, but darker than any other Irish type
Pure Mediterranean	7	63.6 percent swarthy skinned
Keltic	8	very light skinned

Source: Earnest A. Hooton and C. Wesley Dupertuis, *The Physical Anthropology of Ireland* (Cambridge: Peabody Museum of Archaeology, Harvard University, 1955), 166–190.

tuted the bulk of their presentation. Of equal importance for us, however, are their comments on the "sociology" of each racial type. These comments reflect Hooton and Dupertuis's sociocultural perspective on the innate abilities of each type and extend the meaning of the types from mere physical variation to implications of aptitude, achievement, and potential.

Today's physical anthropologists may wish to debate, refute, or refine Hooton and Dupertuis's type categories because their research is now outmoded and largely forgotten. Reconsidering their methods or empirical findings is not important for the archaeological analysis of racialization, though. Much more significant is the connection between the racial categories they constructed and their sociological comments about each category. The correlations they made between racial type, skin color, and education, and between racial type and occupation reveal the subtle continuation of the racialist science that followed Irish people wherever they traveled.

Hooton and Dupertuis unequivocally equated skin color with educational rank. Their educational ranks extend from the Pure Nordics at the top to the Keltics at the bottom (Table 4.4). The skin colors get increasingly darker as one moves down the scale, from the Pure Nordics and East Baltics, who have pink skin, to the Pure Mediterraneans, almost 64 percent of whom were "swarthy." The one-to-one correlation between skin color and education was violated only by the Keltics, who, though "very light skinned," are classified as the lowest in educational rank. The Keltics, who were 90.34 percent Catholic, were also the most illiterate of the eight racial types (Hooton and Dupertuis 1955, 171).

As perhaps may be expected, Hooton and Dupertuis also found a correlation between educational rank and occupation (Table 4.5). This correlation, however, is much less distinct. The Pure Nordics and the East Baltics, who Hooton and Dupertuis ranked 1 and 2 in terms of education (and who both had pink skin), had high proportions of "university men," professionals, and soldiers but few hired laborers or "tinkers." The Keltics, the least educationally prepared of the eight racial types, led in hired laborers, "tinkers," farmers, and herders and included a high number of factory workers. The correlation between educational rank and racial type was not simply a matter of social opportunity, though. On the contrary, the relationship was biological. In their discussion of the high number of skilled tradespeople among the Dinarics (who were ranked fourth educationally), Hooton and Dupertuis observed: "Thus, like the other round-headed types, it [the Dinaric racial type] seems to have a higher occupational status than is characteristic of most of the long-heads" (1955, 176). Religion was not a deciding factor because the Dinarics were 93.5 percent Catholic.

The research Ripley, Coon, and Hooton and Dupertuis pursued spans several decades. The period of American history in which they researched and wrote was one in which thousands of immigrants from eastern and southern Europe arrived in the United States. The Irish had established themselves as "old immigrants" by this time and, as Hooten and Dupertuis noted, had in many instances moved into positions of power and authority. Many men and women of Irish heritage had grown wealthy in America and were no longer considered nonwhite. Writers, artists, and even scientifically trained and dedicated physical anthropologists had portrayed the Irish people in various ways, but overall, the Irish occupants of 472 Pearl Street lived in a time when many of the racial designations in America were still very much in flux. In fact, 100 years later, highly educated anthropologists were still treating the Irish as research subjects. Perceiving them this way meant they could take numerous, sometime quite invasive, measurements of them. The continued prevalence of Irish jokes and caricatures in some quarters (see Curtis 1996) suggests that the racialized position of people of Irish heritage may not be entirely a thing of the past. In any case, to obtain a true picture of the racialization of the Irish residents of 472 Pearl Street during the period of interest, we must develop one final element in the epochal structure within which the immigrants functioned day by day. This concerns how Irish men and women reacted to the racialization process they encountered in the United States. As I have shown, the Irish were racialized at home, but the racialization process continued across the Atlantic, and any attempt to understand the racialization

Table 4.5. Correlation of Hooton and Dupertuis' Irish Educational Rank and Occupations

Racial Type	Educational Rank	Occupations
Pure Nordic	1	high in mercantile workers, semi-skilled trades, professional men, and soldiers; high in farm dependents; no lower agricultural workers, tinkers, fishermen, transport workers, clerks, factory workers
East Baltic	2	highest percentage of university men; only 2.9 percent hired laborers or tinkers; statistically insignificant farm dependents
Predominantly Nordic	3	leads in clerks; high in students, farm dependents; slightly high in skilled trades; low in hired laborers, tinkers, navvies, fishermen
Dinaric	4	slightly high in skilled trades, shopkeepers and assistants, professional workers, soldiers, students; deficient in hired laborers, tinkers, agriculturalists, navvies
Nordic Alpine	5	rather high in agriculturalists, farm dependents; somewhat high in transport workers, the professions, students; low in navvies
Nordic Mediterranean	6	leads in navvies; high in semi-skilled trades, clerks, soldiers; slightly low in tinkers, agriculturalists; low in professional workers
Pure Mediterranean	7	leads in shopkeepers, transport workers, soldiers, but sample is too small to be meaningful
Keltic	8	leads in hired laborers, tinkers, farmers, herdsmen; high in factory workers; second in navvies; deficient in mercantile class, clerks, professional men, soldiers, students

Source: Earnest A. Hooton and C. Wesley Dupertuis, *The Physical Anthropology of Ireland* (Cambridge: Peabody Museum of Archaeology, Harvard University, 1955), 166–190.

of the Irish in America must recognize their reaction to its continuance and renewed form.

Learned Habitus of Race in Irish America

A complete understanding of the full range of attitudes and emotions of the Irish immigrants who reached America is outside the scope of this exploration. My goal in this section is merely to suggest the racialist atmosphere that helped create the epochal racial structure of the United States during the period 1850–1870. Rather than attempt a full-blown and necessarily incomplete account of the racialist environment the Irish encountered in the United States, I focus only on one aspect of this history: the rise of a powerful, albeit short-lived, nativist American organization and the collective reaction of the Irish to it.

The kind of America-first passion that could be aroused in American citizens was expressed most clearly in the 1850s by the institution of the secretive Order of the Star Spangled Banner, better known as the Know Nothing Party. Its members were initially interested in temperance and antislavery measures, but they soon became preoccupied with anti-immigration policy. Much of the growth in Know Nothing membership was related to antipathy to the Irish (Gibson 1951, 78). Party members directed most of their opprobrium toward the so-called famine Irish, those unfortunate families who had fled starvation, disease, and death at home (Brighton 2005, 122–123). Because the Know Nothings were virulently opposed to slavery and Irish immigration, they were also anti-Catholic; they claimed that the archbishop of New York had condoned slavery and praised the practice in Cuba (Anbinder 1992, 45). From here, it was only a short step to argue that Irish immigrants also supported slavery. The vision Know Nothing propagandists promoted was that every person of Irish heritage who stepped on the shores of the United States was a supporter of slavery. This image was an explosive one in the 1850s, when the future of slavery in the United States was hotly contested in every field of national life.

Significantly, some Americans connected the supposedly universal support of slavery among the Irish with their physicality. Nativist authors writing in the early-mid 1850s observed that Irish attitudes were related to their physiognomy, physiology, and cultural norms (Knobel 1986, 131). Arguments such as these easily led to the conceptualization of the Irish "race" as a distinct kind of humanity (Garner 2004, 106–107). Such pronouncements, which took place in the 1850s, were concurrent with the rise of American physical anthropology and the analysis of skulls and other skeletal elements as a route to identifying various human races.

An insight into the Irish reaction to the outrages of the Know Nothings appears in John Mitchel's *Jail Journal* (1918), an account that was first serialized in Mitchel's New York City newspaper. Mitchel was not a neutral observer by any means; radically pro-Irish, he had once been a prisoner of the British. He was vocally anti-English and was a pro-slavery supporter of the Confederacy in the 1860s. Nonetheless, Mitchel's opinion was undoubtedly shared by other Irish immigrants who found themselves being harassed by American nativists. Mitchel (1918, 381) described the Know Nothing Party as a "foolish . . . filthy . . . [and] imbecile" movement. He wrote that though the Irish in New York were "patient and good-humoured," they "could not always endure the outrage." In fact, Irish often fought back, sometimes violently. The greatest affront, according to Mitchel was the "anti-Papist mania" that menaced Irish Catholic immigrants, even as "Irish Orangemen" joined the ranks of the Know Nothings to fight the influx of Catholics into America.

The precise impact of the short-lived Know Nothing Party on anti-Irish sentiment is difficult to gauge; we must leave it to historians to determine this relationship. The Know Nothings and other nativist anti-Irish entities, including newspapers, impugned the Irish as a people for some time, but it seems that many nativists believed that the Irish could be reformed. As historian Dale Knobel (1986, 151–152) notes, several nativists proposed methods for "domesticating" the Irish. This assimilationist agenda included insisting that Irish residents of the United States abandon alliance to a foreign power (the pope), deny any kind of Celtic revival, and become full-fledged American citizens in heart and mind.

During the course of the nineteenth century, the nativist American's view of the Irish was transformed. At the beginning of the century, nativists viewed with horror the influx of rural "peasants" who practiced the Catholic religion and sometimes spoke English poorly or not at all. By the end of the century, many Irish individuals had become prominent as political leaders and powerful business owners. The rise in the fortunes of some Irish men and women meant that the social position of the Irish in the United States was transformed. Whereas nativists initially racialized the Irish as nonwhite because of their customs and beliefs, by the end of the century, when it was clear that the Irish were willing to be Americanized, nativists began to view them as white. Catholicism continued to cause conflicts from time to time, but at least in terms of racial categorization, the Irish had been granted whiteness by the beginning of the twentieth century. Much of this racial transformation came through the field of labor as Irish men and women entered the American working class (Ignatiev 1995; Roediger 1991). As part of claiming whiteness in the United States, some Irish men and women, in espousing their equality to other white "races," concomitantly argued that they were better than all those peoples judged nonwhite (Garner, 2004, 112). This claim of racial superiority tied the Irish with nativist Americans who felt the same way. Thus, while racial category is bestowed on a people from the outside, the Irish example demonstrates that a people also can strive for a racial label through conscious action.

What is important here is the notion that Irish immigrants in America, including those living at 472 Pearl Street in New York City, could and did face anti-Irish prejudice. Protestant America embraced anti-Catholicism; it was said at the time that many Americans were anti-Irish first and anti-Catholic second. Some even argued that "everything Irish" was repugnant to Protestant America (Miller 1985, 323).

Segregating the Irish, New York Style

Spatial segregation constitutes one element of the racialization process. Even melting-pot theorists had to admit in their more empirical studies that various peoples tended to congregate in certain neighborhoods of America's largest cities (e.g., Glazer and Moynihan 1963). While it may be true that the settlement patterns of cities such as New York developed because recent immigrants chose to live alongside older immigrants from their own culture, we cannot totally discount the reality that the "less desirable races" were segregated in locales that were crowded, unsanitary, and unsafe. Such was the case for the Irish immigrants in New York.

Our collective vision of Manhattan today is that it is the center of the world's commerce, an overbuilt terrain of incredibly highly valued real estate. Throughout the eighteenth and early nineteenth centuries, however, the area that became the Five Points was a low-lying wetland area dominated by a small body of water called the Collect Pond. A 1754 map depicts a tannery, a poorhouse, and a "Jews Burial Ground" near the pond (Figure 4.10). The now-famous "Negros Burial Ground" appears on the edge of the pond (Yamin 2000b, 1:8). After the pond was filled in the beginning of the nineteenth century, the area retained much of its quasi-industrial quality. Spatially removed from elite neighborhoods, the area around the old pond, renamed the Five Points because of the intersection of three streets, "offered crowded and unsanitary living conditions to the city's poorest, largely immigrant population" (Brighton 2005, 131). Even Charles Dickens, world-renowned for his concern over the plight of the poor and disfranchised, would not enter the Five Points without a police escort. His description of the area is as evocative as any of his accounts of Old London: "This is a place, these narrow ways, diverging to the right and left, and reeking everywhere with dirt and filth. . . . What place is this, to which the squalid street conducts us? . . . Here, too, are lanes and alleys, paved with mud knee deep" (Dickens 1842, 1:211–215). This is the environment in which Peter McLoughlin built his tenement at 472 Pearl Street, one block south of the intersection of the three streets that gave the district its name.

When McLoughlin built the tenement, the city did not have ordinances requiring standards of construction, so most of the buildings were raised quickly and were substandard, unsafe, and unsanitary. Diseases such as cholera and typhus were common, and some residents colorfully called the tenements the "Gates of Hell" (Brighton 2005, 132). Irish immigrants were packed into such tenements at the middle of the nineteenth century.

It would not be inaccurate to refer to the Irish settlement of the Five Points as an "ethnic enclave" even though not all residents were Irish or Irish American (Pitts 2000, 37). It may be more precise, however, to conceptualize the Five Points as a segregated section of the city, a place of residence for individuals judged racially inferior within the epochal structure of American race. Irish immigrants, struggling to find their place in the racial order, were relegated to low-paying jobs and dangerous living conditions until they could demand society's rewards because of their white skin. For archaeologists, a question of major interest concerns the material dimensions of this racial struggle.

The Material Possessions of the Racialized Irish in a New York Tenement

I have selected an archaeological feature with the mundane name of Feature J to examine, albeit briefly, the material conditions of Irish immigrant racialization in the United States. Archaeologists determined that Feature J was a stone-lined privy pit eleven feet in diameter and approximately five feet deep (see Figure 4.2). It contained a series of fill layers in which were found thousands of household artifacts with dates consistent with the 1850–1870 era. The soil inside the privy was deposited in two strata which, based on the artifacts, archaeologists could segment into two temporal periods: 1850–1860 and 1860–1870. This division of the deposits is significant because it permits us to study material changes that were coterminous with the racialization process the Irish in New York City experienced.

The archaeologists excavating Feature J discovered 447 small finds (e.g., coins, hardware, jewelry) in the late deposit and 2,083 in the earlier deposit. Like much archaeological analysis, however, the greatest interpretive potential appeared to rest in the analysis of the ceramic and glass objects. Archaeologists removed a minimum of 932 ceramic and glass vessels from the Feature J

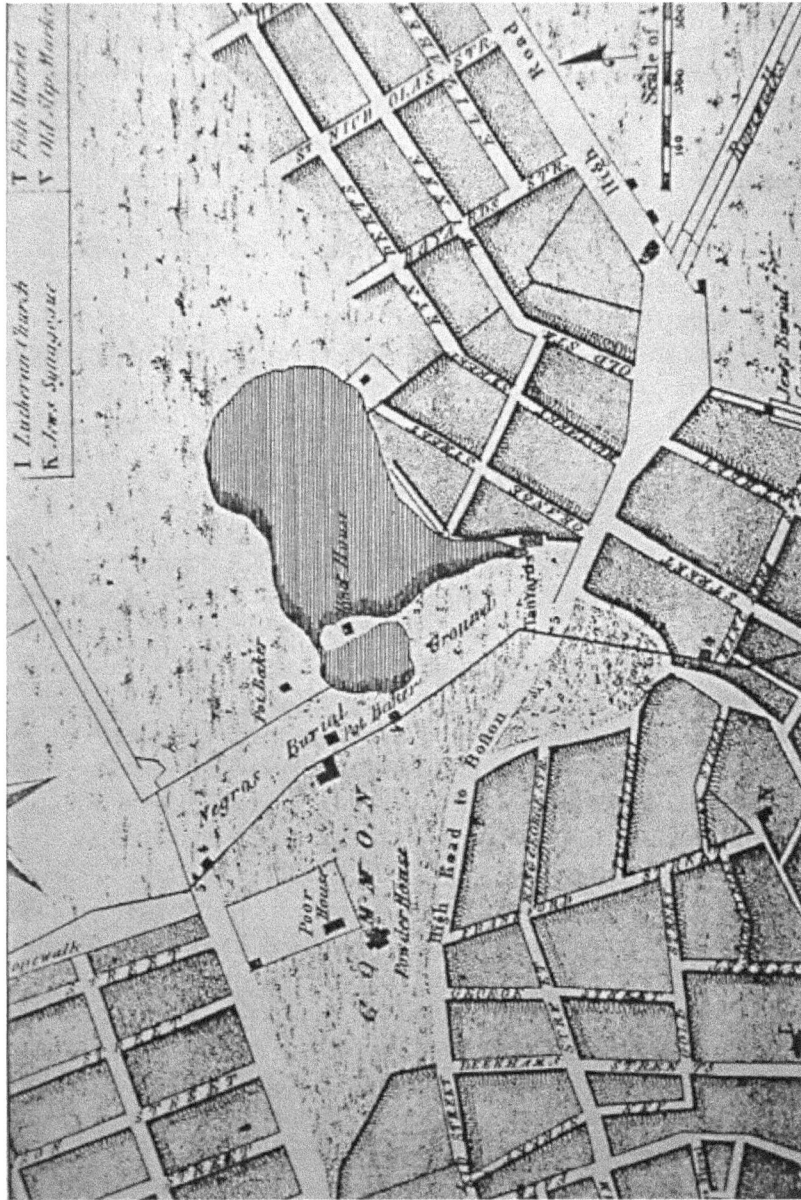

Figure 4.10. Map of northern New York City in 1754. Courtesy of U.S. General Services Administration and John Milner Associates.

privy (396 from the late deposit, 207 ceramic and 189 glass, and 536 from the earlier deposit, 341 ceramic and 195 glass) (Yamin 2000d, 1:A-33–43).

The sheer size of the artifact assemblage from this one feature indicates that people at 472 Pearl Street had ready and routine access to consumer objects. Contemporary advertisements indicate that numerous stores selling ceramic and glass objects were close at hand. Neighborhood merchants proudly proclaimed their acquisition of wares from places as distant as France and England. Nine ceramic dealers were within easy walking distance of the Pearl Street tenement, most of whom sold dishes and glassware at prices that even families living near poverty could afford (Brighton 2000, 11–12). The decorative patterns on the reconstructable ceramic vessels recovered from the tenement's privy indicate the range of consumer products available (Figure 4.11). The earliest deposit yielded thirty-eight distinct decorative motifs, while the later stratum yielded twenty-eight patterns. The patterns present include twenty-six different styles of transfer-printing (in blue, red, and brown), two styles of shell-edged decoration, two varieties of flowing transfer-print (in blue and gray), and twenty styles of molded decorations without applied pigment. The archaeologists also identified at least fourteen miscellaneous patterns. The range of decorative styles means that numerous and varied ceramic and glass consumer products were available to the residents of the 472 Pearl Street tenement. The presence of these items cause us to question how the residents' social position as an in-migrating and racialized people affected their ability to acquire such things.

Brighton's (2005) analysis of the Feature J ceramics and glass compares them with a contemporary assemblage collected at the Greenwich Mews site. This site was also located in Manhattan but was associated with two American-born working-class families. Analytically dividing the assemblage into teaware, tableware, and serving groups, Brighton discovered some differences between the two sites' assemblages but nothing stark enough to indicate extreme social difference. For our purposes, the differences between the collections cannot be related to the artificial (albeit powerful) segmentations created by the racialization process. For example, the two families at Greenwich Mews owned three serving vessels, whereas the residents of 472 Pearl Street probably had only one per family. The Pearl Street assemblage had a higher percentage of teawares than tablewares, while the pattern is just the opposite for the Greenwich Mews site. The difference between the two samples is so minor as to be insignificant. The distinction may relate to simple differences in the buying power (i.e., economic capital) of each family.

To compensate for the analytical problems of having a small number of sites with which to compare and not being able to account for the idiosyncra-

Figure 4.11. Decorated ceramics from 472 Pearl Street. Courtesy of U.S. General Services Administration and John Milner Associates.

cies of buying habits, Brighton examined vessel complexity over time. This kind of analysis was possible because of the stratification of the soils in the privy. His analysis appears to document the racial transformation of Irish immigrants in America during the nineteenth century.

As Brighton notes, the change in the diet of the Irish as they relocated from rural Ireland to urban Manhattan necessitated a change in ceramic and glass vessels. The most notable change between the Old and the New Worlds was the greater availability of meat in America. Rural men and women simply did not consume large quantities of meat in Ireland, whereas the standard American diet included meat. As would be expected, the faunal collections from the sites reflect the introduction of meat into the daily diet. Almost half of the Greenwich Mews faunal collection was composed of beef bones, whereas only about 20 percent of the sample from 472 Pearl Street was beef. This percentage is relatively small, but when taken in conjunction with the bones of sheep, pigs, and chickens in the faunal collection, it shows the variety of the Irish immigrant diet when compared to that of rural Ireland, where potatoes, milk, and sometimes oatmeal were standard fare. The full analysis of the faunal materials from Feature J indicated that the residents of 472 Pearl Street consumed substantial amounts of meat, with pork, the cheapest meat then available, predominating (Milne and Crabtree 2000).

The artifact sample from the Five Points, though large in itself, does not come from enough sites to permit sweeping generalizations. Nevertheless, Irish immigrants in New York obviously had a varied assemblage of ceramic and glass wares. The uppermost deposit in the Feature J privy indicated the emergence of new behaviors that were adopted in the United States organized around social dining. The lower, earliest deposits in the privy were associated with individuals who had recently arrived in America, whereas the uppermost deposits were related to people who had lived in the country for at least a decade. The transformation of the ceramic and glass assemblages probably had much to do with the desire of Irish immigrants to obtain social and economic opportunities in their new home. Clearly, "the Irish were forced to reshape behaviors and world view" to gain acceptance from their American neighbors (Brighton 2005, 233). The conscious change of behavior was part of the Irish effort to conform to the perception of what it meant to be white in the United States.

As noted above, the Five Points was infamous for its unsanitary conditions. Commentators with little compassion sometimes ascribed the poor's lack of sanitation to the "culture of poverty" or even to inborn characteristics that caused them to act like subhuman beasts (Geremek 1997, 239–240). Individuals who held this prejudiced view could easily characterize the poor as also lazy, promiscuous, and immoral. The finer truths did not necessarily matter in the racialization process. If individuals not living in poverty can imagine those in or near poverty as acting in debased ways, then "empirical reality becomes superfluous or not credible" to those not in poverty (Gans 1995, 97). The sanitation choices available in the tenements were made by the landlords, and their major concern was financial. Fixing leaking privies, draining pools of stagnant water, and removing piles of stinking garbage were all costs landlords had to bear, and most of them chose to look the other way if they were not forced to ameliorate the dire conditions.

The unhealthy condition of New York City's tenements led to concerns about staying healthy, and the immigrants who inhabited the dark narrow tenements thus had to find their own means of health care. The excavations at the privy located behind 472 Pearl Street confirm that its Irish and Irish-American residents had to seek their own medical remedies.

Remarkable insights into the health and self-medication of Irish immigrants can be gained by examining the medicinal bottles they left behind in places such as the Feature J privy. The analysis of the Feature J glassware indicates the presence of 17 medicine bottles and 45 vials in the earliest soil horizon. Their combined frequency accounts for 31.8 percent of the glass when categorized by functional group. The more recent soil layer produced 23 medicine bottles and 19 vials, or 22.3 percent of the total glass objects present. Nineteenth-century men and women also considered mineral water to be medicinal, so the 27 mineral water bottles from the upper deposit and the 5 from the deeper deposit must also be included (Yamin 2000d, 1:A-36, A-42). Archaeologists thus removed 136 bottles that probably once held medicines from the privy at 472 Pearl Street. Included in the sample are examples of Udolpho Wolfe's Aromatic

Schnapps (for general invigoration), Mexican Mustang Liniment (for a variety of ailments ranging from cuts and colds to lameness and harness sores), and J. R. Stafford's Olive Tar (for serious maladies, including cancer and cholera) (Brighton 2005, 190).

Archaeologists who have examined nineteenth-century medicines tend to group them into two categories: ethical and proprietary. So-called ethical medicines were those prescribed by a physician, whereas proprietary medicines were those whose ingredients were kept secret and protected by patent (Fike 1987, 3). It is relatively easy to conclude that a high number of prescription medicines might indicate access to a physician, whereas a high number of proprietary medicines might imply a lack of access and the need to self-medicate. Brighton's (2005, 246–247) analysis of the medicine bottles found at the Pearl Street tenement indicates a high percentage of prescription medicine bottles in the 1850–1860 stratum, but about half the amount in the 1860–1870 deposit. Conversely, the later deposit yielded a much higher percentage of proprietary medicine bottles than the earlier stratum. In fact, the percentages of prescription and proprietary bottles in the early Pearl Street deposit almost perfectly match those found in the Greenwich Mews sample of artifacts of American-born residents.

The distribution of prescription medicines and proprietary medicines is especially intriguing because it appears to contradict what we might expect given the racially based epochal structure of the nineteenth-century United States. We might expect that American doctors, perhaps influenced by the fear of immigrants that was spreading throughout the middle and upper classes, would have discouraged immigrants from seeking their help. And, even if immigrants sought their services, nativist doctors may have turned them away. In a racialized environment, we might well expect those people judged to be inferior to have limited access to traditional physicians. Conversely, we also may suppose that individuals judged to be inferior would have sought their own health remedies. The inability of racialized people to find regular medical care is another implication of the epochal structure. Racialist thinking might be seen hiding behind the unequal distribution of reasonable health care.

The linkage between access to health care and racialization was clearly evident when archaeologists examined the artifacts they had excavated from the A.M.E. church in Bloomington, Illinois (Cabak, Groover, and Wagers 1995; see Chapter 2). As was true at Pearl Street, the Wayman Church privy also yielded a large number of medicine bottles. In fact, the assemblage included 562 whole or broken medicine bottles. Fully 447, or 79.5 percent, once held prescription medicines, whereas 115, or 20.5 percent, were proprietary. Included in the collection are bottles whose ingredients were promoted to cure or alleviate headaches, stomach and kidney distress, dysentery and diarrhea, coughs and colds, and pain in general.

In their interpretation of these artifacts, Cabak, Groover, and Wagers concluded that the presence of the bottles represented the efforts of African Americans to level the effects of inequality in health care they confronted in Bloomington: "Given the past discrimination that blacks have experienced in securing medical treatment, the recovered artifacts can potentially be attributed to the segregated health care practices probably present in Bloomington during the late 19th and early 20th century" (1995, 70). The residents' efforts took at least two paths: self-medication through the purchase of proprietary medicines, and visits to the two doctors who were members of the congregation. The discovery of the medicine bottles in the church's privy suggests that the two physicians administered an ad hoc clinic at the church. In addition to the bottles, the archaeologists also found nine test tubes, one glass syringe plunger, and one glass eyedropper inside the privy.

Much the same situation obtained for the Irish immigrants living at 472 Pearl Street. Brighton (2005, 249) notes that the residents of the tenement had access to charitable dispensaries where they could get free medical assistance. He also notes, however, that in the 1860–1870 deposit the number of proprietary medicine bottles increased in concert with the growing stigma of being Irish, Catholic, poor, and sick. These Irish families, who had been in America for over ten years, may have been well acquainted with feeling alienated from the medical community. They thus had to self-medicate with the ineffective and even potentially dangerous concoctions they could purchase on their own. Another possibility, of course, is that the Irish, being forced into low-paying jobs, simply could not afford to visit the doctor. Either way, discrimination, as an element of the racialization process, undoubtedly played a prominent role in the access to medical care.

The occurrence of medicine bottles at the Wayman A.M.E. Church in central Illinois and at the privy behind 472 Pearl Street in Manhattan suggest at least two significant points that may be relevant to an archaeology of racialization. First, the archaeological deposits make it abundantly clear that individuals could supply themselves with medicines (though perhaps of dubious reliability or effectiveness) during the late nineteenth and early twentieth centuries. On its face, this is not news to historical archaeologists. The ability to purchase nostrums and remedies implies some measure of personal agency, and archaeologists know that the proprietary medicine industry was big business in Gilded Age America. More than a few individuals became multimillionaires by selling homemade remedies on street corners and through local newspapers. Irish immigrants living in the Five Points were just like other sick

Americans of modest income. They could visit a local dispensary or merchant who sold proprietary medicine to obtain the medicine they hoped would help them or their loved ones. When examined in finer detail, however, it becomes evident that the act of visiting a patent medicine dealer was less of a choice than it might seem. Individuals denied access to the medical profession—and who were racialized as inferior—had to seek the only cures available to them. That many of these medicines were harmful or worthless only strengthens the connection between health care options and racialized social position.

Second, and equally pertinent to this discussion, is the idea that the ratio of prescription medicine bottles to proprietary medicine bottles in late-nine-teenth-century contexts may constitute one place historical archaeologists might look for the subtle evidence of racialization. Further research must occur to confirm this assessment, but the evidence collected to date at least makes this possibility worth examining in finer detail.

I have long been skeptical of the archaeological search for ethnic markers (e.g., Orser 1991). My lack of belief in the ability of individual artifacts to reflect a social variable as complex as ethnic identity stems from my long experience with African American archaeology. The history of the historical archaeologists' search for African "survivals" in the New World is so well known and so much a part of the discipline's intellectual tradition that an exhaustive discussion is unnecessary here. Suffice it to say that "the strange career of colonoware pottery" (Orser 1996, 117–123) continues to haunt much archaeological research in the American Southeast. Some explanation about colonoware pottery is deemed necessary, however, even though we must briefly depart from Irish immigration and turn to another group of racialized people.

The issues that surround the ethnic (and indeed cultural) affiliations of colonoware pottery raised profound questions about the ability of historical archaeologists to link material objects with ethnic categories. Regarding Africans in the New World specifically, the central issue for historical archaeologists, anthropologists, historians, and others concerned whether the plantations of the New World were effective "melting pots" for enslaved Africans. Africans held in bondage in the southern United States and the Caribbean were drawn from cultures that were scattered along a huge region that stretched from Senegambia to Central Africa. Members of the largest cultures and individuals who were most resistant to enslavement were undeniably able to retain many of their cultural traditions, including many religious beliefs and practices. But in some enclaves, like the British West Indies, enslaved Africans "were spread widely and rarely concentrated on a single plantation" (Higman 1984, 128). What developed in the New World was a pan-African culture—perhaps a "multi-creolization"—that retained elements of diverse

Old World African characteristics. As such, African ethnicity, expressed as a "continental ethnicity," provided an avenue for African American unity in the New World (Stuckey 1987, 3). This cultural development does not mean, of course, that African ethnicity was never significant. It only suggests that members of African cultural ethnicities formed themselves into one large ethnonationalist collective when faced with capture, transportation, and degradation. This collectivity, though pan-ethnic, was also uniquely racial. Its members were bound together through a process that was inherently intended to racialize them as inferior.

The issue of Irish ethnicity, which is rooted in roughly similar terms, was addressed by Heather Griggs (1999), who also examined Feature J at 472 Pearl Street. Griggs questions the past archaeological search for ethnic markers and argues that sociohistorical reality is too complex to permit straightforward correlations between any single object of material culture and past ethnic identity. She correctly observes that the urge to refer to Irish immigrants in America as "the" Irish serves to minimize and even erase the social differences Irish men and women faced at home. This point is important because Griggs is arguing that using the identifier "the Irish" is the same as imposing a racial label on them. When viewed from today's vantage point, it appears to make no difference whether the application of the term is imposed by nineteenth-century Know Nothing bigots or modern-day historical archaeologists. This proposition seems to make abundant sense.

But in attempting to give her Irish subjects cultural dignity by refusing to accept imposed uniformity, Griggs glosses over an important point: that Irish-born people in nineteenth-century America were racialized. Nativists perceived them as a huge, undifferentiated mass of unwashed, uncombed peasants dedicated to following the pope and worshiping idols. As modern-world archaeologists, we cannot ignore the practice of imagined cultural homogenization through racialization, even though we recognize its fallacy. Overlooking this effect of racialization would be analogous to ignoring the effects of Eurocentrism because we do not believe that Eurocentrism was a good practice. When attempting to analyze the racialization process in history, we thus may need to use the folk terminology of the day to grasp even a portion of the complexities of the racialized epochal structure. Griggs's refusal to focus on ethnicity removes aspects of racialization from her analysis as well. She proposes, for example, that the Staffordshire figurines, redware flower pots, and lighting fixtures found in the Feature J privy may have been intended to beautify some tenants' rooms. Other items—celluloid and tortoiseshell hair combs, carved bone toothbrushes, and jewelry with semi-precious stones—

may reflect economic and social differences between tenant families. She further draws attention to the toys found in the privy—including ceramic tea sets, dolls, a miniature cannon, and marbles—and observes that these objects may indicate that the children who lived in the tenement "may not have been required to work or scavenge to supplement the family income, but were allowed freedom to participate in childhood activities" (Griggs 1999, 95). The link between toys and freedom seems strained because it implies that working children—equally as racialized as their parents—never had any time for play. The presence of toys may indicate a resistance to becoming the drones their parents were forced into being.

In a further effort to move away from ethnicity and toward economic capital and consumption, Griggs (1999, 98) mentions material items that are conspicuously absent from the Feature J assemblage. These objects include watches and carpets, consumer goods that may have been purchased by Irish immigrants who were more well-to-do. She further notes that historians have documented that working-class people in nineteenth-century New York City wore watches and that such objects were readily available in the city's many shops. The absence of watches from the 472 Pearl Street privy implies that the residents there could not afford such amenities, or perhaps only that evidence of them has not appeared in the archaeological deposits investigated to date.

Griggs's impression of the economic disparity among the tenement's residents may be correct. Differences in income and buying power (total economic capital) are commonsensical in a capitalist environment where ready access to consumer products widely obtains. But what she misses in her analysis she actually notes in the article's conclusion. She quotes Ignatiev's assessment that one hallmark of racialization is the definition of a people as an undifferentiated mass. Ignatiev's (1995, 1) next two sentences, however, read: "It follows, therefore, that the white race consists of those who partake of the privileges of the white skin in this society. Its most wretched members share a status higher, in certain respects, than that of the most exalted persons excluded from it." Brighton (2005) considers Griggs's concern about ignoring homegrown Irish inequality and includes two central points she missed: the role of race in Ireland and the transformative characteristics of racialization of the Irish in the United States. During the nineteenth century, the racial transmogrification of the Irish in the United States had two phases—the early nonwhite phase and the later white phase. This transformation has attracted the attention of historians, who have been responsible for documenting its significance in the modern American past (Ignatiev 1995; Roediger 1991).

One additional and somewhat problematic item in the Feature J privy de-

Figure 4.12. Father Mathew cup from 472 Pearl Street. Courtesy of U.S. General Services Administration and John Milner Associates.

posit requires comment. This item is a brown transfer-printed handleless cup decorated with the image of Father Theobald Mathew (Figure 4.12). The image on the outside shows Father Mathew addressing an audience of ten men, women, and children who are seated on their knees looking with rapt attention at the standing priest. One woman on Father Mathew's right holds a small infant. In the background are the indistinct peaks and glens of a mountain range rather than the urban skyline of New York. Inside, the cup has an intricate cabled border with an elaborate image. A beehive sits on a low four-legged table in the center of the image made of coiled straw rope in a style that would be familiar to anybody who came to maturity in the Irish countryside (Evans 1957, 206). Several bees buzz around the top of the hive and a short shovel leans against the table. Lying on the ground in front of the table is a rake and a two-pronged pitchfork. Most important, one scroll reading "Temperance and Industry" appears above the hive and table, and another reading "Industry Pays Debts" appears beneath it. The maker's mark on the cup's base indicates that it was manufactured sometime in the 1820–1840 period (Brighton 2005, 255).

Father Mathew was a Capuchin Irish priest who established the Total Abstinence Movement in Ireland in 1838. He visited the United States in 1849 at the request of New York bishop John Hughes and stayed until 1851. History does not record whether Father Mathew visited the Five Points neighborhood, but Brighton (2005, 251–6) is correct to focus attention on this artifact because of its highly charged symbolic meaning. Mathew believed that drunkenness was Ireland's greatest social problem and that it accounted for much of the people's crime and poverty (Stivers 2000, 36). His goal was to make Irish drinkers realize that they could be closer to God if they practiced the more moral habits usually associated with abstinence. In the United States, Father Mathew's plan was perfectly consistent with the Anglo-Saxon ideal, so his message was well received by reformers who sought to elevate the collective social position of Irish immigrants.

We cannot know precisely who owned the Father Mathew cup or guess its meaning to them. It may have simply been a useable cup with an image on it. The cup's users may not have known the significance of Father Mathew or perhaps were not interested in his message even if they had heard of him. Many archaeologists, however, might be inclined to consider the cup as an ethnic marker of Irishness. After all, the image is of Irish people (one of whom is identifiable), the design of the beehive and the two-pronged pitchfork are typical of early-nineteenth-century Ireland and would have been immediately recognized by any Irish-born person, and the mountains in the background evoke the Irish landscape. To interpret the cup properly, we must consider its context in the lowest soil horizon inside the Feature J privy. The cup's appearance in mid-nineteenth-century America (1850–1860) came at a time when the immigrant Irish were struggling to prove their worthiness to be considered white. They were collectively attempting to climb the epochal racial structure of America, and reformers realized that Father Mathew's message would constitute one avenue for the transformation that would be required. From this standpoint, then, the Father Mathew image may represent a statement about Irish racialization rather than or even in addition to Irish ethnicity or the social problems posed by alcoholism. The cup may proclaim Irish aspirations in a land that many did not actually seek and in which their collective position would be determined not by the color of their skin but by the nature of their traditions, customs, and religion. Of course, alternative interpretations are also possible. Since the cup was found inside the privy, it remains possible that someone who rejected the image of Father Mathew and what it meant, simply threw it away to get rid of it. Such a conclusion, however, is also open to a racial interpretation. Discarding the cup in such an apparently callus fashion may represent a rejection of the image of Irish men and women as drunkards in need of salvation from the good priest.

The Irish racial experience in the United States is inherently interesting to race theorists because they were light skinned and European. Their struggle to gain the "birthright" of their perceived light skin in a racialized epochal structure indicates that racialization is not strictly about skin color and physical characteristics. Cultural traits can also be racialized.

5

The Chinese in Northern California

From the New York City Irish living in a crowded tenement, we move across the country to northern California and another urban setting. Here we focus on people who, unlike the Irish, could not claim the "phenotypic birthright" of whiteness within the racialized epochal structure of the United States. Instead, the Chinese in the United States had to struggle against unorganized oppression, which included personal assaults and discrimination, as well as organized repression, which included a series of federal, state, and local ordinances designed to segregate the Chinese from white America. The Chinese in the United States provide another excellent case study of how historical archaeologists can approach the complex subject of racialization and the difficulties they may encounter when conducting this line of inquiry. The archaeological context used in this chapter derives from the excavation of a Chinese laundry in Stockton, California.

Background of Excavation

In this chapter, I focus on the racialization process in one archaeological context, with the understanding that racialization was pursued nationally in the United States. The racialization process was multiscalar in design, scope, and execution within the national setting. In this sense, the United States participated in the global processes of colonialism and imperialism, in which individuals collectively classified as white maintained control and authority over people perceived as nonwhite.

Elsewhere (Orser 2004b, 82–90), I have presented an overview of how other archaeologists have examined Chinese archaeological deposits using a perspective that rests on an understanding of ethnicity. Such overviews are extremely important for helping archaeologists understand the full range of possible research topics. In this context, however, an overview approach would be inadequate for the contextualized investigation an analysis of racialization requires. Because racialization is situationally charged and temporally mutable within the confines of the epochal structures, archaeologists attempting to study it must be willing to tack back and forth between several analytical

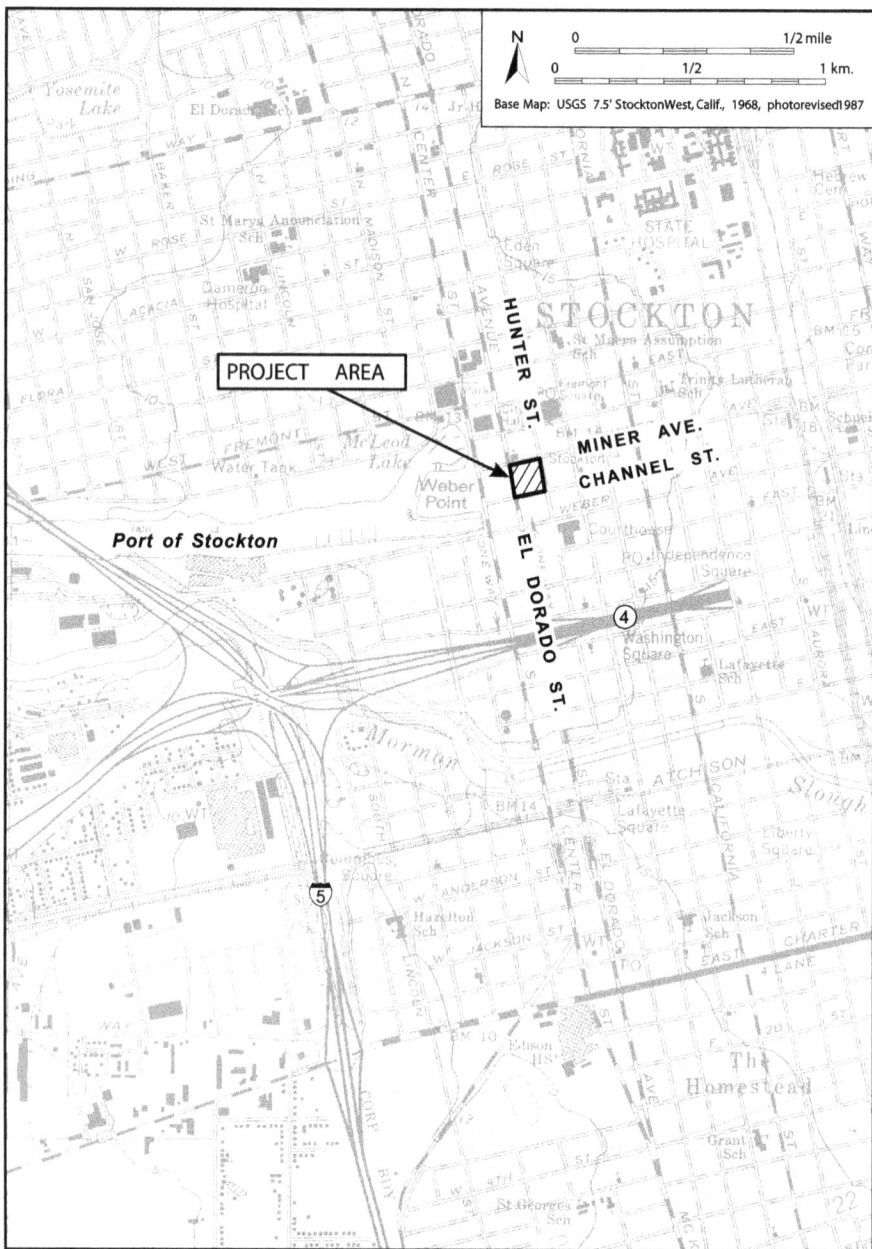

Figure 5.1. Location of 117-123 Channel Street, Stockton, California. Courtesy of the Anthropological Studies Center, Sonoma State University.

scales. This methodology is needed to appreciate the multidimensional character of the epochal structures of the modern world; structures that affect several locales around the world at once but in contextually diverse ways. The archaeological deposit used in this chapter is temporally more recent than the Irish context explored in the previous chapter, but the period of occupation conforms to a time when the residents of the archaeological site were being racialized.

The deposit of interest in this chapter derives from 117-123 Channel Street in Stockton, California (Figure 5.1). In 2000, archaeologists from the Anthropological Studies Center at Sonoma State University spent sixteen days excavating property where a cineplex was slated to be built as part of a downtown redevelopment project. The investigation took place in Lot 6, and the Chinese laundry was discovered in what the archaeologists termed "Analytical Unit B" (Figure 5.2). The archaeological information in this chapter is based on information presented in the site report (Waghorn 2004). As is true of the excavation of the 472 Pearl Street tenement in New York City, the excavation and the reportage is of such a high quality that this information can be used even though I did not assist in either the excavation or the post-excavation analysis. The laundry was clearly a place of work, but the artifacts in the deposit included the kind of material objects used every day by Chinese individuals in northern California during the late nineteenth and early twentieth centuries. As was true of the Irish assemblage, however, the date range of the excavated material conforms to a time when the individuals associated with the artifacts were struggling to create a place within the racialized epochal structures then being enacted and enforced in modern America.

The site I have chosen to explore in this chapter does not contain the most information ever collected from a Chinese-related site, and it is not the most abundant in terms of excavated material culture. I have decided to examine this site in detail specifically because it seems so mundane. The apparently unremarkable nature of this early-twentieth-century northern California site is important because it permits insights into how immigrant individuals seeking only to live their daily lives were inserted into a racialized epochal structure over which they had little if any control. The archaeological deposit from Analytical Unit B at 117-123 Channel Street contained a minimum of 2,044 identifiable items and has a deposition date from about 1894 to about 1937.

The Chinese at 117-123 Channel Street

By 1885, Stockton had twenty-two laundries operated by Chinese immigrants (Waghorn 2004, 14). The historical research conducted as part of the Stockton

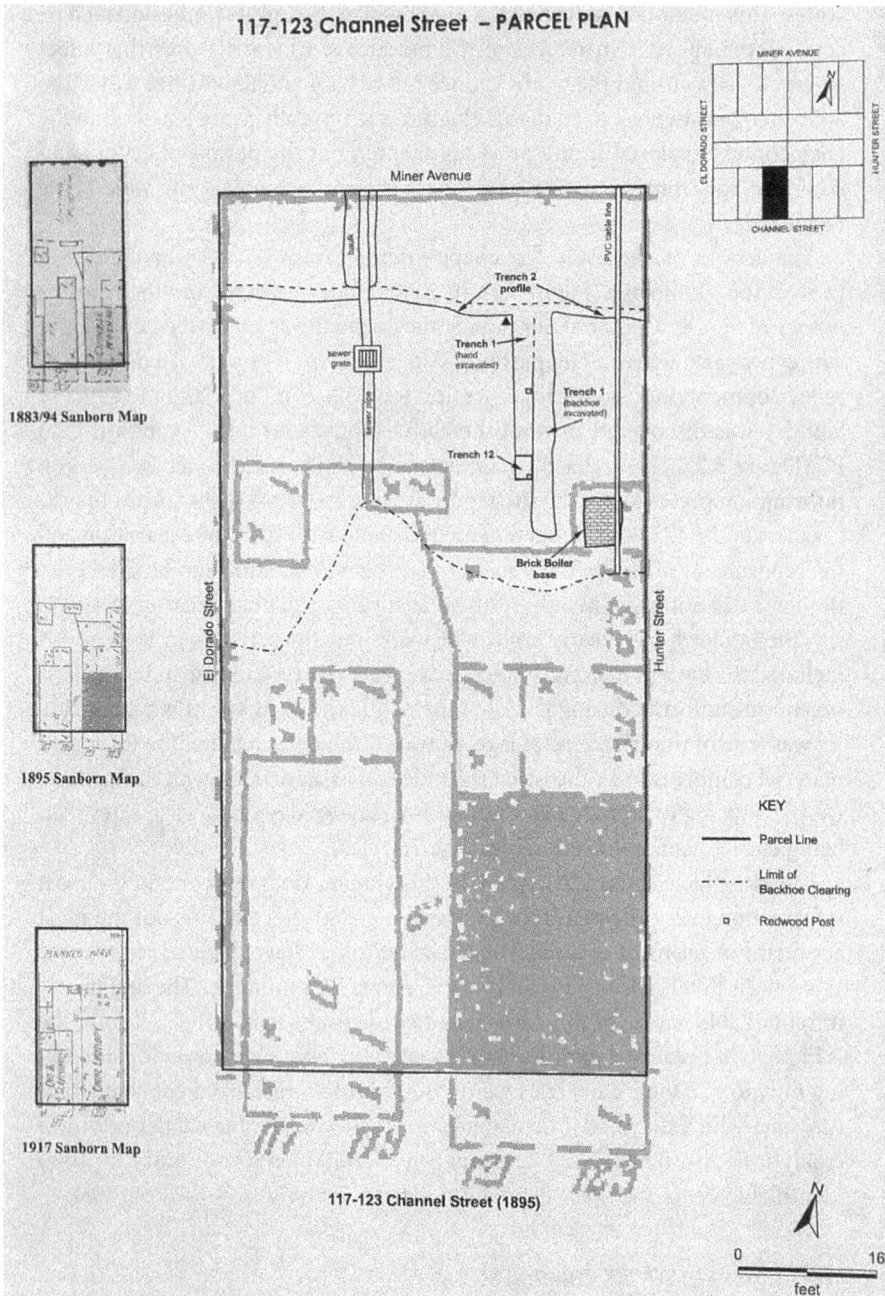

Figure 5.2. Chinese laundry at 117-123 East Channel Street. Courtesy of the Anthropological Studies Center, Sonoma State University.

Table 5.1. Individuals at 123 Channel Street, According to 1900 and 1910 Censuses

Name	Age	Immigration Date	Age at Immigration
1900			
Lee Sing	40	1880	20
Hon Gin	36	1880	16
Hin Bow	44	1881	25
Hon Quong	35	1870	5
Lee Hay (born in California)	25		
Sam Wong (born in Oregon)	33		
1910			
Hung Lee	15	1908	13
Joe Hun	35	1890	15
Shel	19		
Jim Hum	55	1890	35
Wee Wing	45	1890	25
Tuck Fong	35		
Hom Chong	48	1887	25

Source: Annita Waghorn, *Historic Archaeological Investigations of the City Center Cinemas Block Bounded by Miner Avenue and Hunter, El Dorado, and Channel Streets, Stockton California* (Rohnert Park, Calif.: Anthropological Studies Center, Sonoma State University, 2004), 56.

site report indicates that Lot 6 was developed in 1870. A Sanborn insurance map shows that during the period 1883–1894, a "Chinese Wash House" was located on Lot 6. A large drying platform was situated behind the building. According to Waghorn (2004, 50), the Chinese Business Directory of 1900 indicates that the building on the lot was the Sing Lee Laundry at 123 East Channel Street. She also notes that the 1910 U.S. population census lists the head of the household as Lee Sing, a 40-year-old man who immigrated in 1880 (Waghorn 2004, 50). This census record indicates he was literate and spoke English. Six individuals were listed as living within the building. Four of them were immigrants from China and the remaining two were born in the Northwest, one in California and one in Oregon. All were single males who spoke English and were literate (Table 5.1).

An examination of the four individuals listed at the laundry in 1900 shows that they all immigrated in the 1870–1881 period, or before the passage of the discriminatory Chinese Exclusion Act of 1882. Three were young men when they immigrated, and one was a child. By 1910, however, all the residents of the laundry building, except "Sing See" (perhaps really Lee Sing) had arrived during the enforcement of the Chinese Exclusion Act, which was designed to prevent male Chinese laborers from entering the country. Despite the intentions of the act, all of the newer residents of the household in 1910 had been young single men when they immigrated. By 1910, three of the oldest residents were married.

The two married individuals for which information exists in 1910 suggests several marriage patterns within this group. Fifty-five-year-old Jim Hum is reported to have immigrated in 1890 (at age 35) but is recorded as having been married for thirty-one years. This means that he married at age 24 while he was still in China. Hom Chong, however, who is listed as having immigrated in 1887 (at age 25), is reported to have been married for twenty years. He was thus married at age 28 in 1890, after he had migrated to the United States.

The paucity of additional information about the men who labored and lived in the laundry at 123 East Channel Street is indicative of the subtle ways racialization can operate. As Waghorn (2004:56) notes in the site report, the compilers of the town's directories did not include Chinese laundries until 1910. We can only speculate about the reasons for the failure to include all businesses in the directories when the purpose of such directories was to advertise and promote local business. The role of racialization in ignoring such important local businesses is difficult to dismiss.

The Chinese in Northern California

Men and women of Chinese descent have played a seminal role in the cultural history of the United States. Though they were never as numerous as the Irish, the Chinese were a significant cultural force, particularly in the West. Census enumerators listed only 758 foreign-born Chinese in 1853, but ten years later this number had risen to 35,565, or an increase of over 4,500 percent (DeBow 1853, xxxvi; Kennedy 1864, 620). Up through the 1860s almost all Chinese immigrants in America lived in California (Ma 2000, 2), but by 1870, this percentage had shrunk to 75 percent, as the number of Chinese in the United States totaled 62,682 (Walker 1872, 336). This puts the number of foreign-born Chinese in California at just over 47,000 individuals in 1870.

Americans generally tolerated Chinese immigrants when they first appeared in California (Atherton 1914, 282), but the mainstream perspective began to change when it was clear that Chinese laborers were willing to work for relatively low wages and endure harsh living conditions, thus providing competition for white male laborers. Once they were fully racialized, Chinese workers were generally relegated to low-paying, low-status labor positions (Schrieke 1936, 8–9).

The Chinese in the West quickly became associated with the extractive industries of that region. In fact, the discovery of gold in California in 1848 induced the first Chinese immigrants, mostly merchants, to travel to the United States. The new settlers sent stories home of the riches to be made, which encouraged immigration among individuals seeking a better standard of living (Clausen and Bermingham 1982, 13). By the 1850s, about 85 percent of the Chinese in California were engaged in mining, an extractive industry that required no previous experience (Chang 2003, 38). Rising numbers of Asian immigrants in the mines and camps meant increased interethnic conflict, and anti-Chinese sentiment began to grow among nativist Americans. According to one commentator, a root cause of anti-Chinese discrimination in the West resulted from the "economical superiority of the Asiatic" (Atherton 1914, 282). Some Americans apparently resented Chinese immigrants who saved their hard-earned money and sent it home to China. The altruistic use of economic capital appeared to violate the tenets of American consumerism at the same time that it demonstrated that money earned in the United States could be used to raise the standard of living in a distant country.

Industrialists and capitalists outside the American West were as concerned as westerners about the roles Chinese laborers would play in America's workforce. After the emancipation of African American slaves, southern agriculturalists contemplated employing Chinese workers—whom they usually referred to with the derogatory label "coolies"—in their sugar and cotton fields. Contemporary writers commenting on the Chinese as field hands found it impossible to discuss them without racial identifiers, even when attempting to praise them as hard working. One prominent Louisiana planter made a declaration that is representative of the genre:

Much has been said of [C]hinese labor, but few seem to comprehend either the nature of the Asiatic, or our own peculiar condition [in the South]. Some political writers seem to be afraid that the [C]hinese will become a dangerous element of society; others that the mixing of the races would be unavoidable, and that we would soon be Mongolised. Is it possible that we could be so affected, influenced and demoralized by these Celestials? I have yet some faith in the superiority of our race, and in the morality of our people. They will sooner become Americanized, than we Mongolised. The Chinese are peaceful, sober, law-abiding and intelligent, their climate is similar to ours, and they are familiar with the culture of sugar cane and rice. We could not obtain more suitable laborers for the cultivation of our plantations. (Bouchereau 1870, x)

Southern planters facing the uncertainties of reconstruction did not precisely know what to think about "coolies": "Opinions vary as to the character of the Coolie, some authorities describing him as a demoralizing blight to any community; as filthy, thievish and infamously vile; while on the other hand, travelers in Mauritius, California and elsewhere, give him a very good character" (DeBow's Review 1867, 362). Others, like Bouchereau, commended the immigrants from the "Celestial Empire" as good laborers. Still others evaluated them comparatively, stating that the Chinese were "nearly as efficient as Irish laborers" (Wittke 1967, 473).

Most Chinese immigrants to America's west coast arrived as semi-free laborers who had booked passage by entering into a contract of indenture for a set number of years (Almaguer 1994, 154–155). U.S. industrialists welcomed Chinese laborers; they needed cheap labor to build the country's infrastructure, such as railroads. But working-class laborers often saw them as a threat when their numbers grew too large or when they started to move into areas of work that had been historically "white." During the early 1870s, industrialists on the East Coast paid fares for Chinese individuals who were willing to travel from California to be strikebreakers (Wittke 1967, 474). Being indentured and receiving low wages meant, however, that they could seldom pay back the fare. In a famous example, the owners of a shoe factory in North Adams, Massachusetts, hired 100 Chinese workers from California as part of a plan to keep wages lower than their regular workforce was willing to accept (Swinton 1870, 3). The arrival of the Chinese in North Adams represented a "seminal event in American history" because it was the first time Asian workers from the West were used to break a strike east of the Rocky Mountains (Gyory 1998, 60).

In 1876, H. N. Clement, a prominent lawyer from San Francisco, voiced the racialist paranoia that grew directly from the increased presence of Chinese in the cities of California: "The Chinese are upon us. How can we get rid of them? The Chinese are coming. How can we stop them?" (Lee 2003, 23) During the 1870s, Californians intent on "racial purity" organized several anti-Chinese associations and promoted boycotts of Chinese merchants and service providers (Wittke 1967, 476). Anti-Chinese forces in San Francisco had organized as early as twenty years before. An adamantly anti-Chinese naturalized working-class Irish immigrant, Dennis Kearney, is credited with creating the slogan "The Chinese Must Go" (Atherton 1914, 284). Kearney, who led a Vigilance Committee and has been described as "a demagogue of extraordinary power" (McClain 1994, 79), pledged to lynch any person who hired Chinese laborers over American (i.e., white) workers (Coolidge 1909, 115).

The Chinese at Home

Scholars who have investigated Chinese emigration indicate that well over half of all Chinese nationals who entered the United States came from Guangdong Province (Lee 2003, 112). The province is located in the Southern Uplands, a geographical region that includes most of southern China. It encompasses 231,400 square kilometers and stretches along the South China Sea at the southern edge of China (Figure 5.3). It has figured prominently in global history because of the founding on its coast of two important European colonies —Macao by the Portuguese (in 1557) and Hong Kong by the British (in 1841)— on either side of the mouth of the Zhujiang (Pearl) River. The capital city of the province is Guangzhou (Canton). Guangzhou constituted an important node of an intercontinental economic network that stretched to numerous trading centers across the globe. As Frank has explained (1998, 101–104), European maritime trade with the Chinese mainland helped circulate several commodities throughout the world, while silver flowed into Guangzhou. China's important role in international trade reached back into the Sung dynasty (begun in 960). Silk and porcelain were the Chinese exports that were most in demand

Figure 5.3. Guangdong Province, China. Drawing by author.

during this period (Abu-Lughod 1989, 327). Glass beads, though in a considerably smaller market, also constituted a notable commodity of the Guangzhou trade from the Song to the Qing dynasties (960–1911) (Francis 2002, 59).

Modern-world archaeologists are familiar with the important role China has played in the rise of the global marketplace through its production of porcelain, usually referred to as Chinese export porcelain. Dutch, English, and French merchant-traders sought Chinese porcelain beginning in the late seventeenth century. Much archaeological information about the porcelain that originated in Canton's factories has come from the wrecks of ships that were carrying huge cargos but never made it to port. One such example is the *Geldermalsen*, which was shipping 150,000 pieces of porcelain for the Dutch East India Company when it foundered (Jörg 1986).

Canton's kiln owners were wise enough to manufacture pieces for specific markets. For example, porcelain makers produced pieces for Portugal that were decorated with Portuguese themes and patterns (Scammell 1981, 290). By the eighteenth century, all social classes in the United States sought Chinese porcelain and European objects with chinoiserie motifs, including furniture, paintings, carvings, and textiles. The desire to obtain such exotic objects stemmed partly from the appeal of the mysteries of Cathay, an image created long before Americans had to come face to face with the people of China (Goldstein 1991, 51) Recognizing their economic advantage in the global ceramics market, Chinese potters carefully guarded the secrets of porcelain manufacture (Patterson 1979, 24).

Chinese people from all social classes were engaged in a search for luxury goods in the same way as their contemporaries in Europe (Pomeranz 2000, 162–165). The quest for luxury items was fueled by the international market in which Guangzhou (Canton) was situated, and for a while Chinese merchants benefited from the trade. With time, however, the economic relationship between China and the West came to favor the West, and the situation for most nonelite Chinese worsened. Increased taxes, overpopulation, and internal conflicts created tensions and made emigration a viable alternative to a harsh life in China (Lee 2003, 112).

Chinese elites struggled to maintain the status quo in the face of European interest in their port cities, beginning with the Portuguese in the early sixteenth century. For this reason, all ports except Canton were closed to Europeans by imperial decree in 1757. Only in 1842 were four other ports opened (Morse 1966, 59). Two years later, Governor-General Li Shih-Yao wrote "Five Rules to Regulate Foreigners" in Canton (Li Shih-Yao 1969, 29–34). The preface to these regulations indicates three important features of Chinese-European contact in China: the Chinese upper class did not have a high opinion of

Europeans or their cultures; Chinese leaders knew that their own merchants would pursue any course of action that would increase their economic capital; and Chinese elites sought to control Chinese culture by keeping their people and European foreigners as far apart as possible. Li Shih-Yao stated that "since foreigners are outside the sphere of civilization, there is no need for them to have any contact with our people other than business transactions, whenever they come to China for trade purposes." At the same time, he noted that "vulgar persons" in China would violate any regulations that did not have the force of legal statute. He thus wrote the Five Rules for the emperor's consideration:

(1) Foreigners should never be allowed to stay at Canton through the winter;

(2) While in Canton, foreigners should be ordered to reside in Co-hong headquarters so that their conduct could be carefully observed and strictly regulated;

(3) Chinese merchants are not allowed to borrow from foreign traders, nor are foreign traders allowed to hire Chinese servants;

(4) The accumulated abuse of allowing foreigners to hire messengers to transmit communications should be forever eliminated; and

(5) To strengthen inspectional work and to prevent possible disturbances, additional police forces should be introduced in the area where foreign ships are anchored. (Li 1969, 30–33)

Rules 1 and 2 provide insight into how Chinese elites expressed their desire to control trade. Elaborating on Rule 1, Li Shih-Yao stated that "Canton, being the capital of a province, is too important a place to allow foreigners to stay there on a permanent basis, since permanent residence will enable them to spy on our activities." He recommended that foreign traders make contact with the *cohong* merchants (a guild of Chinese merchants who paid the emperor for the right to a monopoly on trade at Canton), exchange their goods as quickly as possible, and leave on the same ship on which they arrived. In the event that they could not make their exchanges fast enough, they should be sent to live in the Portuguese colony of Macao and be made to leave as soon as the next ship from their home country reached port. Explaining Rule 2, Li Shih-Yao specified that all foreign traders should be housed with officially acknowledged *cohong* members, renting other space only if space with *cohongs* was not available. *Cohong* translators were to make lists of all foreign traders among them and keep watch over them so that no "unauthorized, unscrupulous Chinese" could enter the premises "for either social contact or business reasons." To ensure compliance, the *cohong* merchants were to post guards at both front and back entrances of their buildings and lock the doors promptly

at sundown. As a warning to local officials who might be interested in bend-
ing the rules, Li Shih-Yao advised that they should be punished alongside any
European offenders. The ability of these rules to maintain the orderliness of
the Canton market as a global entrepot under Chinese control would be tested
later with the importation of opium to China and the Second Opium War of
1856–1860 (Li 1969, 64–67).

The vast majority of nineteenth-century Chinese have been described as
peasants (Chang 2003, 4–7). Family members worked every day in the fields
and paddies planting vegetables and rice. In the Guangzhou area, the typical
agricultural holding was about an acre in size. Most people lived in small villages inhabited by neighbors much like themselves, and they seldom saw the
upper-class individuals who ruled over them. The sociopolitical organization
extended out from the household to the village or town to the rural district
(Buxton 1929, 73, 164). Some commentators have presented Chinese culture
as homogeneous (e.g., Buxton 1929, 163–164), but more careful research shows
that by the mid-nineteenth century, China's coastal region was developing
as a cultural environment distinct from that of the hinterland. The reasons
for the cultural divergence of the littoral are undoubtedly complex, but the
influence of the West in the area around Guangzhou (Canton) has been cited
as a significant factor (Cohen 1976, 256). Despite some variation, much of
nineteenth-century China was inhabited by small farmers who lived in rural
villages and carried on a way of life that broadly duplicated the lives of their
ancestors.

Referring to China's small farmers as peasants is an oversimplification that
tends to erase the internal distinctions that existed in nineteenth-century rural
life. The practice also tends to erase change over time. In fact, as was true for
the Irish—and for all rural people who tilled the soil as tenant farmers—the
common men and women of the countryside were enmeshed in a hierarchy
of landlord-tenant relations that was quite complex.

Little information is available about Chinese tenancy before the 1930s
(Lin 1997). By that time, the Chinese tenant farming system was composed
of classes that included owner-operators, semi-tenants, tenants, and hired laborers; hired laborers were the least economically secure on this scale. Owners
(who had the greatest total capital) typically acquired their land through in-
heritance, though their individual plots could be quite small and noncontigu-
ous (Latourette 1964, 487). "Institutional landlords" and "secondary landlords"
were prevalent (Lin 1997, 121–128). Institutional landlords, the most powerful and economically endowed members of the rural hierarchy, owned many
types of land—including that occupied by schools and temples—but their
most important lands were lineage lands, or corporate holdings maintained

by an extended kin group, often for many generations. Secondary landlords were the equivalent of Ireland's subtenants. They were farmers who rented land from an institutional landlord and then rented it out to those lower down the agricultural ladder. Although Mary Coolidge (1909, 3–6) provided a image of Chinese rural life as benign to confront the racism of the anti-coolie movement in the United States, tenant farming is never entirely kind to those who are forced into its inherently unequal arrangements.

The increasing dissonance between the number of people on the land and the land's ability to produce food was a major stress in nineteenth-century rural China. Though the population of Guangzhou Province did not increase dramatically until the third decade of the twentieth century, it was true nonetheless that the demand for rice—the Chinese staple equivalent to potatoes in Ireland—outstripped the supply beginning in the sixteenth century. Shortages occurred even though farmers double-cropped rice, making one harvest in mid-July and another in early November (Lin 1997, 45).

By the last half of the nineteenth century, the importation of opium, defeat in the Second Opium War, the designs of foreign powers, and the rise of westernization in general were all exerting stress on every aspect of Chinese life. A perspective on the way many Chinese perceived their situation is provided by a speech K'ang Yu-Wei made on April 17, 1898, before the National Protection Society in Beijing (Li 1969, 229–235). K'ang Yu-Wei began his speech, entitled "The Nation Is in Danger," with these words: "It matters little whether we are rich or poor; we 400 million Chinese are today in serious difficulties. We live in a house which is about to collapse, a boat which, leaking badly, is about to topple over." He elaborated by noting that the Chinese were treated worse than slaves and were pushed around and "cut to pieces" whenever foreigners wished. He said that the Chinese people had forgotten the wisdom of Confucius, and he observed, "Our weakness prompted foreign powers to use coercive methods to press their unreasonable demands." In forty days, foreigners had engineered twenty "national disasters" at China's expense. The first six of the twenty disasters K'ang Yu-Wei enumerated indicate how Chinese identified foreign interference with the problems the nation faced:

(1) Germany demanded the lease of Kiaochow (Jiaozhou);
(2) Britain wanted to impose a loan with 3 percent interest;
(3) Germany wanted to open Kiaochow Bay to trade;
(4) France wanted to open Nanning to trade;
(5) Britain opened all internal rivers to trade; and
(6) France forced China to pay a huge indemnity because the Vietnamese had burned Catholic churches in Saigon.

The continuation of the inherently oppressive tenant-farming system and the tensions caused by the presence of diverse foreign nationals, all of whom were seeking to carve out domains of sole influence, were significant "push" factors that made emigration to the United States appealing to Chinese farmers. Political upheaval, war, and natural disasters also played significant roles in encouraging Chinese farmers to contemplate the opportunities the United States appeared to offer (Almaguer 1994, 154).

It would be inaccurate to think that all Chinese immigrants to America were "backward peasants." Quite the contrary, recent research—some of which has been done by historical archaeologists—has repeatedly demonstrated that Chinese immigrants came from many social classes (Praetzellis 2004, 237–238). A story told by a Chinese merchant at the turn of the twentieth century corroborates this research and demonstrates that not all Chinese immigrants were landless farm laborers. The merchant's son, who had received a formal education in Canton, had been confined in a "pen" upon disembarking in the United States, even though he had arrived as a first-class passenger. The man wired his father in China to tell him of his plight, and the father promptly left for the United States. When the father reached San Francisco, he hired a lawyer to defend his son but soon learned that $100 paid to the right person would fix the situation. The merchant paid the bribe and the son was released from custody (Reynolds 1909, 363–364).

The "pull" factors were almost all related to labor. As a result, when Chinese immigrants entered the United States, they immediately appeared to present a significant threat to American laborers. At the beginning of the twentieth century, one anti-Asian writer noted that Chinese and Japanese workers were destroying the labor market. The reason? The immigrants tended to work longer and harder than their American counterparts. Two examples he gave demonstrate the perceived problem. He said that Chinese butchers worked sixteen-hour days and handled about 75 percent of the pork slaughtered in San Francisco. Their American counterparts would only consent to work ten-hour days, in accordance with the Ten-Hour Law of 1853, signed on May 17 of that year (Eaves 1910, 197). Chinese broom makers would accept $6–$9 per week, whereas American workers doing the same tasks expected $2.50 per day (Yoell 1909, 249–250). American nativists, whether they were knowingly racist or not, quickly grafted a threat to white supremacy onto the economic threat represented by the flood of Chinese laborers into the labor pool.

Epochal Structures of Chinese Racialization in America

U.S. nativists racialized Chinese immigrants regardless of whether they identified them as "good" merchants or "suspicious" (albeit hardworking) "coolies." As was true of the opinions about the Irish, individuals who strongly opposed Chinese immigration sought to present their views both textually and visually. As was also true with nativist views of the Irish, the textual presentations often had a veneer of science and reason. In fact, one fairly consistent element of the racialization process is a seemingly objective examination of the people being racialized. An apparently dispassionate logic seeks to add credence to the claims of racialization and desires to make the practice appear reasonable to people who have inculcated the racialist habitus of the United States during the socialization process.

The arguments presented about the "Chinese question" by three apparently rational commentators demonstrates the nature of the discourse. In their pamphlets and books, these authors state their case about the "question" with the aim of winning converts to the cause of racialization. We cannot know how widely publishers distributed these tracts or how many Americans actually read them. The fact that it is so easy to locate such late-nineteenth-century screeds today suggests that the tracts were common and easily obtainable at the time of their publication. The arguments these three authors made help contextualize the general social environment Chinese immigrants faced when they entered the United States. Common sense also suggests that not all Americans were as violently or as vocally opposed to Chinese immigration as the authors of such works. Nonetheless, as was true of the Irish, Chinese individuals faced a series of challenges and obstacles created by the most visible nativist Americans who saw it as their duty to keep America white.

In *The New Issue: The Chinese-American Question* (1870), John Swinton presented his argument for limiting Chinese immigration into the United States after the first wave of Chinese immigration to the West Coast in the 1850s. After noting that the "Chinese question" had become the "living question of the hour," Swinton decried the use of Chinese immigrants as strikebreakers and lamented the fact that people living in China had lately discovered the "golden hills" of the United States. Observing that "impoverished swarms" of Chinese were interested in migrating, he stated: "I am opposed to this unlimited influx of Chinese immigrants" (5).

Swinton presented his case for limiting Chinese immigration in careful terms and in a manner that is wholly consistent with the logic of American race theory. Swinton rested his argument against Chinese immigration on four factors: race, industry, politics, and morality. His views on industry and politics focused on his conviction that Chinese immigrants were taking jobs from U.S. workers by their willingness to accept unreasonably low wages. Addressing the case of the Chinese strikebreakers employed in the North Adams, Massachusetts, shoe factory, Swinton, noted that in hiring Chinese workers, "manufacturers and capitalists had obtained possession, not of a mere 'Chinese gong,' but of a weapon which, unless wrested out of their hands, would make them absolute dictators of labor in America" (3). Swinton perceived the alliance between cheap Chinese labor and the capitalist power elite as a threat to American democracy.

Swinton's views on race and morality provide important insights into the theoretical underpinnings of the racialization process. He argued that "the deepest dividing line between men is that of race" (6). He believed that racial distinctions are biological and as such more profoundly rooted within the human psyche than differences based on politics, religion, law, or culture. Race, he argued, "enters into the elements of the blood; establishes itself in the forms of the bones, expresses itself through the material and size of the brain." He noted that "the people of the United States are of the white European race," and, while he acknowledged the role of African peoples in the South and Native Americans in the West, he proposed that the European peoples—Germanic, Celtic, and Latin "varieties"—were responsible for creating and maintaining the stability of the United States. Swinton believed that "intermixture" with "the Chinese Mongolian or Yellow race" would lead to the debasement and degradation of the "White American race." In his mind, Chinese were "inferior in organic structure, in vital force or physical energy"; in short, he felt that they had "depraved and debased blood."

Swinton noted that although the "Chinese problem" in the United States began with biology, it quickly transformed into consequences that affect labor. He used a trip to Havana, Cuba, to provide empirical evidence for his argument. When he visited a cigarette factory called La Honradez, Swinton observed "Chinese coolies" at work. He was visibly shocked at the treatment these workers received. Poorly fed and crudely housed, they led a terrible, "impoverished existence" (9). His indignation stemmed not from the conditions the workers suffered but from their willingness to accept them. In his view, the factory's owners—who condemned the workers to horrendous conditions and long hours—were not at fault. The threat he foresaw in this situation was that Chinese laborers could accept similar reprehensible working and living conditions in the United States and thereby undercut the wages and living conditions of American workers. The danger was that "Chinese coolies" did not demand the "necessities of life" always required by "the industrial classes of America."

Another deficiency Swindon perceived among the Chinese was their morality. Because he understood the Chinese as pagans, their "practical immorality" was inherently "fouler by far than that known among any European or Christian people" (13). In terms of both race and morality, Swinton was willing to accept the Irish and their ways as part of white America (an acceptance that, as Chapter 4 shows, was nowhere near being settled in the 1870s when he was writing), but he could not overlook the clear "racial" differences he perceived in the Chinese. He linked the "importation" of "Chinese coolies" with the African slave trade and posited that the U.S. government should intervene and regulate Chinese immigration just as it did in the case of the "importation of African slaves." His mention of African Americans is especially provocative because the United States was then in the midst of reconstruction, and many American elites were concerned about how the white population would deal with emancipated blacks. Many southern plantation owners were in the process of considering whether to hire "coolies" on their vast and largely unreconstructed estates.

Swinton ended his diatribe on a patronizing note: "I have no animosity against the Chinese race. As human beings and children of God, I entertain the most amiable feelings toward them. I would defend them against any wrong, under all circumstances. My indignation has been aroused by the outrages perpetrated upon them in California. We must, in no case, permit anything of the kind toward the Chinese immigrants to these Northern States" (15). This comment, perhaps as well as any, demonstrates the viciously subtle nature of racialization. Swinton argued that he did not dislike the Chinese (though his other comments suggest just the opposite). They were biologically inferior to "whites" (even apparently to the Catholic Irish), to be sure, but even so they deserved a paternalistic pat on the head now and then. Perhaps it would be best if they simply stayed in the West and did not bother to go east. The "Chinese problem" should remain something for the western states to solve on their own.

M. B. Starr's *The Coming Struggle: Or What the People on the Pacific Coast Think of the Coolie Invasion* (1873) is much longer and more developed than Swinton's pamphlet, even though the concepts are familiar. Starr's theme is adequately presented in the book's first sentence: "It is now generally understood and believed that a powerful combination of capital is systematically organized to bring into the midst of the most civilized portions of the world vast hordes of the debased, ignorant, and corrupt heathen races, to fill all positions of industry with servile laborers, to the practical exclusion of working citizens" (7). Starr's position mirrored Swinton's; the "Chinese problem" started with U.S. capitalists who insisted on hiring them. Starr likewise condemned the late practice of American slavery but argued that the Chinese could all too easily be enslaved because they were "among the most corrupt" nationalities on earth. He noted that the Chinese would always work for lower wages than any American (i.e., white) worker and would accept filthy, contaminated living conditions. Starr argued that even if they could be "civilized," the Chinese would refuse to pay taxes to a government not their own and that revolts and feuds undoubtedly will result. To Starr, the Chinese were "a contentious and dissolute race, without conscientious scruples" (9).

Starr did not hide his disdain for Chinese immigrants and laid out in detail the problems he believed they would cause by their presence in America. Like Swinton, Starr saw them as a threat to every aspect of American life, but his position was more clearly rooted in his Christian beliefs. For him, religion constituted the greatest deficiency of the Chinese as a people, because they were "heathens." Comparing the influx of Chinese to the enslavement of Africans, Starr argued that imported Africans were "Americanized" because they were "stripped of their idols." They were not allowed "to perform a single act of . . . stupid worship of material things that would corrupt the children of his master," and they were not permitted "to establish a Fetish temple" (20). Starr argued:

The imported African, robbed of his idols, and under restraints and education of home circles, obliged to hear the Gospel or nothing—stood a hundred times better opportunity than the savage for reformation, and a thousand times better than the pagan, who is permitted to roam night and day, protected and sustained in his idolatry, gambling, and filthy orgies, under less restraint even than the native citizen. Besides, most of the imported Africans are dead, and the descendants are native Americans, speaking our language and worshiping our God, quite all civilized and many are Christians; all are citizens, and intend to *stay* with us. (20–21; emphasis in original)

What really troubled Starr was his belief that because Chinese immigrants were "heathens," they could not be Americanized. He felt that they were simply unwilling to learn new things.

Starr addressed the topic of acculturation again in a one-page section entitled "Is There Any Reasonable Prospect that We Will Ever Bring the Pagans as a Race, in the Condition of Slaves, Up to Our Standards of Morals and Civilization?" (80). Starr here created a scenario in which China, with its population of over "four hundred million," could overwhelm the American citizenry by importing just one-tenth of its population. The Chinese, "unfit to be citizens but under their own government . . . [and] having their own schools and idol temples" would begin to fight for "ascendancy" in America. Restating his case for total acculturation in starker terms, Starr said, "We must bring these people up to our Christianity and civilization, or they will bring our children down to their barbarism and vice." Equivocating somewhat on his earlier position, Starr opined that perhaps Chinese could be Americanized faster and more completely than Americans could be Sinocized, but he had enough doubt to make him wonder. The acculturation of the Chinese in the United States would be unnecessary if the sheer force of their numbers came to overwhelm the smaller numbers of "civilized" workers. Working-class Americans would surely degenerate when confronted with the superior number of Chinese. Tellingly, Starr noted that as long as Americans treated immigrant Chinese as "hewers of wood and drawers of water," they could not be raised up to the level of American civilization. His use of this allusion was heavy with biblical meaning because it evoked an image of conquered people reduced to lowly manual labor (Linebaugh and Rediker 2000, 36–70). His use of this phrase was charged with hidden meaning and undoubtedly was read on a deep cognitive level by his nativist Bible-reading American followers.

Starr believed that the "Chinese problem" could be solved only by stopping immigration and thus ending the unholy alliance between American capitalists and Chinese laborers. Rather than to attack the problem by going after the corporate elite, he found it more sensible to use racist language against poor Chinese laborers.

The Chinese and the Chinese Question (1888), by attorney James A. Whitney, also argued against Chinese immigration. Like Swinton, Whitney said that he had nothing personal against the Chinese. He felt that the problem was that America had been opened up to them in such a reckless manner that their large numbers might eventually ruin the country. Like Swinton and Starr, Whitney framed much of his argument in racialist terms, though he was much more sympathetic to Chinese culture and history than the other two authors. He noted that his argument was based on empirical facts, collected and judged with "the calmness of judicial impartiality . . . without prejudice" (1). Whitney argued that Chinese language, music, government, religion, art, literature, and industry were all created in China, free of external influence. He applauded the creativity of the Chinese at home and noted that "current Caucasian public opinion" had underrated the Chinese intellect and overrated their potential harmful effects on the United States. But Whitney also found that "the Chinese character is strong not only in its positive but in its negative elements; that the very absence of those finer and higher qualities, which are with us believed to be essential to enlightened communities, has given, and will continue to give, a preponderating power to the Chinese in all that relates to merely material success" (40). Whitney observed that "the Chinaman is as subtle and facile in whatever requires intellectual work as he is in the perfor-

mance of manual labor," traits he saw as positive (48). Such innate characteristics were supplemented by "suavity and politeness"—which often stood
in marked contrast to the Caucasian's rudeness and discourteousness—and
were found in all Chinese, "with the ignorant as with the educated, with the
laborer as with the mandarin." It should be noted that Whitney's use of the
word "Caucasian" was calculated and rich with meaning. Nativists at the time
used the word, a pseudo-scientific term with the weight of apparent objective
legitimacy behind it, as a synonym for "assimilable" and "white" (Saxton 1971,
18). They judged non-Caucasians to be just the opposite. By adopting this
perspective, those opposed to Chinese laborers could define themselves as
members of a specific identifiable race that, as these three authors stress, was
under assault by a foreign horde.

Whitney's comments regarding this point lacked the viciousness and con-
descension of Swinton's and Starr's screeds against Chinese immigration and
culture. By applauding Chinese culture—in China—he appeared to attach legitimacy to it and thus imbue it with inherent value. But his argument was
considerably more subtle because he structured his complaint against the
Chinese in terms of late-nineteenth-century thoughts about cultural evolution. This approach appeared to be more scientific and thus more damning
than Swinton's and Starr's attacks. Whitney's racism was not as overt as that of
Swinton and Starr, but it was just as powerful. He argued that Chinese institutions in every sphere were "an extension of those which control the family
in the earliest stages of society" (41). In other words, China had a long and
venerable history, but its progress toward "civilization" had been slow. As a
late-Victorian cultural evolutionist, Whitney believed that the "rise" of China
was incomplete, and this is what he found so troubling and potentially dangerous. He feared the future power of China and the Chinese in all spheres of
quotidian life.

The evolutionary track of China and the Chinese, when added to the
"Physical Nature of the Chinese" (63) made Whitney even more nervous.
Speaking as an environmental determinist, Whitney stated that the Chinese
climate had made its people tough but not physically strong. He compared the
coarseness of their hair with the Europeans' soft hair and noted that "as is the
case with animals," Chinese individuals could recover from all cuts, wounds,
and bruises much faster than Europeans. Whitney further noted that these
physical characteristics could be demonstrated empirically by considering the
construction of the Pacific Railroad. As they performed this hard labor, Chinese outdid Caucasians in endurance, but they could not match the whites'
physical strength. As a result, and given his acceptance of cultural evolution,

he believed himself safe in the conclusion that Caucasians are biologically superior to Chinese.

We may pause here and reflect on the ways in which European and U.S. physical scientists racialized Chinese people in the years before Swinton, Starr, and Whitney wrote their tracts. Each would have been aware of this body of thought and each undoubtedly had learned its basic principles as matters of scientific fact. In 1735, Linnaeus distinguished four varieties of humanity, of which the "Asiatic" was one (Voget 1975, 57). Scientists and polemicists interested in human diversity relied on this classification for decades, and many of them worked to define the genetic, or at least the phenotypic, relations between the four human "races." Most formulations were preconceived and inherently racialist. For example, Comte Joseph Arthur de Gobineau argued in the mid-nineteenth century that the racial hierarchy began with whites and moved down to those with yellow and black skin. According to Gobineau, miscegenation—including Asians with Europeans—had led to physical degeneration and democracy, which for him represented social downfall (Hays 1965, 238–239). One common element of the racialization of the Chinese "race" was the argument that all individuals so classified looked alike, that they had a "sameness of physique," even though Chinese women were a "sickly white" color rather than yellow (Jefferies 1869, 147).

In the late nineteenth century, when Swinton, Starr, and Whitney were writing their "scientific" tracts, the ideas of Samuel Morton, the renowned, albeit misguided, U.S. craniologist, were still current. In *Crania Americana* (1839), his most famous work, Morton accepted a division of humanity into four racial groups, which he attempted to prove using measurements of skull size. He posited that skull size reflects intelligence and that intelligence equates to race. In the presentation of his cranial measurements, he offered a scientific foundation for a polygenetic rendering of human history (Bieder 1986, 83). He attempted to simplify the "science" in his quantitative presentation by providing summaries of the characteristics of each of the four human races. (We now know that his quantitative calculations were wrong; see Gould 1981, 66–67.) His description of "the Mongolian race" is worth quoting in full because it was prevalent in America when thousands of Chinese immigrants were in the process of negotiating the epochal racial structure of their new home:

This great division of the human species is characterised by a sallow or olive colored skin, which appears to be drawn tight over the bones of the face; long, black straight hair, and thin beard. The nose is broad, and short; the eyes are small, black, and obliquely placed, and the eye-brows arched and linear; the lips are turned, the cheek bones broad and flat, and the zygomatic arches salient. The skull is oblong-oval, somewhat flattened at the sides, with a low forehead. (Morton 1839, 5)

Morton concluded: "In their intellectual character the Mongolians are ingenious, imitative, and highly susceptible to cultivation." Just above this assertion—and standing in marked contrast—was his conclusion about the mental capacity of "the Caucasian race": "This race is distinguished of the facility with which it attains the highest intellectual endowments" (5).

Most significant for our present purposes are Morton's comments on "the moral character of the Chinese" (45). Rather than make the pronouncement himself, Morton relied on the comments of "Dr. Morrison," actually Robert Morrison, the first Protestant missionary to China, who had arrived in Macao in 1807. He also cited "Gutzlaff," undoubtedly a reference to Rev. Charles (Karl Friedrich) Gutzlaff, who published a journal in 1834 recounting his three voyages to China as a missionary in 1831–1833. Morton stated that Morrison's information derived from "long and intimate acquaintance" with the Chinese, so his personal knowledge made him a reliable authority. Morrison indicated that "the Chinese" were mild, urbane, reasonable, and industrious. They showed respect to the aged but at the same time expected subordination from their juniors. His gross characterization appeared to be flattering on the surface, but Morrison also saw a dark side to the Chinese character in that they exhibited these attributes only in public; their actions were, he said, "often more show than reality." The more accurate "reality," Morrison said, is that "the Chinese are specious, but insincere; jealous, envious, and distrustful to a high degree. . . . The Chinese are generally selfish, cold-blooded and inhumane." As if this were not enough, Morton included the following characterization from Rev. W. Ellis, who wrote the introduction to Gutzlaff's journal: "[Gutzlaff] might with great propriety have added . . . that in the punishment of criminals, in the infliction of torture, they are barbarously cruel; that human suffering, or human life, are but rarely regarded by those in authority, when the infliction of the one, or the destruction of the other, can be made subservient to the acquisition of wealth or power." Morton added to this his view that in letters, science, and art, the Chinese "are the same now what they were many centuries ago" (45).

The view that the Chinese were in a stalled state of cultural development is not insignificant, given the general intellectual support in the late nineteenth century for the theory of cultural evolution. Any assessment that the Chinese were in a state of cultural suspended animation had clear social implications in a world driven by concepts of teleological cultural progress.

Anti-Chinese writers observed their lack of cultural development in many realms of life. In attempting to relate artistic expression with their intellectual development, for example, Hungarian scholar Francis Pulszky (1857, 201) argued that Chinese art was flat and imitative because "the Chinese is endowed with a sober and dry imagination, . . . cold reason predominates, and . . . the creative power is scarcely developed in him." Chinese art was materialistic and stark rather than beautiful, he argued. Pulszky's essay appeared in a book co-authored by Dr. Josiah C. Nott, a student of Morton who is now regarded as an infamous racist (Bieder 1986, 92).

Whitney's comments in his Chapter XXII, "Injurious Effects of Chinese Immigration in California" (1888, 111–116), are pertinent to our discussion of the racial structure of the United States. Like other commentators who claimed that their overriding interest was the employment of working-class native-born Americans, Whitney's central problem revolves around Chinese immigrants who took jobs from "white labor." He said that the various industries in the Pacific Coast region would have experienced a "normal development" with white workers. But the problem was that most white Americans were unemployed because Chinese workers had taken their places. This situation obtained even for white women and children, who sought to supplement the often-meager salary of male breadwinners with seasonal work. The particular activities Whitney cited as incorporating Chinese labor were picking hops and berries, weaving, gathering fruit, digging potatoes, tending gardens, dairying, caning chairs, and laundering. But Whitney felt that the "Chinese problem" was even more potentially damaging. Once these unskilled jobs were filled, unemployed Chinese would look to enter other occupations. U.S. employers, who were only too eager to oblige these inexpensive workers, would rapidly hire them, thus forcing more Americans out of work. This prediction was not just hyperbole. In San Francisco, for example, the owners of the Mission Woolen Mills had hired 550 Chinese. And at a nearby mattress factory, "not a single white man found work" (113). A mine company in Oroville had about 4,000 Chinese in its employ. The social implication of widespread white unemployment was that teenagers would suffer moral decline and become hoodlums. The root of the problem as Whitney saw it was that the Chinese simply were not like Americans: they were generally single, they worked for low wages, they intended to go back to China with their American "riches" in their pockets, and they would accept vile living conditions that Caucasians would refuse in disgust.

Whitney's comments about the living conditions of Chinese immigrants in San Francisco are especially pertinent to this archaeological study. His views on the conditions in San Francisco are even more apposite because of my argument that part of the process of understanding racialization in U.S. history rests on an understanding of physical segregation in concert with the material effects of the racialized social structure, the socio-spatial dialectic.

Whitney stated that at the time of his writing, "sixty thousand of the Chinese are crowded into six or seven blocks of buildings" in San Francisco (115–116). He said that the buildings, originally constructed with twelve-foot ceilings, were often subdivided into two intermediate floors, in effect making three stories. He was silent about who actually made the alterations—landlords seeking to increase their economic capital or Chinese residents seeking to do the same—but the floors, he said, were completely occupied by Chinese. In a description that is remarkably similar to that of the Five Points provided by Dickens and others, Whitney said: "The streets in that portion of the city are connected from one side to the other by subterranean passages, so that the occupants of the houses pass underground from building to building. Sometimes the upper stories of the structures are built outward over the street until, at some distance from the ground, they approach within two feet of each other" (116). Whitney said that this part of the city included four or five thousand Chinese women, "of whom not more than one in twenty is other than the vilest of the vile." His late-Victorian sensibilities kept him from identifying these women as prostitutes, but the label was certainly implied.

The crowded, unclean settlement that Whitney abhorred, the nation's first Chinatown, was created in response to the California legislature's enaction of the Foreign Miners License Law in 1850. This law decreed that people who were not native-born Americans, excluding Native Americans, had to pay $20 per month for the right to mine. Rather than pay the fee, some Chinese miners left the mining camps and settled in San Francisco (Coolidge 1909, 29–30). Many miners, Chinese and otherwise, stayed in the camps until the more-easily-mined stream deposits were played out. Chinatowns thus developed as places where Chinese miners and former miners, as well as other immigrants, could obtain goods and services newly arrived from China (Mary Praetzellis, pers. comm.).

Swinton, Starr, and Whitney all believed that Chinese immigrants in the United States represented a substantial threat to the economic health of the nation. All three stressed that U.S. workers were in grave danger because Chinese workers, who viewed themselves as only temporary visitors to the United States, were willing to live simply and accept wages that were well below the U.S. standard. However, these wages could represent a substantial cache of economic capital when the immigrants finally returned home. Under a veil of concern for the native-born working class, each writer harbored disdain for the immigrants that was rooted in racial theory. Each couched his argument differently, and Whitney even wrote about the antiquity and grace of Chinese culture. But the place for Chinese culture was across the Pacific in China, not in the United States. Each author believed that Chinese people and their culture should stay home.

As was the case with attitudes toward the Irish in New York City, we cannot know with certainty how many Americans shared these three writers' negative sentiments about Chinese immigrants. The idea that the Chinese "race" was uniquely homogeneous—more so than the peoples of Europe, India, and the Near East—was expressed well into the twentieth century (e.g., Buxton 1929, 44; Latourette 1964, 440). The writings of Swinton, Starr, and Whitney suggest that an audience did exist for these ideas.

The racialized situation Chinese immigrants faced is drawn into even sharper focus by considering the drafting and passage of statutes intended to restrict Chinese immigration. The presence of such legislation suggests, at a minimum, that many politicians believed in the restrictions themselves or supported them to gain their constituents' votes.

The 1858 Treaty of Tien-Tsin between the United States and China established formal amicable relations between the two nations. Most of the treaty explained economic relations, elucidated the rights of American citizens in Chinese ports, and enumerated certain conditions of commerce. For our purposes, two clauses of the treaty deserve mention. Article XI specifies that American citizens in China who conducted themselves peacefully and lawfully should be placed on an equal legal footing with the people of China. The treaty thus banned discrimination against Americans. This clause was patently hypocritical on the part of the United States. By the time the treaty was negotiated, the number of Chinese immigrants to the U.S. Pacific Coast had significantly increased and local prejudice had begun "to crystallize against the newcomers" (Jones 1909, 352). The United States had no intention of treating Chinese residents in the United States with the courtesy it demanded for its own citizens in China. Article XXIX enunciated that Americans in China who practiced Christianity should not be molested during their services and devotions. It specified that the same also should hold true for Chinese converts to Christianity. Yet Chinese immigrants in the United States were commonly referred to as "heathens" and "pagans."

The Burlingame Treaty, signed in 1868, welcomed Chinese immigrants into the United States. Article V stated that all people in the world had the right to change their place of residence and even their allegiance and that Chinese would be welcome in the United States. This formal declaration of unrestricted immigration also made the case that Chinese in America should expect to be free from discrimination and violence (McClain 1994, 30).

The 1880 Treaty Regulating Immigration from China was the first attempt the U.S. government made to limit the number of Chinese laborers in the nation. The main feature of this treaty was that the United States reserved the right to regulate, limit, or even suspend the entrance and residence of Chinese in America whenever their presence represented a threat. The treaty was aimed at unskilled laborers; individuals who wanted to emigrate as teachers, students, merchants, or merely as tourists were excluded from its purview. Article III said that the government would seek to offer Chinese in America all the protections accorded to its citizens. A cynic could propose that the federal government made this statement of civil equality in the full knowledge that most of the protections that could be offered would need to originate from state and local agencies rather than from Washington. Federal civil rights legislation would not come until many years later.

The 1880 treaty was transformed into a formal act two years later in the infamous Chinese Exclusion Act of 1882. The preamble to this act left no doubt about its conclusion regarding the influx of Chinese laborers into the United States: "In the opinion of the Government of the United States the coming of Chinese laborers to this country endangers the good order of certain localities within the territory." To show its resolve, Congress imposed a stiff fine on any ship captain found guilty of attempting to import Chinese workers: not more than $500 for each immigrant laborer and possible imprisonment for as long as one year. Congress decreed that the provisions of the act would last for ten years. It further stated that any Chinese person who was in the United States before November 17, 1880, the date of the treaty, or who arrived in the country before the expiration of the ninety-day grace period after the treaty was passed had the freedom to come and go as they wished. The framers of the act established severe penalties for violation for all individuals, not just ship captains. Any person found guilty of trying to import Chinese could face a fine not to exceed $1000 and one year's imprisonment. Section 14 specified that individual states could not attempt to circumvent the act by admitting Chinese individuals to citizenship. Chinese diplomats and their servants were exempted from the provisions of the act, but to make their position absolutely clear, the act explicitly stated that "the words 'Chinese laborers,' wherever used in this act, shall be construed to mean both skilled and unskilled laborers and Chinese employed in mining." This qualification is noteworthy because it implied the assumption that clever American importers would attempt to outwit the law by classifying all incoming Chinese as skilled laborers. The act's creators slammed the door on this possibility, just as they slammed the door on Chinese immigration (Gyory 1998).

The exemption of teachers, students, merchants, and tourists provided a loophole in the act that Chinese immigrants could exploit. Erika Lee (2003, 2–5) recounts the way her grandfather, Lee Chi Yet, entered the United States during the exclusion era. Because he had been a farmer all his life, Lee's grandfather was unable to enter the United States as a member of the exempted class. As a result, he had to purchase papers from another immigrant that named him as the immigrant's son. To become a "paper son," Lee Chi Yet had to surrender his name and become Yee Shew Ning, son of the merchant Yee Yook Haw. His new "kinship" meant that he had to memorize the names, ages, and other pieces of personal information about his new "family." The deception was no easy matter, especially when the "father" and the "son" were interrogated separately by immigration officials. The inspector who interviewed Lee Chi Yet/Yee Shew Ning asked him 145 questions, most of which required a detailed knowledge of the Lee family and their home village in China. Lee Chi Yet passed the test and was permitted to remain in the United States as the son of the exempted merchant.

The Chinese Exclusion Act was in effect from 1882 until 1943. The Chinese were the first immigrant group to be denied entrance to the United States because of their racial classification (Almaguer 1994, 6). The creation of the discriminatory statute obviously emboldened local authorities to enact equally harsh ordinances. Such laws could be written to obscure their racially defined bias. An example is an ordinance passed by the San Francisco city government prohibiting the operation of laundries in wooden buildings without the prior approval of the board of supervisors. Laundries in brick or stone buildings were exempt; the supposed purposed of the ordinance was to prevent potentially devastating urban fires.

Chinese laundry workers were so prevalent in California's urban centers that they became the stereotypic "Chinaman," in the same way that equestrian Plains hunters became the stereotypic "Indians." When San Francisco's Chinese laundry owners, who typically owned wooden buildings as their place of business, petitioned the board of supervisors for licenses, the were invariably refused. Yet the board approved all but one license request by a non-Chinese laundry owner who inhabited a wooden building.

One Chinese owner, Yick Wo, was denied a permit but continued to operate his laundry anyway. He was promptly arrested and convicted of violating the ordinance. The board of supervisors used the claim of public safety concerns to pursue what was for all intents and purposes an element of the process of racialization. Yick Wo fought the case all the way to the U.S. Supreme Court, which reversed his conviction. Writing for the Court, Justice Stanley Matthews decreed in *Yick Wo v. Hopkins* in 1886 that the problem was not that the city ordinance was discriminatory against Chinese—the Chinese Exclusion

Act already had approved discrimination—but that the city administered the ordinance in a discriminatory manner, thus violating the Fourteenth Amendment (Chang 2003, 139).

The San Francisco Board of Supervisors had received petitions as early as 1870 from the city's Anti-Coolie Association demanding that they do something about the unsanitary conditions in Chinatown. Writers who described San Francisco's Chinatown sometimes specifically equated it with the New York City of the Irish: "The unsanitary condition of Chinatown—for many years the horror of the press and the thunder of the politician—was after all a mere matter of profit for the landlord. Chinatown property, like the property formerly leased to immigrants on the East Side in New York, was let with the stipulation that the tenant must make all repairs" (Coolidge 1909, 413). In the face of rising anti-Chinese sentiment in the city, the board authorized ordinances that made it illegal to rent any apartments or rooms that contained less than 500 cubic feet of airspace per adult. At the same time, the board made it a criminal act to dwell or sleep in such cramped spaces. The Anti-Coolie Association also encouraged the board to enact an ordinance requiring Chinese peddlers to obtain licenses and wear badges proving that they indeed had the proper license (McClain 1994, 44–46).

The various federal statutes and the local and state ordinances enacted to restrict, control, and limit the freedom of Chinese in the United States had a demonstrable and clear affect on Chinese immigrant life. Public opinion undoubtedly was shaped by these laws and the rigor with which they were enforced. These rules and regulations demonstrate how nativist American officials created, refined, and maintained a racially based epochal structure. Archaeologists attempting to conceptualize the power of racialization in historic America must not diminish the importance of this structure on daily life.

We should also not neglect how public opinion—the prevailing and situational habitus—can be constructed by elements of popular culture, especially cartoons, that specifically are intended to shape public opinion. Because they are visible on the street every day, these pictorial representations may have more immediate racial consequences than laws enacted in faraway statehouses and federal courts. Just as they did with public images of the Irish, cartoonists helped shape the racialized image of the "Chinaman."

Thomas Nast was by far the most important political cartoonist of the nineteenth century. As a cartoonist for *Leslie's Illustrated*, the *New York Illustrated News*, and, perhaps most famously, *Harper's Weekly*, Nast's opinionated drawings were regularly seen by thousands of readers (Keller 1968, 8). As a political commentator, Nast was a fervent supporter of the Union during the Civil War and a biting and remarkably effective opponent of political corruption. The

Figure 5.4. "Pacific Chivalry." *Harper's Weekly*, August 7, 1869, 512.

graft and nepotism of Tammany Hall—at the hands of Irish Americans William "Boss" Tweed, Peter "Brains" Sweeny, and Richard "Slippery Dick" Connolly—was one of his favorite targets (Vinson 1967, 5–22). Nast was also adept at illustrating the social environments America's minorities faced, including Chinese immigrants. Four of his illustrations will demonstrate both his perspective on the "Chinese question" and his belief that Chinese immigrants were being discriminated against in America. Considered chronologically, his images indicate at least three features that are important here: his depiction of Chinese immigrants in ways that made them readily identifiable to his non-Chinese readers; his ability to show how Chinese individuals were perceived by nativist Americans; and his caricature of many of the Chinese antagonists as stereotypic, simian Irishmen.

Nast's August 7, 1869, illustration entitled "Pacific Chivalry: Encouragement to Chinese Immigration" shows two individuals (Figure 5.4). One is a stereotypic Chinese coolie, with broad-brimmed straw hat, thick-soled cotton shoes, broad trousers, long loose-fitting coat, and long black queue. The second figure is a fierce-looking white man (obviously American) who violently yanks the first man's queue straight back with his left hand while raising a cat-o'-nine-tails over his head with his right hand. He clearly intends to strike the coolie with this whip. The railroad tracks behind the second man indicates that the coolie was probably employed as a laborer for the Central Pacific

Figure 5.5. "The Chinese Question." *Harper's Weekly*, February 18, 1871, 149.

Railroad. The second man's hatband reads "California," and the wall of a shed in the background reads "Courts of Justice Closed to Chinese. Extra Taxes to 'Yellowjack.'"

In a second drawing, published on February 18, 1871, Nast presents a complex picture that is as notable for its text as for the people depicted (Figure 5.5). In the foreground, a Chinese man sits on the ground, holding his head in his left hand. Lady America, a quintessential white maiden wearing a long white gown, stands over him in a protective posture. A crown rests on her head that reads "U.S.," and at her breast is an American crest. She looks defiantly over her shoulder at an angry mob, whose members hold short clubs, pistols, and rocks. The apparent leader of the mob is a stereotypic simian-faced Irishman in classic "Irish" dress: a waistcoat, a coat with tails, a top hat with short du-deen pipe in the band, and a bottle in his pocket. Members of the crowd hold signs reading "Our Rights," "Blood," "Strike," "We Rule," and "If Our Ballots Will Not Stop Them Coming to Our Country, the Bullet Must." In the background behind the mob is a destroyed "Colored Orphan Asylum." Lying on the ground between the mob and the two figures in the foreground are two broadsheets. One reads "Crimes and Drunkenness. Riots by Pure White Strik-ers. Europeans Are the Bulk of Our 'American' Pauperism. Prisons. Work-houses." The second paper reads "Public Institutions Filled with Europeans." The texts on these two papers is difficult to read, but the numerous broad-sheets pasted on the wall behind the Chinese man and Lady America are impossible to ignore. Perhaps more than anything else, this textual material explains the racialized conditions Chinese immigrants faced at the hands of nativist Americans. From top to bottom the signs read:

1. Coolie, Slave, Pauper, Rat-Eater;
2. The Chinese Question. "The Chinaman Works Cheap Because He Is a Barbarian and Seeks Gratification of Only the Lowest, the Most Inevitable Wants." Wendell Phillips;
3. The Lowest and Vilest of the Human Race. I (a White Man) Am Op-posed to Him on Grounds of—1, Race; 2, Industry; 3, Politics; 4, Mo-rality. White [unreadable];
4. Trades—Unions. Meeting. "Resolved [unreadable scribbles] Impor-tation of Chinese Barbarians into the Country Must Be Stopped by the Ballot or Bullet." Workingmen (?);
5. No Family Virtues "Such as We Have" (White Purity);
6. "They Are Dishonest and False, Vicious, Immoral, and Heathenish." Heathen Immorality of the Chinese Race Is Beyond Description;
7. "Degraded Labor of Asia." "European Immorality Is Virtue When Compared with Chinese Immorality.";
8. John Chinaman Is an Idolater and Heathen. Servile Laborers from Asia. Joss Houses in our Midst.";
9. "Chinese Paganism Has, by Its Fruits [,] a Practical Immorality Fouler by Far Than That known among Any European or Christian People."

These broadsheets communicate much about the nativist habitus that was be-ing created in the United States around the influx of Chinese laborers. The posters indicate that some U.S. residents expressed great hostility toward Chi-nese because they were not Christians and because they agreed to work for

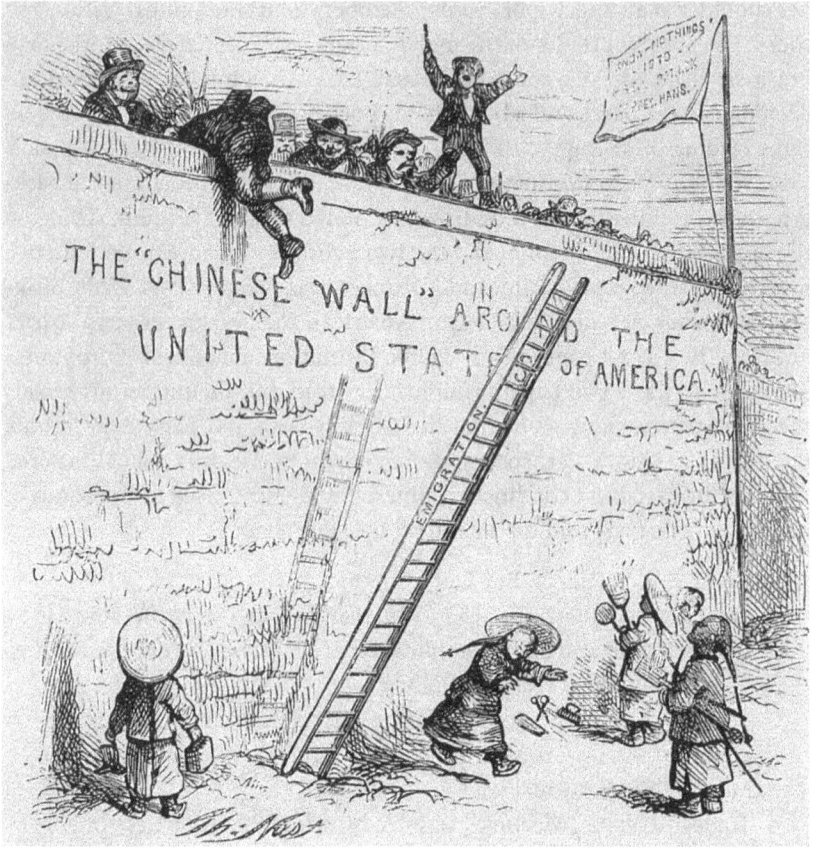

Figure 5.6. "Throwing Down the Ladder by Which They Rose." *Harper's Weekly*, July 23, 1870, 480.

low wages. They also demonstrate that some Americans were willing to use physical violence and armed terrorism to fight the "Asian horde." Billboard number 3 repeats Swinton's claims against the Chinese verbatim, so it is likely that his tract was widely known at the time.

The epithet "rat-eater" used to describe the Chinese is especially vicious and determinedly tenacious. When Emory Bogardus was conducting the Pacific Coast Race Relations Survey in 1925, he interviewed a well-educated African American gentleman who told him that "he dislikes the Chinese to this day, because when he was a boy he was told that the Chinese ate rats" (Bogardus 1928, 46). The use of the term "rat-eater" was extremely powerful in the first broadside, and it would have had profound resonance with many readers viewing Nast's drawing.

In a third cartoon, published on July 23, 1870, Nast shows the problems Chinese immigrants face when attempting to enter the United States (Figure

Figure 5.7. "E Pluribus Unum (Except the Chinese)." *Harper's Weekly*, April 1, 1882, 207.

5.6). He shows four coolies at the bottom of a high stone wall that reads "The 'Chinese Wall' around the United States of America." A flag flies from the corner of the wall that reads, in part, "Know Nothings—1870." A tall ladder that reads on its side "Emigration" is about the crash down on the Chinese at the bottom of the wall, and a number of men, some with simian-Irish features, stand triumphantly at the top of the wall.

In a fourth drawing, Nast reconfirms the message of the third cartoon. He pursues the idea that Chinese immigrants are being unfairly refused entry into the United States. This image, entitled "E Pluribus Unum (Except the Chinese)," is dated April 1, 1882 (Figure 5.7). Nast represents the United States as a crenellated fortress with an arched gateway, a portcullis, and an open drawbridge. The words "The Temple of Liberty" are emblazoned over the gateway, and the gate is guarded by two armed soldiers standing at attention. Two imperial-looking American officers—wearing the broad hats worn during the Napoleonic Era—stand at the end of the drawbridge. One of them holds a huge piece of paper reading "Passport. U.S." A Chinese man standing in front of the officer is being denied entry into the fortress. The would-be Chinese immigrant wears the stereotypic Chinese dress, but Nast has replaced the typical straw "coolie" hat with a more-refined-looking silk cap. The man's queue extends to the ground. The Chinese Exclusion Act was passed one month after the appearance of this cartoon, so Nast's goal here is to suggest visually what was about to happen to Chinese immigrants. In the first cartoon they are being terribly mistreated; in the last cartoon they are being turned away.

Learned Habitus of Race in Chinese America

The Chinese faced a series of contrived racial obstacles they had to negotiate and overcome in order to survive. The same was true of all immigrant groups who entered the United States in the last half of the nineteenth century. Survival, of course, meant finding ways to survive economically, but linked to the need for money in America's Gilded Age capitalist environment was the need to find ways to survive within a racialized social system. The process of negotiation was not uniform throughout Chinese America, just as it differed within each immigrant community. We are fortunate with this case study of a Chinese laundry in Stockton, California, to have access to an in-depth consideration of the Chinese community in nearby Oakland. This study, completed by L. Eve Armentrout Ma (2000), is especially valuable because Ma relies on both textual sources and personal memories. Her investigation thus provides special insights into the daily realities of the lives of Chinese immigrants in northern California at a time when the effort to racialize them was in full swing.

Ma refers to the late nineteenth and early twentieth centuries as the period of "attack" (37). Her term signifies that after a period of initial "promise," when Chinese nationals entered the United States seeking funds that would allow them and their families to survive—either back in China or in their new home—anti-Chinese sentiment crystallized into an active, vocal, and oftentimes violent movement. As feelings against Chinese (and Japanese) workers increased, they were forced out of the more lucrative areas of mining and agriculture and into a small number of jobs, including the laundry business.

Asian immigrants formed themselves into spatially discrete Chinatowns, even though non-Asians commonly visited them and frequented their many business establishments. While it has been commonplace to suppose that America's Chinatowns were totally cut off from the non-Chinese communities around them, recent research by archaeologists has refuted this idea by showing how Chinese communities were tied into numerous and complex social and economic networks that stretched beyond the boundaries of Chinatown (Praetzellis 2004; Voss 2005). However, Ma (2000, 55) argues that by the beginning of the twentieth century, the Chinese community in Oakland "had become almost totally isolated." Ma's comments, when juxtaposed with the convincing arguments of the archaeologists who find that Chinese communities were not isolated, may derive from her informants, since her contention is not footnoted. If this interpretation is indeed that of her informants, it may suggest that many of Oakland's Chinatown residents felt a sense of isolation even though they had frequent personal contact with non-Asian Americans. The sense of personal isolation is one implication of being racialized as inferior within the dominant overarching epochal structure.

Ma (2000, 45–46) notes that in Oakland, intercommunity relations took diverse forms. The Lincoln School, founded in 1872, opened with 400 students (most of whom were Irish), but only four years later, most of the students were Chinese. Five Christian associations had established themselves within Chinatown and taught English using the Bible as the main text. At the same time, Chinese entrepreneurs opened curio shops, an interpreter's agency, and herbalist shops outside Chinatown. Many laundries were also situated outside Chinatown to be near their non-Chinese customers (Mary Praetzellis, pers. comm.)

The picture of daily life in Oakland's Chinatown Ma (2000, 48) paints supports the idea that its residents worked long hours in demanding jobs. Laundering in China was considered women's work, and many of the men who entered the laundries of the United States had held teaching and non-laboring jobs in China (Praetzellis 2004, 251). Recently immigrated Chinese laundry workers were generally farmers or laborers from the tenant farms of southeast China (Siu 1987, 107). Many of them entered new occupations in the United States; by the 1920s, 48 percent of Chinese immigrants were engaged in small businesses, including laundries, whereas only 11 percent worked in agriculture. Twenty-seven percent worked as domestic servants (Lee 2003, 273n).

The Chinese Laundry in Northern California

Laundries figure prominently in the history of Chinese racialization in America (Figure 5.8). The case of *Yick Wo v. Hopkins* was only one piece of a larger politico-cultural process that swirled around the laundry business. Nativists'

Figure 5.8. "The Old Chinese Wash House" by Ralph O. Yardley (c. 1924–1952). Courtesy of The Haggin Museum, Stockton, California, Museum number LB67-7406-46.

assaulted laundries in particular partly because of the large numbers of Chinese men and women who entered this business and who, in the process, gained something of a monopoly. But another important aspect of the nativist assault concerned the way Chinese launderers had the audacity to unite themselves into a number of powerful labor guilds (McClain 1994, 47). These guilds illustrated organization and resistance from people who were judged to be racially inferior to white Americans. Their presence both worried American labor leaders and increased anti-Chinese resentment and harassment (Roediger 2005, 81–82). The laundryworker's guild, established first in San Francisco and then in other cities, was called Tongxingtang (Tung Hing Tong) (Praetzellis 2004, 245). Its job was to set standard prices for all laundries and collect money to hire lawyers to fight discriminatory ordinances.

Wherever they were located, Chinese laundries were targets of angry nativists, who often burned them to the ground during anti-Asian riots (McClain 1994, 99–100). Local newspapers tended to perpetuate the hatred by refusing to find any merit in the laundries or give any respect to their workers. Newspaper reporters and editors therefore were accomplices to promoting the racialization process by projecting the racial otherness of the laundry workers.

Residents of Oakland, California, remembered how, during the early years of the twentieth century, local gangs of young people attacked Chinese laundries and harassed their workers. Chinese laundries in the city had to barricade their doors and windows as a defense against rocks hurled against them (Praetzellis 2004, 248–249). Chinese laundry workers, often members of the same families or onetime residents of the same village in China, often lived in the laundries rather than in Chinatown. This settlement pattern has ramifications for archaeological interpretation because it means that such locales, though not in Chinatown, may be considered of Chinatown. Archaeologists exploring such complex sociohistorical processes as racialization thus may be required to broaden their perception of the space under study (Orser 1996, 136–141).

Sociologist Paul Siu (1987) compiled a compelling and important examination of Chinese laundry workers. His study, completed in 1953 as a doctoral dissertation but begun fifteen years earlier, which has been largely overlooked by scholars, is being revived by historical archaeologists interested in the social milieu of the Chinese laundry. Siu (Xiao Chenpang) was himself an immigrant, having been born just southwest of Guangzhou, the region that sent most immigrants to the United States during the nineteenth century. As a student of the Chicago School of Sociology, Siu used the city of Chicago as a laboratory for study. A sociologist with an interest in history, he was able to combine interviewing with historical documentation to provide an analysis that, though dated, is consistent with the methods of much historical archaeology. Siu presented information about the placement of activity areas inside the typical laundry (ironing beds, laundry shelves, washing machine) and documented the work week for the typical laundry worker (one day sorting, three days washing, and three days ironing). His informants told him that work in a laundry was demanding and exhausting. Siu (1987, 114) recounted the observation of a former herbalist in China who was displeased with the workload and daily commitments in the Chicago laundry:

I had no idea that we Chinese people have to work like this in this country. The very first day, I had to begin to work. What is hard for me is to get up so early—five o'clock in the morning! I have not been accustomed to that in China. In China, life has been easy for me. I usually slept until nine or ten o'clock as I pleased. . . . Now I am here. I begin to feel America is work, work, work. It is nothing to get excited about.

Siu also documented the social life of the typical laundry worker and offered insights into the personal conflicts individuals of Chinese descent experienced in America, including the tensions inherent in celebrating traditional festivals rather than American holidays and the negotiation of filial obligation versus American individualism. He did not dwell on the topic of discrimination, but he noted that "Orientals" were "ostracized because of color" (Siu 1987, 270). One comment Siu recorded from a non-Chinese American, however, speaks volumes about the longevity of some Americans' attitudes about the Chinese, their role as laborers in America, and their place in racialized American society: "The Chinks are all right if they remain in their place. I don't mind their working in the laundry business, but they should not go any higher than that. After all, there aren't even enough jobs for us whites, without them butting in. Besides, we could never compete with them. They naturally work harder than us, and for much less pay" (22). This comment was made near the middle of the twentieth century in Chicago, not in late-nineteenth-century northern California. U.S. residents expressed their rejection of Chinese immigrants in other ways as well; laundry owners in Alameda County in northern California, continued to fight against Chinese laundries into the 1930s by arguing that most Chinese immigrants who worked in laundries were illegals (Lee 2003, 234).

A key theoretical point Siu broached deals with the "sojourner thesis." This thesis is of central importance here because of how Siu frames it as a survival tool in the face of racial discrimination. The basic idea of the sojourner thesis is that Chinese immigrants designed their presence in America as temporary. Most entered the country, often alone and single, with the idea of finding a job and amassing enough money to return home. Once back home they could live more comfortably than they could if they had not visited the United States. Isolating themselves from mainstream U.S. culture was one mechanism used by Chinese immigrants who saw themselves as sojourners.

As Mary Praetzellis (2004, 237–238) notes, however, most revisionist historians have discarded this model—as have historical archaeologists working with Chinese materials—by showing quite convincingly that not all Chinese immigrants saw themselves as sojourners. Many entered the United States with the goal of establishing a business or finding a job and staying. But what is significant is Siu's (1987, 295) argument that Chinese immigrants may have behaved "like a sojourner because this conduct represents a solution to a race problem." Siu, himself something of a sojourner, was a firm assimilationist; he believed that Chinese immigrants should attempt to become as Americanized as possible. But he noted that the Chinese laundry worker clung to his (the vast majority of them were male) culture, in effect creating a "racial colony." Chinese immigrants in America may have admired the material goods of the nation, but because they made no attempt to understand the American way of life, they tended to view things with biased eyes. As a result, the Chinese individual in the United States was a marginalized person, as anyone professing to be a sojourner might well admit. As a confirmed believer in the concept of the American melting pot, Siu tended to see the sojourner as something of a social misfit. He noted that the sojourners' collective construction of "we/they" categories worked against any real assimilation with the dominant culture (Siu 1987, 297).

Rather than agree with Siu that the "psychological satisfaction" of the we/ they creation is simply an indication of immigrant ethnocentrism, it may be more profitable to perceive the construction of the we/they dyad as a racial identifier, as categories originating in the dominant society. Thus, if a sojourner mentality did exist among Chinese immigrants, we might understand it as an adaptation to the epochal structure of race in the United States. Without question, discriminatory statutes and laws—at all levels of government—established the Chinese in America as "they." Theories of physical race tended to reify the racial categories and justify the harshness (and "rightness") of such laws.

The spatial inclusion of Chinese residents in the non-Asian community— because laundries were not necessarily located in Chinatown—has significant ontological importance for archaeological interpretation. At the very least, it causes us to broaden our notion of the spatialization of segregation. Local, state, and federal ordinances enacted by nativists against Chinese immigration in general and Chinese people specifically informed the Chinese in the United States that they were under attack because of who they were. Subtle acts of resentment and discrimination, coupled with violent events of repression and hatred, let Chinese immigrants fully understand their assigned place in racialized America. Whether they all would accept their structural position is another matter entirely.

The Chinese laundry is one site that lends itself especially well to an archaeological consideration of the racialization process for at least two reasons. First, laundries were symbolic physical places upon which nativist, white Americans could focus their attention and hatred. The laundry, thus conceived, is a sociospatial locus of racialized activity that is in agreement with the American ideology of hard work and industry. Accordingly, laundries are sites where the racialization process may be particularly evident in the material culture. Second, the Chinese laundry, a racialized site often located outside the physical limits of Chinatown, permits us to broaden the notion of segregation in a racialized epochal structure. In other words, as archaeologists examining the racialization process, we are forced out of the physical boundaries of Chinatown. This leads us to the conclusion that Chinatown is also a cognitive racial site whose boundaries are free to change situationally and over time. Understanding Chinatown's spatial open-endedness allows us to accept, for example, that the boys' teasing and harassing of Chinese laundry workers outside Oakland's Chinatown (Praetzellis 2004, 248) also represents the harassment of people within Chinatown, albeit indirectly. Such indirect discrimination foregrounds the idea that the racialization process, though perhaps not always obvious, is nonetheless active in various ways within the epochal structure of racialized America.

The Materiality of Chinese Racialization in Stockton

Historical documents yield an immediate indication of the sometimes-indirect nature of the racialization process. The historical research conducted as part of the Stockton redevelopment project, from which the archaeological material used in this chapter derives, indicates that Chinese businesses were not mentioned in the city directories until 1926 (Waghorn 2004, 56–57). The Lee Sing Laundry at 123 East Channel Street is first mentioned then. The reasons for not reporting the laundries in the directories may be diverse. Business owners may have had to pay to be listed and the owners of the Chinese laundries may have chosen not to participate. Perhaps the preparers of the directories thought the laundries too unworthy to be mentioned, or perhaps they perceived them as too temporary (even though in reality many laundries had great longevity, including the one at 123 East Channel). Or maybe the failure to list the laundries in the late nineteenth and early twentieth centuries is a reflection of the racialization process. The recorders, not wishing to give the Chinese proprietors any respect as legitimate shop owners, simply discriminated against them. Whatever the actual reason, the failure to include the laundries in city directories significantly reduces our ability to research them today. Large segments of their histories thus are effectively erased, and so archaeological research provides an important avenue into the past life of the Chinese in the United States.

   The archaeological deposits examined in this chapter consisted of a complex sequence of layers of fill. The nature of these layers told the archaeologists that the artifacts had been deposited in a series of episodes (Waghorn 2004, 75). Included in the stratification were layers of ash, which contained the artifacts, and layers of clay that may represent periods of flooding (Figure 5.9). Analytical Unit B was composed of these thin layers, a wooden post (perhaps the remains of one of the laundry's drying racks), a substantial brick feature that was rectangular and hollow (most likely the support base for the laundry's boiler), and a pit feature (possibly related to the destruction and removal of the building after 1948).

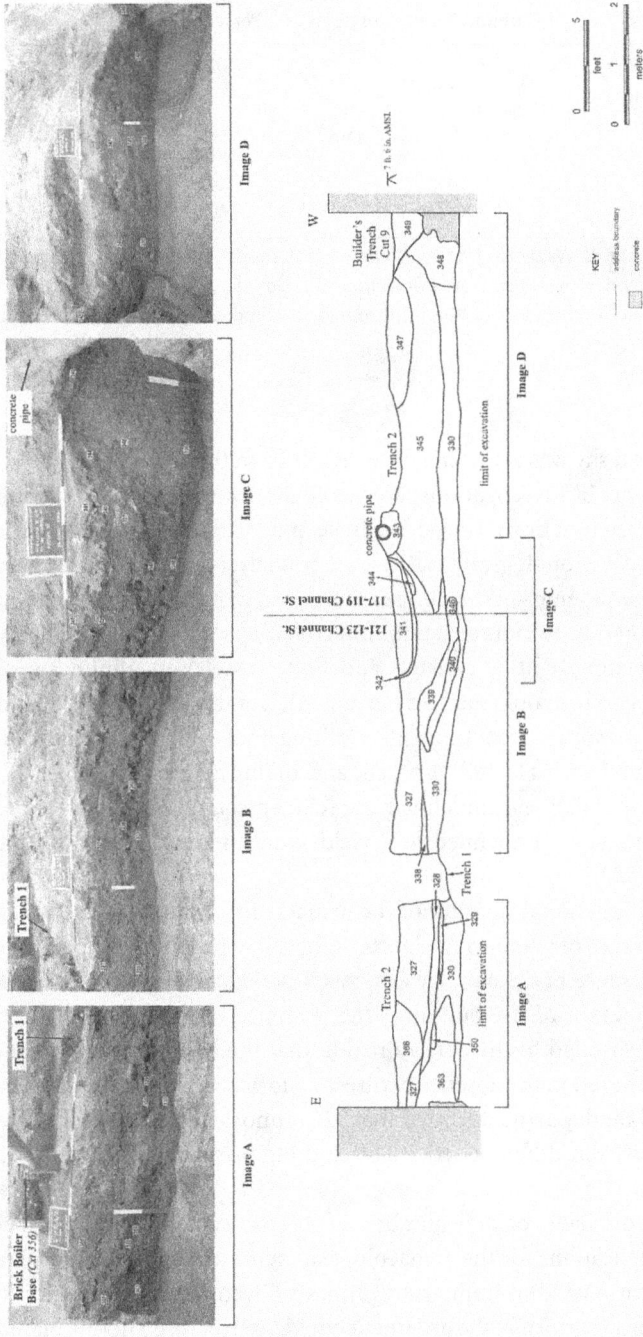

EXCAVATION PROFILE
121–123 and 117–119 Channel Street, Trench 2

Image A Image B Image C Image D

Brick Boiler
Base (Cut 356)

Trench 1

Trench 1

concrete
pipe

W

Builder's
Trench
Cut 9

7 ft. 6 in. AMSL

348

348

347

345

330

343

concrete pipe

344

117–119 Channel St.

121–123 Channel St.

341

342

339

327

333

338

328

Trench 1

329

Trench 2

327

330

350

Trench 2

366

367

363

E

limit of excavation

limit of excavation

Image A Image B Image C Image D

KEY

stratum boundary

concrete

0 feet 5

0 meters 2

Figure 5.9. Soil stratification at the Sing Lee laundry. Courtesy of the Anthropological Studies Center, Sonoma State University.

Table 5.2. Artifacts by Group from 117-123 Channel Street

Category	Minimum Number of Items	Percentage
Activities	55	2.7
Domestic	237	11.6
Indefinite Use	212	10.4
Laundry	1,045	51.1
Personal	495	24.2
Total	2,044	100.0

Source: Annita Waghorn, *Historic Archaeological Investigations of the City Center Cinemas Block Bounded by Miner Avenue and Hunter, El Dorado, and Channel Streets, Stockton, California* (Rohnert Park, Calif.: Anthropological Studies Center, Sonoma State University, 2004), 99.

When she was analyzing the artifacts from the Analytical Unit in the original report of investigations, archaeologist Annita Waghorn organized them into seven functional categories, in keeping with the usual methods employed by the Anthropological Studies Center analysts. The categories are: activities (commerce, entertainment, firearms, tools, writing); domestic (food containers, food preparation/consumption containers, food storage objects, furnishings, heating/lighting artifacts, indefinite vessels); indefinite (mostly objects for which a use could not be determined); laundry (advertising, clothing, hardware); personal (accouterments, clothing, footwear, grooming/health, objects associated with alcohol, tobacco, and opium); structural objects (hardware and materials); and undefined use (cinder, slag). Leaving out those artifacts categorized as "undefined use" yields a minimum number of 2,044 objects (Table 5.2).

The functional division of the artifacts from the laundry indicates a preponderance of laundering objects, followed in proportion by personal objects. The presence of the laundry artifacts is not surprising; it merely indicates the past function of the building. The presence of these artifacts undoubtedly would have led to the determination that the building once functioned as a laundry even in the absence of direct historical documentation. A breakdown of the laundry artifacts shows that 926 (almost 90 percent of the category) are buttons from different articles of clothing or safety and straight pins (Table 5.3).

The discovery of large numbers of objects related to commercial laundering has implications for the archaeological identification of the racialization process as it related to immigrant Chinese. Given the sociohistorical context of northern California, the argument could be structured in this manner: secure in the knowledge that large numbers of Chinese individuals were engaged in

Table 5.3. Laundry Artifacts from 117-123 Channel Street

Subcategory	Item	Frequency	Percentage
Advertising	buttons	6	0.6
Clothing	buttons	523	50.0
	buckles	8	0.6
	cuff links	9	0.9
	other fasteners/objects	11	1.1
Clothing Maintenance	sad irons	1	0.1
	pins	403	38.5
	bluing balls/bottles	65	6.2
	dying bottles	1	0.1
	clothes pins	10	1.0
	scissors	1	0.1
	clothes markers	4	0.4
	other objects	2	0.2
Hardware	boiler parts	3	0.3
Total		1,047	100.1

Source: Annita Waghorn, *Historic Archaeological Investigations of the City Center Cinemas Block Bounded by Miner Avenue and Hunter, El Dorado, and Channel Streets, Stockton, California* (Rohnert Park, Calif.: Anthropological Studies Center, Sonoma State University, 2004), 93–95.

laundering in the late nineteenth and early twentieth centuries, coupled with the knowledge that 91.7 percent of the laundries in Stockton were operated by Chinese workers (22 out of 24 in 1885; Waghorn 2004, 14), archaeologists would have 92 percent confidence that the archaeological site yielding these objects was related to Chinese laundry laborers. Having made this interpretation, the archaeologists could then link this supposition with the historical context of discrimination and racism against Chinese individuals in Gilded Age and pre–World War II America. Such inferential reasoning, however, is not necessary in this case study because the historical materials uncovered by the team from the Anthropological Studies Center have substantiated the presence of Chinese laundry workers at 123 East Channel Street. Nonetheless, the large presence of laundry-related artifacts would have made this supposition entirely reasonable.

Determining the function of the site is not the major concern here. The more pertinent question concerns what we might be able to posit from the artifact assemblage as it pertains to social identity in general and to racial categorization specifically.

The association of specific artifacts with past identity, initially beginning with ethnicity, reaches far back in the history of historical archaeology. As noted previously, when historical archaeologists first began to examine social identity with artifacts, one obvious place to begin was the antebellum plantations of the American South. Disciplinary interest in social variables coincided in time with the development of plantation archaeology, so the interest in identifying the material components of ascribed statuses there was somewhat inevitable (see Orser 1990). And given that many American historical archaeologists were intent on demonstrating the anthropological relevance of their field, some of them used plantations as a research locus to investigate the presence of cultural survivals. The idea of survivals has a long anthropological pedigree extending all the way back to E. B. Tylor (Hodgen 1931), but the concept entered historical archaeology's lexicon through the anthropologically trained archaeologists' knowledge of the work of Melville Herskovits (1930). The process of applying Herskovits's ideas to material culture, and the controversy it engendered, are today so well known that discussion here is unnecessary. Suffice it to say that identifying clear-cut African survivals in the New World generally has frustrated archaeologists, though a few have suggested that blue beads, some pottery forms and styles, mortuary practices, and religious symbolisms may have served in that capacity.

The archaeologically collected material survival most often associated with the overseas Chinese has been opium smoking paraphernalia. The link between immigrant Chinese and opium smoking has meant that the excavation of opium pipes and pipe pieces generally has been used to indicate Chinese presence. Archaeologists at the 117-123 Channel Street excavation did find at least seven objects associated with opium smoking (Waghorn 2004, 104).

Though Chinese healers had used the opium poppy for generations, widespread usage of opium as a narcotic is a feature of the colonial period of China's history (Li 1969, 52). The First Opium War (1839–1842) significantly impacted the area around Guangzhou (Canton) and created severe tensions in Chinese-European and Chinese-American relations (Barnett 1976, 163). Since most of the nineteenth-century immigrants to America originated in Guangzhou or nearby, many undoubtedly were familiar with opium use (Wylie and Fike 1993, 257). Many anti-Chinese nativist agitators did not consider this knowledge incidental, and many of them used it as a negative aspect of the Chinese character in the racialization process. For example, the editor of the Fresno, California, *Republican* noted that the opium dens, or "hop joints," of Chinatown attracted white men who "are the dregs of creation" (Rowell 1909, 226). The California legislature made opium smoking illegal in 1881 (Ma 2000, 16, 44). Anti-Chinese activists obviously knew that opium smoking was not restricted to the Chinese. Opium dens were indeed established in Chinatown, but any concrete interpretive connection between opium paraphernalia and people of Chinese descent would be specious unless supported by other information.

Table 5.4. Serving and Tableware Ceramics from 117-123 Channel Street

Category	Asian	Non-Asian
Serving	9	14
Tableware	65	8
Total	74	22
	(77.1 percent)	(22.9 percent)

Source: Annita Waghorn, *Historic Archaeological Investigations of the City Center Cinemas Block Bounded by Miner Avenue and Hunter, El Dorado, and Channel Streets, Stockton, California* (Rohnert Park, Calif.: Anthropological Studies Center, Sonoma State University, 2004), 89–90.

Today's historical archaeologists have grown significantly more sophisticated in understanding the linkage between artifact usage and social meaning, and most have abandoned the search for single identity markers (see Orser 1998, 662). Archaeologists now accept the mutability of artifact meaning and the strong importance of situational context. On the surface, this understanding might appear to preclude the search for artifactual evidence of racialization. Social identity seems much too complex and fluid to permit any sort of social identification through material objects. The fixity of identity in archaeology is a serious matter that I consider in the next chapter. The artificial construction of race, racial markers, and the color line, however, means that the racialization process is amenable to archaeological examination.

A close examination of the serving and tableware ceramics collected from the Stockton laundry site reveals that most of them (77.1 percent) are identified as Asian objects (Chinese or Japanese) (Table 5.4). Taken as a discrete collection, then, we might be able to conclude, in the absence of supporting historical documentation, that the site was inhabited either by immigrant Asians or by nonnativist Americans who were comfortable buying and using Asian-made products.

An examination of the artifacts categorized as serving vessels reveals that only nine of the twenty-three (39.1 percent) are Asian in manufacture. This collection includes at least three Chinese porcelain bowls, five Chinese porcelain teapots, and one Japanese porcelain teapot. Fourteen of the serving vessels (60.9 percent) are made of the improved white earthenware common throughout the United States during the period of the laundry's existence and probably used in almost every home in the country. An examination of the tableware vessels, however, reveals the opposite distribution. Here, 65 of the 73 vessels (or 89.0 percent) are Asian, whereas only eight (or 11.0 percent) are non-Asian. The Asian collection includes Chinese porcelain bowls, plates, dishes, and spoons and a Japanese porcelain bowl and bowl cover.

The distribution of serving and tableware ceramics, though minor in terms of the entire context of Chinese life in America, is nonetheless provocative because it bears directly on the nature of archaeological interpretation. Upon viewing the relative presence of these ceramics, archaeologists trained years ago undoubtedly would have concluded that the unequal distribution probably represents some measure of acculturation. They perhaps would interpret the smaller presence of non-Asian wares as an attempt by the laundry workers to conform to their surroundings by "Americanizing" their food preparation and consumption practices. Their acquisition of local American wares—although they would have been foreign to them—would serve to signal this effort. Pragmatic skeptics might counter that this interpretation was not necessarily true. Perhaps Chinese consumers in the laundry simply purchased objects that were close at hand. Ceramic vessels imported from Asia were clearly available in Stockton (and archaeological research substantiates that the same was true everywhere Chinese immigrants settled), but so were non-Asian wares. When he or she broke a Chinese vessel or merely wanted to have another small bowl, the Chinese consumer may have purchased a non-Asian piece because it was readily available. This circumstance is pragmatism born of necessity that has no deeper social meaning.

Examining the artifact assemblage from the laundry further, we note that in no category do Asian artifacts constitute the only materials found. In other words, all categories of artifacts show a mixture of Asian and non-Asian objects. This finding substantiates the argument that immigrant Chinese in the United States were not as isolated as some commentators have stressed (Voss 2005). The multicultural nature of the material goods demonstrates that Chinese men and women in Stockton appear to have consumed the same basic items as their non-Asian neighbors. In her interpretation of the excavation for the site report, Annita Waghorn (2004) explored the ways in which Asian and non-Asian objects co-occur.

In terms of medical care, for example, the deposits at the laundry indicate that the workers there used both traditional Chinese and modern American cures. Archaeologists found over fifty medicine bottles from the burgeoning nationwide patent-medicine industry, including bottles for tonics, liniment, blood purifiers, soda water, and bitters. The two most common cures in the collection were Dr. J. Hostetter's Stomach Bitters and Lash's Kidney and Liver Bitters. Hostetter's Stomach Bitters, represented by at least twenty bottles, was one of the most widely used patent medicines in America in the late nineteenth century and was first available in 1853 (Fike 1987, 36). The Hostetter headquarters were in Pittsburgh, but the firm also maintained a distributor in San Francisco. Lash's Kidney and Liver Bitters, represented in the collection by at least thirteen bottles, was a New York business that also keep an office in San Francisco. Like all good patent medicines, Lash's Kidney and Liver Bitters was touted as a powerful cure-all. An advertising card describes it as "Positively without an equal for all diseases arising from a disordered condition of the kidneys and liver—A mild cathartic and sure cure for constipation, indigestion, biliousness, dyspepsia, chills and fever, nervous or sick headache" (Watson 1965, after 16).

In self-administering such widely available medicines, the Chinese immigrants working and living at the laundry appear to have been no different from thousands of other people living in the United States—both foreign- and native-born. From a pragmatic perspective, then, we might wish to conclude that at least one of the Chinese laundrymen fell ill and, in an attempt to feel better, obtained widely available over-the-counter medicines as a curative. This action was not at all unusual during the late nineteenth and early twentieth centuries.

At the same time, however, we can wonder whether the situation also does not contain elements of a process Mullins (1999c) identified in his study of African American consumers in Annapolis, Maryland. Upon finding evidence of national brand-name consumption at the Maynard-Burgess site, Mullins concluded that purchasing prepackaged branded products may have represented the peoples' attempt to avoid purchasing loose goods from local merchants. At the time, many African Americans in the city believed that white merchants selling loose goods harbored racist views and thus were shorting the packages they sold to them. Many black consumers found it economically more responsible to purchase prepackaged items. In a similar process, Chinese immigrants may have purchased the same patent medicines as thousands of native-born Americans, but for a wholly different reason. Like all non-first-class passengers arriving on the shores of America, the first Americans Chinese immigrants met were medical examiners. Between 1903 and 1906, immigration doctors employed the humiliating Bertillon system to examine newly arrived immigrants. This system, created by a French scientist and detective, subjected all immigrants to a series of nude measurements that Bertillon believed would allow investigators to identify criminals. The immigration service was enthusiastic about using this system of measurement to decrease the number of Chinese immigrants by disallowing the entry of "undesirables." Officials discontinued using the Bertillon system after only three years, but medical examiners still made numerous observations of all Chinese immigrants at the time of entry (Lee 2003, 84–85, 211–212). None of the identified individuals who lived and worked at Sing Lee's laundry apparently had entered the United States during the time Bertillon's system was used. It remains possible, none-

Figure 5.10. Medicine vials from the Sing Lee laundry. Courtesy of the Anthropological Studies Center, Sonoma State University.

theless, that Chinese immigrants, understanding how they were perceived by nativist Americans and having been subjected to a possibly humiliating medical examination upon entry, simply preferred not to make contact with another American doctor if they could self-medicate instead.

One important distinction appears in the medicinal collection from 117-123 Channel Street. The Chinese workers who lived there used traditional cures in addition to patent medicines. During the excavations, the archaeologists found vials exhibiting Chinese characters painted on their outside surfaces (Figure 5.10). Bottle collectors often refer to such small vials as "opium bottles," but in truth they usually held homemade homeopathic medicines that may have contained some opium (Waghorn 2004, 273). Also found were three Chinese stoneware apothecary jars. These jars usually contained medicines, and one of the recovered bottles retained its paper label reading, in Chinese, ". . . ee Sang . . . Drug Company" of San Francisco.

Figure 5.11. Bottle with crow bones from the Sing Lee laundry. Courtesy of the Anthropological Studies Center, Sonoma State University.

The most evocative of the traditional medicines was a common brown bottle found to contain the remains of five American crows (*Corvus macrorhynchus*) (Waghorn 2004, 271–272) (Figure 5.11). Chinese herbalists commonly used crows to prepare traditional medicines to help ameliorate spasms and breathing problems as well as epilepsy, headaches, and dizziness. Analysis of the materials mixed with the crow bones indicated the presence of five herbs, three of which could be identified: albizia bark, notopterygium root, and red sage root. These herbs were thought to be useful, respectively, for insomnia and blood circulation, rheumatism and arthritis, and nervousness and blood circulation. Many of the American-made patent medicines found in the collection claimed to help or heal the same complaints. The use of an American species of crow in place of one traditionally used in China is a clear example of adaptation (Waghorn 2004, 272).

The laundry workers' reuse of medicine bottles to hold bluing dye constitutes an important caveat to their use of American patent medicines. The practice of Chinese laundry workers reusing bottles has been documented

Figure 5.12. Medicine bottle used to hold bluing at the Sing Lee laundry. Courtesy of the Anthropological Studies Center, Sonoma State University.

at another laundry site (Staski 1993, 134), and the Stockton laundry substantiates that this practice was widespread. Waghorn (2004, 274) reports that fifty-seven of the bitters bottles found at the laundry had bluing residue inside them, whereas twenty-one had no such residue (Figure 5.12). The lack of residue, of course, does not mean that the laundry workers would not have used them to hold bluing; it may only indicate that they had not done so by the time the laundry was abandoned. Still, the broad array of patent medicine bottles discovered at the site suggests that Chinese immigrants used American patent medicines.

Table 5.5. Faunal Remains from 117-123 Channel Street

Species	Pounds Present	Percentage
beef	66.0	20.5
mutton	20.5	6.4
pork	213.8	66.3
cat	2.0	0.6
rabbit	3.0	0.9
fowl	17.0	5.3
Total	322.3	100.0

Source: Annita Waghorn, *Historic Archaeological Investigations of the City Center Cinemas Block Bounded by Miner Avenue and Hunter, El Dorado, and Channel Streets, Stockton, California* (Rohnert Park, Calif.: Anthropological Studies Center, Sonoma State University, 2004), 85.

The faunal remains excavated from the laundry site also provide important information about the lives of Chinese immigrants in Stockton, California. When analyzed, it was clear that beef and pork provided well over 80 percent of the meat eaten by the residents of the laundry (Table 5.5). Chinese at home preferred pork to other meats, although they also consumed beef, mutton, fish, and fowl (Gust 1993, 185, 188), all of which are represented in the laundry collection. What stands out, however, are two cats, representing 2.0 pounds of total meat at the laundry. The consumption of cat, though never a major part of the diet, constitutes an element of the stereotypic image of the Chinese in America and helps to set them apart from their American neighbors.

Race and the Chinese Laundry Workers in Stockton

The excavation of the Sing Lee laundry in Stockton, California, is an important endeavor for several reasons. Perhaps the most immediate is that it adds another body of information to the expanding database of archaeological sites affiliated with the overseas Chinese in America. Archaeologists have excavated and analyzed several sites associated with immigrant Chinese, in both urban and rural settings (Praetzellis 2004, 239). These data constitute an important resource for understanding a significant segment of America's ethnic history, even though at least one archaeologist has argued that this research area remains understudied and somewhat marginal (Voss 2005). One notable feature of the archaeological research on the immigrant Chinese is that it is currently restricted to the western United States. Of the fifty-two projects in the United States Mary Praetzellis (2004, 239) listed in her careful overview of the archaeology of the overseas Chinese, fully thirty-eight (or 73.1 percent) are located in California. As of 2004, four projects have been completed in Idaho, three each in Arizona and Nevada, and two each in Oregon and Texas.

The unequal distribution of archaeological research on immigrant Chinese sites in California and the American West is perhaps not surprising; Chinese first entered the United States from the West, establishing many Chinatown enclaves throughout California's major cities. But the spread of Chinese immigrants throughout the nation is also deserving of archaeological analysis. The American West, and California specifically, was the main site of contact, conflict, and accommodation between immigrant Chinese and native-born Americans, but census records confirm that individuals of Chinese descent settled throughout the cities of the eastern United States during the nineteenth and twentieth centuries. Paul Siu (1987, 23) noted that the first Chinese-operated laundry in Chicago opened in 1872, only one year after the devastating, city-wide fire. Chinese immigrants moved farther east than Chicago. In 1880, only 748 Chinese lived in Manhattan, but only a few years later Chinese proprietors operated about 2,000 laundries in the New York metropolitan area (Chang 2003, 102). In Brooklyn in 1890, Chinese immigrants reacted strongly against the passage of the Geary Act—which extended the Exclusion Act for an additional ten years—and formed an organization called the Chinese Equal Rights League (McClain 1994, 205–206).

Archaeological research into the Chinese immigrant experience, however, is a practice relegated to the American West. This unequal distribution must change before historical archaeologists can claim any substantive understanding of the material conditions of Chinese immigrants and the racialization process as it pertains to them. The current situation is reminiscent of the not-too-distant past, when the archaeology of African American life was restricted to antebellum plantations in the American South. The archaeology of African America is a much more mature field of study today, and archaeologists are examining sites associated with Americans of African descent throughout the country. This research increasingly focuses on non-slave-holding sites. Paul Mullins's research is an example of the dramatic transformation in African American archaeology that might be used as a model for the further development of the archaeology of the overseas Chinese in America. His ongoing efforts, first in Annapolis and now in Indianapolis, violate all the precepts of African American archaeology as it was first designed and practiced: it deals with twentieth-century sites (and thus with modern-day issues), it concentrates on an urban environment, it finds its research locale outside the Deep South, and it foregrounds the significant role of the racialization process in daily life.

As an economic and social institution, the Chinese laundry offers a perfect micro-environment in which to investigate the larger macrosocial process of racialization. That the Chinese in America were identified as a race is irrefutable. Not only did they originate in a country far from the shores of America, they retained traditions and practiced customs that were entirely foreign to native-born Americans. They also dressed differently and the men wore their hair in a long braid. Perhaps most damning in a nation that professed Christian godliness, the Chinese believed in a set of religious tenets that were undeniably foreign and un-Christian. Added to their lack of Christian credentials, the Chinese looked different than native-born Americans and transplanted Europeans, so they could not argue for a birthright bestowed by whiteness. Quite the contrary; they were members of the "yellow horde" that was too easily stereotyped and ostracized. A widely read American weekly caricatured the typical "Chinaman's" speech, at the same time making a statement about his role in American labor: "Mellican man, Lettee Chinaman landee—me washee, washee, and me workee cheapee" (Gyory 1998, 144). The racial epochal structure reached all the way to the federal government in the form of the Chinese Exclusion Act. When U.S. Representative Horace F. Page of California argued before the House's Committee on Education and Labor in 1882 that the Chinese had no wish to assimilate in the United States, he was playing to a fear of difference (Coolidge 1909, 168). Nativist Americans unalterably opposed to "race mixing" ignited fears in U.S. society.

National laws and state and local statutes mandated discriminatory practices on a broad scale, and specific practices expressed how these laws affected the racial milieu in U.S. society. The archaeological problem is how to identify the racialization process in the material culture. Specific objects that exhibit Chinese writing—ceramic bowls and plates with pecked Chinese characters (Michaels 2005; Voss 2005), patent-medicine bottles with Chinese labels (Staski 1993, 135–136), and homeopathic medicine vials (Waghorn 2004, 273)—perhaps provide the best nontextual evidence for Chinese presence.

One intriguing line of possible investigation into the racialization process might involve the juxtaposition of Chinese and Japanese porcelains in the laundry. The Sino-Japanese War of 1894–1895 should have been sufficient to convince U.S. residents that China and Japan were separate nations with distinct cultural identities. Many Americans, however, grouped Chinese and Japanese immigrants together as "Asiatics" or "Orientals." As late as 1941, but only two weeks after the attack on Pearl Harbor, *Time* magazine published an article entitled "How to Tell Your Friends from the Japs." The goal of the article was to educate the magazine's readers about how to separate their friends—the

Chinese—from their new enemies—the Japanese. The author said that the Chinese grew fat when they were prosperous, but the Japanese seldom did, that the Chinese were not as hairy as the Japanese, and that the eyes of the Japanese individual were set closer together. But, the author concluded, telling Chinese and Japanese individuals apart was difficult because they represented the "same racial strain" (Chang 2003, 223).

It would be merely supposition to suppose that Chinese-Japanese tensions existed in Stockton, or elsewhere in the United States, without detailed historical research, but the presence of the Chinese and Japanese porcelains at the Stockton laundry is interesting nonetheless. One line of future investigation might be to learn whether U.S. merchants indiscriminately sold Japanese and Chinese porcelains as "china" merely because of their paste. Chinese purchasers of porcelain undoubtedly recognized the difference between the porcelain made in their homeland versus that made in Japan, but the issue is whether they cared.

The archaeological recognition of the racialization process as Chinese immigrants experienced it must include an expanded concept of segregation. Chinese laundries need not have been situated directly in Chinatown to be part of its cultural force.

The racialization of the Chinese in America is an important element of U.S. history. At the same time, it presents special problems for an archaeology of the racialization process because of the significance archaeologists have attached to ethnicity. The Chinese were racialized in America and even legislated against, and as archaeologists, we will only come to understand the importance of the racialization process, and accept its material dimensions as observable, when we acknowledge this historical reality.

6

Modern-World Archaeology and Racialization

In the "Forethought" to *The Souls of Black Folk*, W.E.B. Du Bois stated that "the problem of the Twentieth Century is the problem of the color-line" (Du Bois 1903/1999, 5). Du Bois was correct in his assessment then, but he would still be correct had he written these words 100 years later. Issues of race continue to haunt modern life around the globe including in the United States, a nation founded on ideals of liberty and freedom but with a palpable and undeniable backdrop of racial inequality. Initial confrontations with Native Americans on the eastern shore led to later battles with them in the Midwest, the Plains, and finally in the West. The importation and enslavement of thousands of men, women, and children of African descent took place at the same time as the growing concern over the "Indian problem." Their presence in the United States led many to an intense, internally wrenching philosophical turmoil over the "Negro problem." As American citizens struggled to resolved this "problem," they also confronted the "Irish problem." The presence of Irish immigrants raised questions of religion, since vast numbers of immigrants from the Emerald Isle were "papists" who, Americans feared, bore greater allegiance to Rome than to Washington. The "Chinese problem" developed later, and by the mid-twentieth century, the "new immigrant problem" appeared. U.S. history, it seems, has been characterized by a constant conversation about race. The essence of the discourse has not changed in the early years of the twenty-first century. As I write, Americans are worrying about a new immigrant "problem"—this one stemming not from Europe or Asia as in the past, but from Mexico and Central America. Much of the debate and many of the op-ed pieces in newspapers duplicate attitudes and biases expressed in the past about other immigrants. The stereotypical caricatures are missing from the mainstream media, but they can probably be found in fringe literature, probably much as they were presented 100 years ago.

Large-scale controversies of the United States provide a significant and meaningful backdrop to the specific but often more spatially confined conflicts that occur over race and racialization. The mainstream news media are consumed, at the time of writing, with the story of the alleged rape of a dancer by a number of athletes at a prominent southern university. The resolution of this legal case is far from known at this time, but the media are presenting it as having occurred within a complex milieu that incorporates race, class, region, and history; it represents Old South vs. New South, elite vs. nonelite, black vs. white. Just like the immigrant "problems" Americans have imagined, this rape case, though extremely localized in space, has far-reaching racial connections that stretch across space and through time. The case is a metaphor for the racial history of the United States and the nation's continuing conflict over race.

The categorization of the human "races," the maintenance of the racial epochal structure, and the racialization process all permeate every social action in American life. In fact, race was the impetus for the development of American archaeology. The resolution of the controversy over the Moundbuilders was as much a racial as an academic success, and it was a success made by archaeologists who decided to confront a controversial issue the history and meaning of race in the nineteenth-century. Cyrus Thomas put the Moundbuilder controversy to rest in the decade the American frontier was deemed closed by historian Frederick Jackson Turner (1893). With the vast majority of Native Americans safely relegated to reservations, the true story of the Moundbuilders could be told. What is important, though, is that the "problem" presented by the ancient builders of America's earthen mounds was a precursor to the "problems" many in the nation would soon perceive with immigrant populations.

Issues of race and racialization also haunt every aspect of American historical archaeology. Race has been a powerful vector of social inequality since about 1500, and we have no reason to expect that archaeological practice should be immune from its impact. The examination of racialization should not be divorced from the archaeology of America's history. Paradoxically, though, the archaeological study of race is a fairly recent practice. Why is this so?

Perhaps we should not be surprised by the twentieth-century archaeologists' general avoidance of racialization as a subject for analysis. After all, racial identity is inherently difficult to examine materially. As Paul Mullins (2006) insightfully notes, race is a formidable topic for archaeologists because its very investigation seems to essentialize it. As soon as archaeologists set out to determine the material conditions of the racialization process, they appear to provide credence to the concept that race exists as a biological reality. The search for the material conditions of race appears to offer epistemological reality to the Linnean project. This conclusion, of course, is spurious. The exact reverse also can be claimed: that the avoidance of racialization in archaeology makes it appear invisible. Mullins's plan to overcome this problem is to promote an overtly engaged archaeology that has the power and the intellectual will to articulate a political philosophy that mirrors that pursued by scholars of the African diaspora. This group of writers and equal rights advocates openly urges the development of an anti-racist discourse. Drawing on the insights of novelist Richard Wright, Mullins understands that this perspective unabashedly goes against the grain of dominant representations in the field of archaeology and is thus controversial.

Mullins's reference to diaspora research helps foreground the role of immigration in the U.S. racial structure. In this book, I have examined two immigrant communities as a microcosm for an archaeology of racialization. I selected Irish and Chinese groups because of their immigrant past rather than for their perceived phenotypic characteristics. Both examples provide dramatic insights into American race, but they are not truly unique in a broad sense. With every new wave of immigrants, American nativists racialized the newcomers by slotting them into the hierarchical epochal structure. Since many scientists of the early twentieth century upheld the biological reality of the racial hierarchy, the process of designation was naturalized. Racism was misrecognized as nature.

The Role of Structure

The model I use in this book examines how U.S. elites (whites) created and maintained an epochal racial structure. They placed each new immigrant group within that structure based on racialized characterizations. The immigrants' desire to make a better life in America or to acquire enough funds to allow them to return home joined with their need to work to survive. Immigrants usually had to work for lower wages than the group who proceeded them in the same segments of the labor market. The epochal structure of race, as reinforced by the science of the day, installed whites at the top and nonwhites below. First Native Americans and then immigrants were place in subordinate positions within the epochal structure. Whites and nonwhites were divided by a color line, but this line was neither as simple nor as rigid as early twentieth-century racial scientists suggested (see Orser 2004b, 145–146). The case of the Irish, as explained by Roediger (1991) and Ignatiev (1995), demonstrates how one group could move up by pushing another group down. The Irish also used their birthright of white skin to nudge the process forward. But fiction writers such as Harriet Beecher Stowe were not operating in an ideological vacuum when they made the stereotypical evil overseer on an antebellum slave plantation an Irishman. His position is truly liminal: he stands between the white owner and the black enslaved, economically, culturally, and racially.

Places on the racial hierarchy below whiteness were not fixed in U.S. history, and this circumstance is what terrified U.S. workers in the West when the Chinese came among them. In the eyes of nativist Americans, Chinese immigrants, who were racialized as inferior and seemed willing to accept any terms from white employers, had the potential to upset the epochal structure, perhaps by sheer numbers alone.

The structural model of hierarchical race denies the perspective that race is purely psychological. An explanation of racism based solely on psychology does not provide a useful way to understand the historic and enduring project of racialization from an archaeological perspective. My argument, largely taken from Bonilla-Silva's (1997), is similar to Lodziak's (1995) argument against sociocultural interpretations that rely on psychological interpretation alone. Racialization had clear, physical implications to those people both experiencing it and enforcing it. Racial theory is here modeled as a dominant ideology fixed in the hierarchical structure of the United States. As a concept, it clearly had psychological elements, because people thought it, but its effects were quite real.

The Fixity of Identity

The epochal structure of American society as modeled here appears to run counter to much current thinking in archaeology. Elsewhere (Orser 2004b, 78–82) I have explored the mutability of ethnicity as an archaeological concept. Specifically, I noted that ethnicity is a self-defined social variable that varies through time and space. I used the work of sociologists to support this idea by noting that some people associated with an ethnic group may wish to deny this group while they are young but embrace it when they get older. Identifying ethnicity is difficult in living populations because of the many shifts and transformations that are possible. I observed that using archaeological materials to assign ethnic identity is considerably more difficult. My observation was not new to social archaeologists; this case had been made decades earlier (McGuire 1982).

A huge body of data collected by scholars in diverse disciplines indicates that social identity is mutable. The changeability of identity is apparent even in sociohistorical settings where the identities seem clear-cut and obvious. Contemporary Northern Ireland provides a perfect example. Americans who hear about the "troubles" in Northern Ireland are usually told by the mainstream media that Catholics are in conflict with Protestants. The binary opposites are easily recognized and immediately understood because they appear to be well defined and obvious. A individual's church membership and theological perspective seems neatly to define their allegiance. This facile understanding often leads people who know nothing about Northern Ireland to wonder why the factions cannot co-exist since both religions are Christian.

Insights into the inherent power of the essentialization of identity come from embedded ethnographic research. William Kelleher's (2003) ethnographic observations collected in a midsized town in Northern Ireland amply demonstrates the initial appeal of essentializing a group's identity. Kelleher notes that the inclination of outsiders is to conceptualize the two groups (Protestants and Catholics) as binary opposites organized around the historical terms of "colonizer" (Protestant) and "colonized" (Catholic). Many readings of Irish history openly support this supposition. But Kelleher discovered when he looked deeply into the social realities of Northern Ireland that the neat binary opposites are much too facile to explain the intricacies of daily life. Relying on participant observations made in a glass factory as well as numerous interactions with people from the various communities, Kelleher was able to map the diversity of identities. He described, for example, how the apparently straightforward expressions of class are played out over a diverse and overlapping network of social relations. These relations include vectors of location, religion, demography, economy, politics, and family that, through their articulation, create distinct discourses (154–155). These various discourses frustrate an easy interpretation of everyday life in Northern Ireland.

The categories people have created over the past several decades in the north of Ireland have clear meanings and visible impacts on social practice. Individuals are definitely marked by both. Because Northern Ireland is administratively part of the United Kingdom, the social space of Kelleher's town was constructed largely as Protestant space. From the perspective of the effort to build an archaeology of racialization, Kelleher's discovery of this point is most salient. What he actually describes in the town is the construction of a racialized epochal structure. Because the central religico-political authority is British, it is coded as "Protestant" in the same way that "American" is coded as white, Anglo, and middle class (78–79). As a result, the Catholics in town experienced the double consciousness Du Bois (1903/1999) identified among African Americans.

Kelleher (2003, 79) argued that the world created in Northern Ireland is a racialized one. In a modern nation-state, ethnicized difference is perceived as positive, while racialized difference is viewed negatively. The daily practices Kelleher observed in his study area were racialized in many ways, one of which was spatial. In today's Northern Ireland, the spatialized areas traditionally are marked by often-elaborate murals painted on building walls, flags (the Irish tricolor, the British Union Jack), and painted streets and curbs (see Rolston 1992, 1998).

The individuals in Kelleher's town enmeshed in the social order know their "place" socially because of the intersection of habitus, capital, and field, and they know their "place" physically because of the socio-spatial dialectic. The racialized positions are structural.

The racial structure is also tenacious. The staying power of Chinese racialization, for example, is aptly shown by comments that "no Americans" appear in the movie *The Joy Luck Club* and headlines that read "American Beats Kwan" when figure skater Michelle Kwan, born in Torrance, California, lost to Tara Lipinski, born in Philadelphia (Chang 2003, 392–393). Kwan is apparently not American enough for the reporter. More important, did he or she or the readers even notice the absurd racial slur?

The structural nature of the racialized American hierarchy provides immense opportunities for archaeologists because the nature of the racial structure changes slowly, if at all. Using historical sources, we can contextualize the ways in which the epochal structure of race was created, expressed, and maintained in America at any point in history. And because the focal point of social archaeology is the group rather than the individual, we can derive collective understandings of the ways in which people within the sociohistorical formation expressed their racialized identities or had them designed for them. Excavated material culture, when linked with contemporary drawings, writings, and legislation, provides rich detail about the operation of racialization in historic America.

The two case studies presented in this book have been constructed with a strong reliance on historical sources. The archaeological material may appear somewhat supplemental or merely tangential. But I believe that it only indicates the subtle nature of the material dimensions of the racialization process. As noted in Chapter 3, some homogenization of the material culture between the "American races" is to be expected given the prevalence and success of the capitalist project. Similarities in material culture became inevitable as Americans became fully embedded within the market as consumers.

By adopting a structural perspective of racialization and by emphasizing the power of the capitalist marketplace, I do not mean to imply that individual Americans are mere automatons incapable of freedom of thought or action. On the contrary, plenty of room exists for personal abilities, achievements, and acquisitions within the system. Part of the flexibility in the system derives from the operation of the social networks immigrants created and maintained.

Both Irish and Chinese immigrants to the United States stayed in touch with people back home, and many of them hoped eventually to return. Immigrants to America had to adapt their homegrown habitus to their new surroundings in the field of American race as they attempted to increase their total volume of capital. Amassing capital of all kinds was made difficult because of the American racial hierarchy. This structure was created and actively reaffirmed by nativist public sentiment if possible, and if not possible with informal means, then through the enactment and enforcement of racially inspired statutes and laws.

Irish and Chinese immigrants in America, like all those who came before and after them, found themselves enmeshed within a new socio-spatial dialectic. Their movements out of the physical spaces created for them usually were accompanied by their attempts to change their racial designation. The movement of Irish immigrants from New York's fetid tenements to the grandeur and power of Tammany Hall represented more than a spatial change; it also signaled a transformation of the racial order, even if the structure itself remained intact. Conversely, Chinese immigrants who moved their laundries outside Chinatown appeared to violate this process because their spatial relocation was not accompanied with a concomitant change in racial position.

The analyses presented in Chapters 4 and 5 are necessarily brief and incomplete. Much more research probably will be pursued with the collections I have used. As noted earlier, my goal is not to provide a definitive interpretation of the sites or their residents; these presentations are much better made by the sites' chief investigators. My goal was to use the two archaeological deposits to examine how the racialization process affected Irish immigrants in New York City and Chinese immigrants in Stockton, California, with the eventual hope being that material elements of the process could be identified. No question exists that both peoples were racialized. They were racialized in different ways, and experienced diverse outcomes, but the inherent nature of the process was remarkably similar throughout.

No unambiguous material evidence exists to indicate racialization, but we should not be surprised. Much of its material dimension is hidden within the capitalist project, as Irish and Chinese men and women entered the great American marketplace. Thus, white clay smoking pipes and fine earthenware objects with Irish motifs and bottles containing Chinese characters appear to indicate ethnicity at its most basic level. The items indeed do suggest cultural affiliation, but their presence must be situated within a historical context that recognizes the racialization process. Objects with cultural motifs did not exist in any more isolation than the individuals who used them. The artifacts and their owners were embedded within a structured, though not entirely rigid, racialized environment not of their making. Once contextualized, apparent ethnic artifacts acquire racial meaning.

Composing an archaeology of racialization in historic America is neither easy nor straightforward. Concrete conclusions will take years to formulate as greater numbers of excavators shed light on the process. Multiscalar analysis must focus on both the broad trends in racial theory, as well as on local representations in many forms, extending from print media to material culture. American historical archaeologists must be willing to confront the difficult subject of racialization if they are to claim any concrete understanding of their nation's and the wider world's human history.

Bibliography

Abbott, Edith, ed. 1924. *Immigration: Select Documents and Case Records*. Chicago: University of Chicago Press.

Abu-Lughod, Janet L. 1989. *Before European Hegemony: The World System, A.D. 1250–1350*. New York: Oxford University Press.

Allen, Theodore W. 1994. *The Invention of the White Race*. Vol. 1. *Racial Oppression and Social Control*. London: Verso.

Almaguer, Tomás. 1994. *Racial Fault Lines: The Historical Origins of White Supremacy in California*. Berkeley: University of California Press.

Anbinder, Tyler. 1992. *Nativism and Slavery: The Northern Know Nothings and the Politics of the 1850s*. New York: Oxford University Press.

Arensberg, Conrad M. 1937. *The Irish Countryman: An Anthropological Study*. New York: Macmillan.

Arensberg, Conrad M., and Solon T. Kimball. 1940. *Family and Community in Ireland*. Cambridge, Mass.: Harvard University Press.

Ascher, Robert, and Charles H. Fairbanks. 1971. "Excavation of a Slave Cabin: Georgia, U.S.A." *Historical Archaeology* 5:3–17.

Ashmore, Wendy. 2002. "Decisions and Dispositions: Socializing Spatial Archaeology." *American Anthropologist* 104:1172–1183.

Atherton, Gertrude. 1914. *California: An Intimate History*. New York: Harper and Brothers.

Babson, David W. 1987. "The Tanner Road Settlement: The Archaeology of Racism on Limerick Plantation." M.A. thesis, University of South Carolina, Columbia.

———. 1990. "The Archaeology of Racism and Ethnicity on Southern Plantations." *Historical Archaeology* 24, no. 4:20–28.

———. 1997. "Introduction." *Historical Archaeology* 31, no. 3:5–6.

Baker, Lee D. 1998. *From Savage to Negro: Anthropology and the Construction of Race, 1896–1954*. Berkeley: University of California Press.

Baker, Vernon G. 1978. *Historical Archaeology at Black Lucy's Garden, Andover, Massachusetts: Ceramics from the Site of a Nineteenth Century Afro-American*. Andover, Mass.: Robert S. Peabody Foundation for Archaeology, Phillips Academy.

———. 1980. "Archaeological Visibility of Afro-American Culture: An Example from Black Lucy's Garden, Andover, Massachusetts." In *Archaeological Perspectives on Ethnicity in America: Afro-American and Asian American Culture History*, ed. Robert L. Schuyler, 29–37. Farmingdale, New York: Baywood.

Banton, Michael. 1987. *Racial Theories*. Cambridge: Cambridge University Press.

Barnard, Toby. 2004. *Making the Grand Figure: Lives and Possessions in Ireland, 1641–1770*. New Haven, Conn.: Yale University Press.

Barnett, Suzanne Wilson. 1976. "National Image: Missionaries and Some Conceptual Ingredients of Late Ch'ing Reform." In *Reform in Nineteenth-Century China*, ed. Paul A. Cohen and John E. Schrecker, 160–180. Cambridge, Mass.: Harvard University Press.

Beames, Michael. 1983. *Peasants and Power: The Whiteboy Movement and Their Control in Pre-Famine Ireland*. Sussex: Harvester Press.

Beddoe, John. 1885. *The Races of Britain*. Bristol: J. W. Arrowsmith.

Belgrave, Ronald. 1990. "Black People and Museums: The Caribbean Heritage Project in Southampton." In *The Politics of the Past*, ed. Peter Gathercole and David Lowenthal, 63–73. London: Unwin Hyman.

Benedict, Ruth. 1942. *Race and Racism*. London: Routledge.

Bieder, Robert E. 1986. *Science Encounters the Indian, 1820–1880: The Early Years of American Ethnology*. Norman: University of Oklahoma Press.

Blakey, Michael L. 1988. "Racism through the Looking Glass: An Afro-American Perspective." *World Archaeological Bulletin* 2:46–50.

———. 1990. "American Nationality and Ethnicity in the Depicted Past." In *The Politics of the Past*, ed. Peter Gathercole and David Lowenthal, 38–48. London: Unwin Hyman.

———. 1997. "Past Is Present: Comments on 'In the Realm of Politics: Prospects for Public Participation in African-American Plantation Archaeology.'" *Historical Archaeology* 31, no. 3:140–145.

Blaut, J. M. 1993. *The Colonizer's Model of the World: Geographical Diffusionism and Eurocentric History*. New York: Guilford Press.

Bogardus, Emory S. 1928. *Immigration and Race Attitudes*. Boston: D. C. Heath.

Bonilla-Silva, Eduardo. 1997. "Rethinking Racism: Toward a Structural Interpretation." *American Sociological Review* 62:465–480.

———. 1999. "The Essential Social Fact of 'Race.'" *American Sociological Review* 64:899–906.

———. 2003. *Racism without Racists: Color-Blind Racism and the Persistence of Racial Inequality in the United States*. Lanham, Md.: Rowman and Littlefield.

Bouchereau, L. 1870. *Statement of the Sugar and Rice Crops, Made in Louisiana in 1869–70*. New Orleans: Young, Bright.

Bourdieu, Pierre. 1977. *Outline of a Theory of Practice*. Trans. Richard Nice. Cambridge: Cambridge University Press.

———. 1984. *Distinction: A Social Critique of the Judgement of Taste*. Trans. Richard Nice. Cambridge, Mass.: Harvard University Press.

———. 1986. "The Forms of Capital." In *Handbook of Theory and Research for the Sociology of Education*, ed. John G. Richardson, 241–258. New York: Greenwood Press.

———. 1987. "What Makes a Social Class? On the Theoretical and Practical Existence of Groups." *Berkeley Journal of Sociology* 32:1–18.

———. 1988. *Homo Academicus*. Trans. Peter Collier. Stanford, Calif.: Stanford University Press.

———. 1990. *The Logic of Practice*. Trans. Richard Nice. Stanford, Calif.: Stanford University Press.

———. 1993. *The Field of Cultural Production: Essays on Art and Literature.* Trans. Randal Johnson. New York: Columbia University Press.

Bourdieu, Pierre, and Loïc J. D. Wacquant. 1992. *An Invitation to Reflexive Sociology.* Chicago: University of Chicago Press.

Brace, C. Loring. 2005. *"Race" Is a Four-Letter Word: The Genesis of the Concept.* New York: Oxford University Press.

Braudel, Fernand. 1967. *Capitalism and Material Life, 1400–1800.* Trans. Miriam Kochan. New York: Harper and Row.

———. 1977. *Afterthoughts on Material Civilization and Capitalism.* Trans. Patricia M. Ranum. Baltimore, Md.: Johns Hopkins University Press.

———. 1985. *The Structures of Everyday Life: The Limits of the Possible.* Trans. Siân Reynolds. New York: Harper and Row.

Breen, T. H. 2004. *The Marketplace of Revolution: How Consumer Politics Shaped American Independence.* New York: Oxford University Press.

Brighton, Stephen A. 2000. "Prices that Suit the Times: Shopping for Ceramics at Five Points." In *Tales of the Five Points: Working-Class Life in Nineteenth-Century New York., Volume 2. An Interpretive Approach to Understanding Working-Class Life,* ed. Rebecca Yamin, 11–30. West Chester, Pa.: John Milner Associates.

———. 2005. "An Historical Archaeology of the Irish Proletarian Diaspora: The Material Manifestations of Irish Identity in America, 1850–1910." Ph.D. diss., Boston University, Boston.

Brinton, Daniel G. 1890. *Races and Peoples: Lectures on the Science of Ethnography.* New York: N. D. C. Hodges.

Bunche, Ralph J. 1936/1968. *A World View of Race.* Port Washington, N.Y.: Kennikat Press.

Buxton, L. H. Dudley. 1929. *China: The Land and the People.* Oxford: Clarendon Press.

Cabak, Melanie A., Mark D. Groover, and Scott J. Wagers. 1995. "Health Care and the Wayman A.M.E. Church." *Historical Archaeology* 29, no. 2:55–76.

Campbell, George. 1879. *White and Black: The Outcome of a Visit to the United States.* London: Chatto and Windus.

Chang, Iris. 2003. *The Chinese in America: A Narrative History.* New York: Viking.

Childe, V. Gordon. 1926. *The Aryans: A Study in Indo-European Origin.* New York: Alfred A. Knopf.

———. 2004. "Archaeology as a Social Science: Inaugural Lecture." In *Foundations of Social Archaeology: Selected Writings of V. Gordon Childe,* ed. Thomas C. Patterson and Charles E. Orser Jr., 81–90. Walnut Creek, Calif.: Altamira Press.

Chippendale, Chris. 1989. "'Social Archaeology' in the Nineteenth Century: Is It Right to Look for Modern Ideas in Old Places?" In *Tracing Archaeology's Past: The Historiography of Archaeology,* ed. Andrew L. Christenson, 21–33. Carbondale: Southern Illinois University Press.

Clark, Graham. 1964/1939. *Archaeology and Society: Reconstructing the Prehistoric Past.* London: Methuen.

Clausen, Edwin, and Jack Bermingham. 1982. *Chinese and African American Profession-*

als in California: A Case Study of Equality and Opportunity in the United States. Washington, D.C.: University Press of America.

Cohen, Paul A. 1976. "The New Coastal Reformers." In Reform in Nineteenth-Century China, ed. Paul A. Cohen and John E. Schrecker, 255–264. Cambridge, Mass.: Harvard University Press.

Coleman, Anne. 1999. Riotous Roscommon: Social Unrest in the 1840s. Dublin: Irish Academic Press.

Conley, Dalton. 1999. Being Black, Living in the Red: Race, Wealth, and Social Policy in America. Berkeley: University of California Press.

Coolidge, Mary Roberts. 1909. Chinese Immigration. New York: Henry Holt.

Coon, Carleton S. 1939. The Races of Europe. New York: Macmillan.

Cox, Oliver C. 1970/1948. Caste, Class, and Race: A Study in Social Dynamics. New York: Monthly Review Press.

Curtis, Liz. 1996. Nothing But the Same Old Story: The Roots of Anti-Irish Racism. Belfast: Sásta.

Curtis, L. Perry. 1971. Apes and Angels: The Irishman in Victorian Caricature. Washington, D.C.: Smithsonian Institution Press.

Danaher, Kevin. 1964. In Ireland Long Ago. Cork: Mercier Press.

———. 1972. The Year in Ireland. Cork: Mercier Press.

Dawdy, Shannon Lee. 2006. "Thinker-Tinkers, Race and the Archaeological Critique of Modernity." Archaeological Dialogues 12:143–164.

DeBow, J. D. B. 1853. The Seventh Census of the United States: 1850. Washington, D.C.: Robert Armstrong.

DeBow's Review. 1867. "Department of Immigration and Labor." DeBow's Review 4:357–364.

Delle, James A. 1998. An Archaeology of Social Space: Analyzing Coffee Plantations in Jamaica's Blue Mountains. New York: Plenum Press.

Delle, James A., Stephen A. Mrozowski, and Robert Paynter, eds. 2000. Lines that Divide: Historical Archaeologies of Race, Class, and Gender. Knoxville: University of Tennessee Press.

Dickens, Charles. 1842. American Notes for General Circulation. 2 vols. London: Chapman and Hall.

Domínguez, Virginia A. 1986. White by Definition: Social Classification in Creole Louisiana. New Brunswick, N.J.: Rutgers University Press.

Donham, Donald L. 1999. History, Power, Ideology: Central Issues in Marxism and Anthropology. Berkeley: University of California Press.

Douglas, Mary, and Baron Isherwood. 1979. The World of Goods. New York: Basic.

Drucker, Lesley M. 1981. "Socioeconomic Patterning at an Undocumented Late 18th Century Lowcountry Site: Spiers Landing, South Carolina." Historical Archaeology 15, no. 2:58–68.

Du Bois, W. E. B. 1939/1973. Black Folk Then and Now: An Essay in the History and Sociology of the Negro Race. New York: Octagon.

———. 1903/1999. The Souls of Black Folk. Ed. H. L. Gates, Jr., and T. H. Oliver. New York: W.W. Norton.

Eaves, Lucile. 1910. *A History of California Labor Legislation, with an Introductory Sketch of the San Francisco Labor Movement*. Berkeley: The University Press.

Edelstein, Art. 2001. *Fair Melodies: Turlough Carolan, An Irish Harper*. East Calais, Vt.: Noble Stone Press.

Egmond, Florike, and Peter Mason. 1997. *The Mammoth and the Mouse: Microhistory and Morphology*. Baltimore, Md.: Johns Hopkins University Press.

Ellis, Eilish. 1977. *Emigrants from Ireland, 1847–1852: State-Aided Emigration Schemes from Crown Estates in Ireland*. Baltimore, Md.: Genealogical Publishing.

Epperson, Terrence W. 1987. "'Thus in the Beginning All the World was America': Class Formation and the Social Construction of Race in the Chesapeake, 1675–1740." Research proposal submitted to the Carter G. Woodson Institute for Afro-American Studies, University of Virginia, Charlottesville.

———. 1988. "Archaeologies of Race and Resistance in British Colonial America." Paper presented at the annual meeting of the Society for American Archaeology, Phoenix, Arizona.

———. 1990a. "Race and the Disciplines of the Plantation." *Historical Archaeology* 24, no. 4: 29–36.

———. 1990b. "'To Fix a Perpetual Brand': The Social Construction of Race in Virginia, 1675–1750." Ph.D. diss., Temple University.

———. 1996. "The Politics of 'Race' and Cultural Identity at the African Burial Ground Excavations, New York." *World Archaeological Bulletin* 7:108–117.

———. 1999. "The Contested Commons: Archaeologies of Race, Repression, and Resistance in New York City." In *Historical Archaeologies of Capitalism*, ed. Mark P. Leone and Parker B. Potter, Jr., 81–110. New York: Kluwer Academic/Plenum.

———. 2001. "'A Separate House for the Christian Slaves, One for the Negro Slaves': The Archaeology of Race and Identity in Late Seventeenth-Century Virginia." In *Race and the Archaeology of Identity*, ed. Charles E. Orser, Jr., 54–70. Salt Lake City: University of Utah Press.

———. 2004. "Critical Race Theory and the Archaeology of the African Diaspora." *Historical Archaeology* 38, no. 1:101–108.

Evans, E. Estyn. 1957. *Irish Folkways*. London: Routledge and Kegan Paul.

———. 1992. *The Personality of Ireland: Habitat, Heritage, and History*. Dublin: Lilliput.

Fagan, Brian. 2001. *Graham Clark: An Intellectual Life of an Archaeologist*. Boulder, Colo.: Westview.

Fanon, Frantz. 1968. *The Wretched of the Earth*. Trans. Constance Farrington. New York: Grove Press.

Feagin, Joe R. 2000. *Racist America: Roots, Current Realities, and Future Reparations*. New York: Routledge.

Ferguson, Niall. 2002. *Empire: The Rise and Demise of the British World Order and the Lessons for Global Power*. New York: Basic.

Fields, Barbara J. 1982. "Ideology and Race in American History." In *Region, Race, and Reconstruction: Essays in Honor of C. Vann Woodward*, ed. J. Morgan Kousser and James M. McPherson, 143–177. New York: Oxford University Press.

Fike, Richard E. 1987. *The Bottle Book: A Comprehensive Guide to Historic, Embossed Medicine Bottles*. Salt Lake City, Utah: Peregrine Smith.

Fitts, Robert K. 1996. "The Landscapes of Northern Bondage." *Historical Archaeology* 30, no. 2: 54–73.

Folkmar, Daniel. 1911. *Dictionary of Races or Peoples*. Washington, D.C.: Government Printing Office.

Francis, Peter, Jr. 2002. *Asia's Maritime Bead Trade: 300 B.C. to the Present*. Honolulu: University of Hawai'i Press.

Frank, Andre Gunder. 1998. *Reorient: Global Economy in the Asian Age*. Berkeley: University of California Press.

Franklin, Maria. 1997. "'Power to the People': Sociopolitics and the Archaeology of Black Americans." *Historical Archaeology* 31, no. 3:36–50.

———. 2001. "A Black Feminist-Inspired Archaeology?" *Journal of Social Archaeology* 1:108–125.

Fredrickson, George M. 2002. *Racism: A Short History*. Princeton, N.J.: Princeton University Press.

Gans, Herbert J. 1995. *The War against the Poor: The Underclass and Antipoverty Policy*. New York: Basic.

Garman, James C. 1994. "Viewing the Color Line Through the Material Culture of Death." *Historical Archaeology* 28, no. 3:74–93.

Garner, Steve. 2004. *Racism and the Irish Experience*. London: Verso.

Gathercole, Peter, and David Lowenthal, eds. 1990. *The Politics of the Past*. London: Unwin Hyman.

Geremek, Bronislaw. 1997. *Poverty: A History*. Trans. Agnieszka Kolakowska. Oxford: Blackwell.

Gero, Joan M. 2000. "Troubled Travels in Agency and Feminism." In *Agency in Archaeology*, ed. Marcia-Anne Dobres and John Robb, 34–39. London: Routledge.

Gibson, Florence E. 1951. *The Attitudes of the New York Irish toward State and National Affairs, 1848–1892*. New York: Columbia University Press.

Ginzburg, Carlo. 1980. *The Cheese and the Worms: The Cosmos of a Sixteenth-Century Miller*. Trans. John Tedeschi and Anne Tedeschi. Baltimore, Md.: Johns Hopkins University Press.

Glazer, Nathan, and Daniel Patrick Moynihan. 1963. *Beyond the Melting Pot: The Negroes, Puerto Ricans, Jews, Italians, and Irish of New York City*. Cambridge, Mass.: MIT Press and Harvard University Press.

Goldberg, David Theo. 1993. *Racist Culture: Philosophy and the Politics of Meaning*. Oxford: Blackwell.

Goldstein, Jonathan. 1991. "Cantonese Artifacts, Chinoiserie, and Early American Idealization of China." In *America Views China: American Images of China Then and Now*, ed. Jonathan Goldstein, Jerry Israel, and Hilary Conroy, 43–55. Bethlehem, Pa.: Lehigh University Press.

Gordon, Milton M. 1964. *Assimilation in American Life: The Role of Race, Religion, and National Origins*. New York: Oxford University Press.

Gossett, Thomas F. 1963. *Race: The History of an Idea in America*. Dallas, Tex.: Southern Methodist University Press.

Gould, Stephen Jay. 1981. *The Mismeasure of Man*. New York: W.W. Norton.

Gradwohl, David M., and Nancy M. Osborn. 1984. *Exploring Buried Buxton: Archaeology of an Abandoned Iowa Coal Mining Town with a Large Black Population*. Ames: Iowa State University Press.

Green, Sally. 1981. *Prehistorian: A Biography of V. Gordon Childe*. Bradford-on-Avon: Moonraker.

Griggs, Heather J. 1999. "Go gCuire Dia Rath Agus Blath Ort (God Grant that You Prosper and Flourish): Social and Economic Mobility Among the Irish in Nineteenth-Century New York City." *Historical Archaeology* 33, no. 1:87–101.

Gust, Sherri M. 1993. "Animal Bones from Historic Urban Chinese Sites: A Comparison of Sacramento, Woodland, Tucson, Ventura, and Lovelock." In *Hidden Heritage: Historical Archaeology of the Overseas Chinese*, ed. Priscilla Wegars, 177–212. Amityville, N.Y.: Baywood.

Gyory, Andrew. 1998. *Closing the Gate: Race, Politics, and the Chinese Exclusion Act*. Chapel Hill: University of North Carolina Press.

Hale, Grace Elizabeth. 1999. *Making Whiteness: The Culture of Segregation in the South, 1890-1940*. New York: Vintage.

Hamilton, William Tighe, and W. R. Wilde. 1843. *Report of the Commissioners Appointed to Take the Census of Ireland for the Year 1841*. Dublin: Alexander Thom.

Hammil, Jan. 1987. "Cultural Imperialism: American Indian Remains in Cardboard Boxes." *World Archaeological Bulletin* 1:34–36.

Hannaford, Ivan. 1996. *Race: The History of an Idea in the West*. Baltimore, Md.: Johns Hopkins University Press.

Harrington, Michael. 1963. *The Other America: Poverty in the United States*. Baltimore, Md.: Penguin.

Harrington, Spencer P. M. 1993. "Bones and Bureaucrats: New York City's Great Cemetery Imbroglio. *Archaeology* 46, no. 2:28–35, 38.

Harris, Fred R., and Lynn A. Curtis, eds. 1998. *Locked in the Poorhouse: Cities, Race, and Poverty in the United States*. Lanham, Md.: Rowman and Littlefield.

Hays, H. R. 1965. *From Ape to Angel: An Informal History of Social Anthropology*. New York: Alfred A. Knopf.

Herskovits, Melville. 1930. "The Negro in the New World: The Statement of a Problem." *American Anthropologist* 32:145–155.

Herzog, Don. 1998. *Poisoning the Minds of the Lower Orders*. Princeton, N.J.: Princeton University Press.

Higman, B. W. 1984. *Slave Populations of the British Caribbean, 1807-1834*. Baltimore, Md.: Johns Hopkins University Press.

Hodder, Ian. 2002. "Two Approaches to an Archaeology of the Social." *American Anthropologist* 104:320–324.

Hodgen, Margaret T. 1931. "The Doctrine of Survivals: The History of an Idea." *American Anthropologist* 33:307–324.

———. 1971. *Early Anthropology in the Sixteenth and Seventeenth Centuries.* Philadelphia: University of Pennsylvania Press.

Holmes, T. Rice. 1899. *Caesar's Conquest of Gaul.* London: Macmillan.

Hooton, Earnest A., and C. Wesley Dupertuis. 1955. *The Physical Anthropology of Ireland.* Cambridge, Mass.: Peabody Museum of Archaeology and Ethnology, Harvard University.

Hull, Katherine L. 2004. "Material Correlates of the Pre-Famine Agri-Social Hierarchy: Archaeological Evidence from County Roscommon, Republic of Ireland." Ph.D. diss., University of Toronto.

Ignatiev, Noel. 1995. *How the Irish Became White.* New York: Routledge.

Ignatiev, Noel, and John Garvey, eds. 1996. *Race Traitor.* New York: Routledge.

Jeffries, John P. 1869. *The Natural History of the Human Race.* New York: Edward O. Jeffries.

Jones, Chester Lloyd. 1909. "The Legislative History of Exclusion Legislation." *Annals of the American Academy of Political and Social Science* 34:351–359.

Jörg, C. J. A. 1986. *The Geldermalsen: History and Porcelain.* Groningen: Kemper.

Joseph, J. W. 1993. "White Columns and Black Hands: Class and Classification in the Plantation Ideology of the Georgia and South Carolina Lowcountry." *Historical Archaeology* 27, no. 3:57–73.

Kelleher, William F., Jr. 2003. *The Troubles in Ballybogoin: Memory and Identity in Northern Ireland.* Ann Arbor: University of Michigan Press.

Keller, Morton. 1968. *The Art and Politics of Thomas Nast.* New York: Oxford University Press.

Kennedy, Joseph C. G. 1864. *Population of the United States in 1860.* Washington, D.C.: Government Printing Office.

Kennedy, Líam, Paul S. Ell, E. M. Crawford, and L. A. Clarkson. 1999. *Mapping the Great Irish Famine: A Survey of the Famine Decades.* Dublin: Four Courts Press.

Kingsley, Charles. 1892. *Charles Kingsley: His Letters and Memories of His Life, as Edited by His Wife.* London: Macmillan.

Knobel, Dale T. 1986. *Paddy and the Republic: Ethnicity and Nationality in Antebellum America.* Middletown, Conn.: Wesleyan University Press.

Knox, Robert. 1850. *The Races of Men: A Fragment.* London: Henry Renshaw.

Kroeber, A. L. 1948. *Anthropology.* New York: Harcourt, Brace.

LaRoche, Cheryl J., and Michael L. Blakey. 1997. "Seizing Intellectual Power: The Dialogue at the New York African Burial Ground." *Historical Archaeology* 31, no. 3:84–106.

Latourette, Kenneth Scott. 1964. *The Chinese: Their History and Culture.* 4th ed. New York: Macmillan.

Lee, Erika. 2003. *At America's Gates: Chinese Immigration during the Exclusion Era, 1882–1943.* Chapel Hill: University of North Carolina Press.

Lefebvre, Henri. 1979. "Space: Social Product and Use Value." In *Critical Sociology: European Perspectives,* ed. J. W. Freiberg, 285–295. New York: Irvington.

———. 1991. *The Production of Space.* Trans. Donald Nicholson-Smith. Oxford: Blackwell.

Leiman, Melvin M. 1993. *Political Economy of Racism*. London: Pluto Press.

Leone, Mark P., Parker B. Potter Jr., and Paul A. Shackel. 1987. "Toward a Critical Archaeology." *Current Anthropology* 28:283–302.

Lesser, Alexander. 1961. "Social Fields and the Evolution of Society." *Southwestern Journal of Anthropology* 17:40–48.

Li, Dun J., ed. 1969. *China in Transition, 1517–1911*. New York: Van Nostrand Reinhold.

Lin, Alfred H. Y. 1997. *The Rural Economy of Guangdong, 1870–1937: A Study of the Agrarian Crisis and Its Origins in Southernmost China*. London: Macmillan.

Linebaugh, Donald W. 2005. *The Man Who Found Thoreau: Roland W. Robbins and the Rise of Historical Archaeology in America*. Durham: University of New Hampshire Press.

Linebaugh, Peter, and Marcus Rediker. 2000. *The Many-Headed Hydra: Sailors, Slaves, Commoners, and the Hidden History of the Revolutionary Atlantic*. Boston: Beacon Press.

Li Shih-Yao. 1969. "Five Rules to Regulate Foreigners (1759)." In *China in Transition, 1517–1911*, ed. Dun J. Li, 29–34. New York: Van Nostrand Reinhold.

Little, Barbara J., ed. 2002. *Public Benefits of Archaeology*. Gainesville: University Press of Florida.

Lodziak, Conrad. 1995. *Manipulating Needs: Capitalism and Culture*. London: Pluto.

Lowenthal, David. 1990. "Conclusion: Archaeologists and Others." In *The Politics of the Past*, ed. Peter Gathercole and David Lowenthal, 302–314. London: Unwin Hyman.

Lydon, J. F. 1994. "The Medieval English Colony (13th and 14th Centuries)." In *The Course of Irish History*, ed. T. W. Moody and F. X. Martin, 144–157. Rev. ed. Niwot, Colo.: Roberts Rinehart.

Ma, L. Eve Armentrout. 2000. *Hometown Chinatown: The History of Oakland's Chinese Community*. New York: Garland.

Malins, Edward, and the Knight of Glin. 1976. *Lost Demesnes: Irish Landscape Gardening, 1660–1845*. London: Barrie and Jenkins.

Marx, Karl. 1967. *Capital: A Critique of Political Economy*. Vol. 1. New York: International.

Matthews, Christopher N. 2002. *An Archaeology of History and Tradition: Moments of Danger in the Annapolis Landscape*. New York: Kluwer Academic/Plenum.

McCall, Leslie. 1992. "Does Gender Fit? Bourdieu, Feminism, and Conceptions of Social Order." *Theory and Society* 21:837–867.

McClain, Charles J. 1994. *In Search of Equality: The Chinese Struggle against Discrimination in Nineteenth-Century America*. Berkeley: University of California Press.

McConville, Michael. 1986. *Ascendancy to Oblivion: The Story of the Anglo-Irish*. London: Phoenix Press.

McDavid, Carol. 1997a. "Descendants, Decisions, and Power: The Public Interpretation of the Archaeology of the Levi Jordan Plantation." *Historical Archaeology* 31, no. 3:114–131.

———. 1997b. "Introduction." *Historical Archaeology* 31, no. 3:1–4.

McGuire, Randall H. 1982. "The Study of Ethnicity in Historical Archaeology." *Journal of Anthropological Archaeology* 1:159–178.

———. 1988. "White American Attitudes Concerning Burials." *World Archaeological Bulletin* 2:40–45.

Meltzer, David J. 1998. "Introduction: Ephraim Squier and Edwin Davis, and the Making of an American Archaeological Classsic." In *Ancient Monuments of the Mississippi Valley by Ephraim G. Squier and Edwin H. Davis*, ed. David J. Meltzer, 1–95. Washington, D.C.: Smithsonian Institution Press.

Meskell, Lynn, Chris Gosden, Ian Hodder, Rosemary Joyce, and Robert Preucel. 2001. "Editorial Statement." *Journal of Social Archaeology* 1:5–12.

Michaels, Gina. 2005. "Peck-Marked Vessels from the San José Market Street Chinatown: A Study of Distribution and Significance." *International Journal of Historical Archaeology* 9:123–134.

Miles, Robert. 1989. *Racism*. London: Routledge.

Miller, Daniel. 1987. *Material Culture and Mass Consumption*. Oxford: Basil Blackwell.

Miller, Kerby A. 1985. *Emigrants and Exiles: Ireland and the Irish Exodus to North America*. Oxford: Oxford University Press.

Milne, Claudia, and Pamela Crabtree. 2000. "Revealing Meals: Ethnicity, Economic Status, and Diet at Five Points, 1800–1860." In *Tales of Five Points: Working-Class Life in Nineteenth-Century New York*, ed. Rebecca Yamin, 130–196. Vol. 2. West Chester, Pa.: John Milner Associates.

Min, Pyong Gap, and Rose Kim. 2000. "Formation of Ethnic and Racial Identities: Narratives by Young Asian-American Professionals." *Ethnic and Racial Studies* 23:735–760.

Mitchel, John. 1918. *Jail Journal*. Dublin: Gill and Son.

Mitchell, Frank, and Michael Ryan. 1998. *Reading the Irish Landscape*. Dublin: Town House.

Montagu, Ashley. 1942. *Man's Most Dangerous Myth: The Fallacy of Race*. New York: Columbia University Press.

Moore, Thomas. 1857. *The Poetical Works of Thomas Moore*. New York: Leavitt and Allen.

Morris, Alan G. 1989. "Discussing Race in a Racist Society." *World Archeological Bulletin* 3:71–75.

Morse, Hosea Ballou. 1966. *The Gilds of China, with an Account of the Gild Merchant or Co-Hong of Canton*. Taipei: Ch'eng-Wen.

Morton, Samuel George. 1839. *Crania Americana: Or, a Comparative View of the Skulls of Various Aboriginal Natives of North and South America*. Philadelphia, Pa.: J. Dobson.

Mullins, Paul R. 1996. "The Contradictions of Consumption: An Archaeology of African America and Consumer Culture." Ph.D. diss., University of Massachusetts, Amherst.

———. 1999a. *Race and Affluence: An Archaeology of African America and Consumer Culture*. New York: Kluwer Academic/Plenum Press.

———. 1999b. "'A Bold and Gorgeous Front': The Contradictions of African America and Consumer Culture." In *Historical Archaeologies of Capitalism*, ed. Mark P. Leone and Parker B. Potter, Jr., 169–193. New York: Kluwer Academic/Plenum Press.

———. 1999c. "Race and the Genteel Consumer: Class and African-American Consumption, 1850–1930." *Historical Archaeology* 33, no. 1:22–38.

———. 2001. "Racializing the Parlor: Race and Victorian Bric-a-Brac Consumption." In *Race and the Archaeology of Identity*, ed. Charles E. Orser, Jr., 158–176. Salt Lake City: University of Utah Press.

———. 2004. "Ideology, Power, and Capitalism: The Historical Archaeology of Consumption." In *A Companion to Social Archaeology*, ed. Lynn Meskell and Robert W. Preucel, 195–211. Malden, Mass.: Blackwell.

———. 2006. "Excavating America's Metaphor: Race, Diaspora, and Vindicationist Archaeologies." Unpublished draft in possession of the author.

Muwakkil, Salim. 2005. "The Persistent Taint." *In These Times* 29, no. 7:13.

Nurse, G. T. 1989. "Rejoinder to 'Discussing Race in a Racist Society.'" *World Archeological Bulletin* 3:75–77.

O'Callaghan, Sean. 2000. *To Hell or Barbados: The Ethnic Cleansing of Ireland*. Dingle: Brandon.

O'Donoghue, David. 1998. *Hitler's Irish Voices: The Story of German Radio's Wartime Irish Service*. Belfast: Beyond the Pale.

O'Dowd, Anne. 1991. *Spalpeens and Tattie Hokers: History and Folklore of the Irish Migratory Agricultural Worker in Ireland and Britain*. Dublin: Irish Academic Press.

Ollman, Bertell. 2003. *Dance of the Dialectic: Steps in Marx's Method*. Urbana: University of Illinois Press.

Omi, Michael, and Howard Winant. 1983. "By the Rivers of Babylon: Race in the United States." *Socialist Review* 13:31–65.

———. 1986. *Racial Formation in the United States: From the 1960s to the 1980s*. New York: Routledge.

———. 1994. *Racial Formation in the United States: From the 1960s to the 1990s*. New York: Routledge.

Orser, Charles E., Jr. 1984. "The Past Ten Years of Plantation Archaeology in the Southeastern United States." *Southeastern Archaeology* 3:1–12.

———. 1988a. "The Archaeological Analysis of Plantation Society: Replacing Status and Caste with Economics and Power." *American Antiquity* 53:735–751.

———. 1988b. *The Material Basis of the Postbellum Tenant Plantation: Historical Archaeology in the South Carolina Piedmont*. Athens: University of Georgia Press.

———. 1990. "Archaeological Approaches to New World Plantation Slavery." In *Archaeological Method and Theory*, ed. Michael B. Schiffer, 111–154. Vol. 2. Tucson: University of Arizona Press.

———. 1991. "The Archaeological Search for Ethnicity in the Historic United States." *Archaeologia Polona* 29:109–121.

———. 1996. *A Historical Archaeology of the Modern World*. New York: Plenum.

———. 1998. "The Challenge of Race to American Historical Archaeology." *American Anthropologist* 100:661–668.

———. 1999. "Negotiating Our 'Familiar' Pasts. In *The Familiar Past?: Archaeologies of Later Historical Britain*, ed. Sarah Tarlow and Susie West, 273–285. London: Routledge.

———, ed. 2001. *Race and the Archaeology of Identity.* Salt Lake City: University of Utah Press.

———. 2004a. *Historical Archaeology.* 2nd ed. Upper Saddle River, N.J.: Prentice Hall.

———. 2004b. *Race and Practice in Archaeological Interpretation.* Philadelphia: University of Pennsylvania Press.

———. 2004c. "The Archaeologies of Recent History: Historical, Post-Medieval, and Modern-World." In *A Companion to Archaeology,* ed. John Bintliff, 272–290. Oxford: Blackwell.

———. 2005. "Symbolic Violence, Resistance, and the Vectors of Improvement in Early Nineteenth-Century Ireland." *World Archaeology* 37:392–407.

———. 2006a. "Symbolic Violence and Landscape Pedagogy: An Illustration from the Irish Countryside." *Historical Archaeology* 40, no. 2:20–36.

———, ed. 2006b. *Unearthing Hidden Ireland: Historical Archaeology at Ballykilcline, County Roscommon.* Bray, Ireland: Wordwell.

Orser, Charles E., Jr., and Annette M. Nekola. 1985. "Plantation Settlement from Slavery to Tenancy: An Example from a Piedmont Plantation in South Carolina." In *The Archaeology of Slavery and Plantation Life,* ed. Theresa A. Singleton, 67–94. Orlando: Academic Press.

Orser, Charles E., Jr., Douglas W. Owsley, and J. Richard Shenkel. 1986. "Gaining Access to New Orleans' First Cemetery." *Journal of Field Archaeology* 13:342–345.

Orser, Charles E., Jr., and Thomas C. Patterson. 2004. "V. Gordon Childe and the Foundations of Social Archaeology." In *Foundations of Social Archaeology: Selected Writings of V. Gordon Childe,* ed. Thomas C. Patterson and Charles E. Orser, Jr., 1–23. Walnut Creek, Calif.: Altamira Press.

Otto, John Solomon. 1975. "Status Differences and the Archaeological Record: A Comparison of Planter, Overseer, and Slave Sites from Cannon's Point Plantation (1794–1861), St. Simons Island, Georgia." Ph.D. diss., University of Florida, Gainesville.

———. 1977. "Artifacts and Status Differences: A Comparison of Ceramics from Planter, Overseer, and Slave Sites on an Antebellum Plantation." In *Research Strategies in Historical Archaeology,* ed. Stanley South, 91–118. New York: Academic Press.

———. 1980. "Race and Class on Antebellum Plantations." In *Archaeological Perspectives on Ethnicity in America: Afro-American and Asian American Culture History,* ed. Robert L. Schuyler, 3–13. Farmingdale, N.Y.: Baywood.

———. 1984. *Cannon's Point Plantation, 1794–1860: Living Conditions and Status Patterns in the Old South.* Orlando, Fla.: Academic Press.

Patterson, Jerry E. 1979. *Porcelain.* Washington, D.C.: Cooper-Hewitt Museum.

Patterson, Nerys. 1994. *Cattle-Lords and Clansmen: The Social Structure of Early Ireland.* 2nd ed. Notre Dame, Ind.: University of Notre Dame Press.

Patterson, Thomas C. 1995. *Toward a Social History of Archaeology in the United States.* Fort Worth, Tex.: Harcourt Brace.

———. 2001. *A Social History of Anthropology in the United States.* Oxford: Berg.

Paynter, Robert. 1990. "Afro-Americans in the Massachusetts Historical Landscape." In *The Politics of the Past,* ed. Peter Gathercole and David Lowenthal, 49–62. London: Unwin Hyman.

———. 1992. "W.E.B. Du Bois and the Material World of African Americans in Great Barrington, Massachusetts." *Critique of Anthropology* 12:277–291.

Pitts, Reginald H. 2000. "'A Teeming Nation of Nations': Heyday of Five Points, 1830 to 1865." In *Tales of the Five Points: Working-Class Life in Nineteenth-Century New York, Volume I, A Narrative History and Archaeology of Block 160*, ed. Rebecca Yamin, 37–66. West Chester, Pa.: John Milner Associates.

Pomeranz, Kenneth. 2000. *The Great Divergence: China, Europe, and the Making of the Modern World Economy*. Princeton, N.J.: Princeton University Press.

Praetzellis, Mary. 2004. "Chinese Oaklanders: Overcoming the Odds." In *Putting the "There" There: Historical Archaeologies of West Oakland*, ed. Mary Praetzellis and Adrian Praetzellis, 237–259. Rohnert Park, Calif.: Anthropological Studies Center, Sonoma State University.

Price, David H. 2004. *Threatening Anthropology: McCarthyism and the FBI's Surveillance of Activist Anthropologists*. Durham, N.C.: Duke University Press.

Pulszky, Francis. 1857. "Iconographic Researches on Human Races and Their Art." In *Indigenous Races of the Earth, or New Chapters of Ethnological Inquiry*, by Josiah C. Nott and George R. Gliddon, 87–202. Philadelphia: J. B. Lippincott.

Radcliffe-Brown, A. R. 1940. "On Social Structure." *Journal of the Royal Anthropological Society of Great Britain and Ireland* 70:1–12.

Reynolds, James Bronson. 1909. "Enforcement of the Chinese Exclusion Law." *Annals of the American Academy of Political and Social Science* 34:363–374.

Ripley, William Z. 1899. *The Races of Europe: A Sociological Study*. New York: D. Appleton.

Roediger, David R. 1991. *The Wages of Whiteness: Race and the Making of the American Working Class*. London: Verso.

———. 2005. *Working toward Whiteness: How America's Immigrants Became White, The Strange Journey from Ellis Island to the Suburbs*. New York: Basic Books.

Rolston, Bill. 1992. *Drawing Support: Murals in the North of Ireland*. Belfast: Beyond the Pale.

———. 1998. *Drawing Support 2: Murals of War and Peace*. Belfast: Beyond the Pale.

Rousseau, Jean-Jacques. 1984. *A Discourse on Inequality*. Trans. Maurice Cranston. London: Penguin.

Rowell, Chester H. 1909. "Chinese and Japanese Immigrants: A Comparison." *Annals of the American Academy of Political and Social Science* 34:223–230.

Rutman, Darrett B. 1971. *The Morning of America, 1603–1789*. Boston: Houghton Mifflin.

Sarich, Vincent, and Frank Miele. 2004. *Race: The Reality of Human Differences*. Boulder, Colo.: Westview Press.

Saxton, Alexander. 1971. *The Indispensable Enemy: Labor and the Anti-Chinese Movement in California*. Berkeley: University of California Press.

Scammell, G. V. 1981. *The World Encompassed: The First European Maritime Empires: c. 800– 1650*. London: Methuen.

Schlereth, Thomas J. 1991. *Victorian America: Transformations in Everyday Life, 1876–1915*. New York: HarperCollins.

Schrieke, B. 1936. *Alien Americans: A Study of Race Relations*. New York: Viking.

Shackel, Paul A. 2000. *Archaeology and Created Memory: Public History in a National Park*. New York: Kluwer Academic/Plenum.

———. 2003. *Memory in Black and White: Race, Commemoration, and the Post-Bellum Landscape*. Walnut Creek, Calif.: AltaMira Press.

Shackel, Paul A., and Erve J. Chambers, eds. 2004. *Places in Mind: Public Archaeology as Applied Anthropology*. New York: Routledge.

Shackel, Paul A., and David L. Larson. 2000. "Labor, Racism, and the Built Environment in Early Industrial Harpers Ferry." In *Lines that Divide: Historical Archaeologies of Race, Class, and Gender*, ed. James A. Delle, Stephen A. Mrozowski, and Robert Paynter, 22–39. Knoxville: University of Tennessee Press.

Shackel, Paul A., Terrance J. Martin, Joy D. Beasley, and Tom Gwaltney. 2004. "Rediscovering New Philadelphia: Race and Racism on the Illinois Frontier." *Illinois Antiquity* 39, no. 1:3–7.

Shanklin, Eugenia. 1998. "The Profession of the Color Blind: Sociocultural Anthropology and Racism in the 21st Century." *American Anthropologist* 100:669–679.

Shanks, Michael, and Christopher Tilley. 1987. *Re-Constructing Archaeology*. Cambridge: Cambridge University Press.

Shennan, Stephen J. 1989a. "Introduction: Archaeological Approaches to Cultural Identity." In *Archaeological Approaches to Cultural Identity*, ed. Stephen J. Shennan, 1–32. London: Unwin Hyman.

———. ed. 1989b. *Archaeological Approaches to Cultural Identity*. London: Unwin Hyman.

Shermer, Michael, and Alex Grobman. 2000. *Denying History: Who Says the Holocaust Never Happened and Why Do They Say It?*. Berkeley: University of California Press.

Sigerson, George. 1871. *History of the Land Tenures and Land Classes of Ireland*. London: Longmans, Green, Reader, and Dyer.

Silverberg, Robert. 1970. *The Mound Builders*. Athens: Ohio University Press.

Simmel, Georg. 1978. *The Philosophy of Money*. Trans. Tom Bottomore and David Frisby. London: Routledge and Kegan Paul.

Singleton, Theresa A. 1991. "The Archaeology of Slave Life." In *Before Freedom Came: African-American Life in the Antebellum South*, ed. Edward D. C. Campbell Jr. and Kym S. Rice, 155–175. Richmond: The Museum of the Confederacy.

Siu, Paul C. P. 1987. *The Chinese Laundryman: A Study of Social Isolation*. Ed. John Kuo Wei Tchen. New York: New York University Press.

Slater, Don. 1997. *Consumer Culture and Modernity*. Cambridge: Polity Press.

Smaje, Chris. 1997. "Not Just a Social Construct: Theorising Race and Ethnicity." *Sociology* 31:307–327.

Smedley, Audrey. 1993. *Race in North America: Origins and Evolution of a Worldview*. Boulder, Colo.: Westview.

———. 1998. "'Race' and the Construction of Human Identity." *American Anthropologist* 100:690–702.

Soja, Edward W. 1980. "The Socio-Spatial Dialectic." *Annals of the Association of American Geographers* 70:207–225.

———. 1989. *Postmodern Geographies: The Reassertion of Space in Critical Social Theory.* London: Verso.

Squier, Ephraim G., and Edwin H. Davis. 1847. Ancient Monuments of the Mississippi Valley Comprising the Results of Extensive Original Surveys and Explorations. Washington, D.C.: Smithsonian Institution.

———. 1848/1998. *Ancient Monuments of the Mississippi Valley.* Ed. David J. Meltzer. Washington, D.C.: Smithsonian Institution Press.

Starr, M. B. 1873. *The Coming Struggle: Or, What the People on the Pacific Coast Think of the Coolie Invasion.* San Francisco: Bacon and Company.

Staski, Edward. 1993. "The Overseas Chinese in El Paso: Changing Goals, Changing Realities." In *Hidden Heritage: Historical Archaeology of the Overseas Chinese,* ed. Priscilla Wegars, 125–149. Amityville, N.Y.: Baywood.

Stivers, Richard. 2000. *Hair of the Dog: Irish Drinking and Its American Stereotype.* Rev. ed. New York: Continuum.

Stocking, George W., Jr. 1987. *Victorian Anthropology.* New York: The Free Press.

Stout, Matthew. 1997. *The Irish Ringfort.* Dublin: Four Courts Press.

Stuckey, Sterling. 1987. *Slave Culture: Nationalist Theory and the Foundations of Black America.* New York: Oxford University Press.

Swartz, David. 1997. *Culture and Power: The Sociology of Pierre Bourdieu.* Chicago: University of Chicago Press.

Swinton, John. 1870. *The New Issue: The Chinese-American Question.* New York: American News.

Taylor, Walter W. 1948. *A Study of Archaeology.* Washington, D.C.: American Anthropological Association.

Terkel, Studs. 1992. *Race: How Blacks and Whites Think and Feel about the American Obsession.* New York: New Press.

Thomas, Cyrus. 1894. "Report on the Mound Explorations of the Bureau of Ethnology." *Twelfth Annual Report of the Bureau of Ethnology to the Secretary of the Smithsonian Institution, 1890–91.* Washington, D.C.: Government Printing Office.

Thrift, Nigel J. 2002. "On the Determination of Social Action in Space and Time." In *The Spaces of Postmodernity: Readings in Human Geography,* ed. Michael J. Dear and Steven Flusty, 106–119. Oxford: Blackwell.

Trouillot, Michel-Rolph. 1995. *Silencing the Past: Power and the Production of History.* Boston: Beacon Press.

Turner, Frederick Jackson. 1893. "The Significance of the Frontier in American History." *Annual Report of the American Historical Association,* 199–227.

Ucko, Peter. 1987. *Academic Freedom and Apartheid: The Story of the World Archaeological Congress.* London: Duckworth.

Vinson, J. Chal. 1967. *Thomas Nast: Political Cartoonist.* Athens: University of Georgia Press.

Voget, Fred W. 1975. *A History of Ethnology.* New York: Holt, Rinehart, and Winston.

Voss, Barbara L. 2005. "The Archaeology of Overseas Chinese Communities." *World Archaeology* 37:424–439.

Waghorn, Annita. 2004. *Historic Archaeological Investigations of the City Center Cinemas Block Bounded by Miner Avenue and Hunter, El Dorado, and Channel Streets, Stockton, California.* Rohnert Park, Calif.: Anthropological Studies Center, Sonoma State University.

Walker, Francis A. 1872. *The Statistics of the Population of the United States.* Washington, D.C.: Government Printing Office.

Warner, Mark S. 1998. "Food and the Negotiation of African American Identities in Annapolis, Maryland, and the Chesapeake." Ph.D. diss., University of Virginia, Charlottesville.

Wasserman, Stanley, and Katherine Faust. 1994. *Social Network Analysis: Methods and Applications.* Cambridge: Cambridge University Press.

Watson, Richard. 1965. *Bitters Bottles.* New York: Thomas Nelson.

Webster, Yehudi O. 1992. *The Racialization of America.* New York: St. Martin's Press.

Wells, Peter S. 2001. *Beyond Celts, Germans, and Scythians: Archaeology and Identity in Iron Age Europe.* London: Duckworth.

Whelan, Kevin. 1999. "Emigration." In *The Blackwell Companion to Modern Irish Culture,* ed. W. J. McCormack, 195–197. Oxford: Blackwell.

Whitney, James A. 1888. *The Chinese and the Chinese Question.* 2nd ed. New York: Tibbals.

Whybrow, Peter C. 2005. *American Mania: When More Is Not Enough.* New York: W.W. Norton.

Williams, Stephen. 1991. *Fantastic Archaeology: The Wild Side of North American Prehistory.* Philadelphia: University of Pennsylvania Press.

Wilson, Bobby M. 2005. "Race in Commodity Exchange and Consumption: Separate but Equal." *Annals of the Association of American Geographers* 95:587–606.

Wilson, David A. 1998. *United Irishmen, United States: Immigrant Radicals in the Early Republic.* Ithaca, N.Y.: Cornell University Press.

Wilson, William J. 1980. *The Declining Significance of Race: Blacks and Changing American Institutions.* 2nd ed. Chicago: University of Chicago Press.

Wittke, Carl. 1967. *We Who Built America: The Saga of the Immigrant.* Rev. ed. Cleveland, Ohio: The Press of Case Western Reserve University.

Wurst, LouAnn, and Robert K. Fitts, eds. 1999. "Confronting Class." *Historical Archaeology* 33, no. 1:1–195.

Wylie, Jerry, and Richard E. Fike. 1993. "Chinese Opium Smoking Techniques and Paraphernalia." In *Hidden Heritage: Historical Archaeology of the Overseas Chinese,* ed. Priscilla Wegars, 255–303. Amityville, N.Y.: Baywood.

Yamin, Rebecca. 1997. "New York's Mythic Slum: Digging Lower Manhattan's Infamous Five Points." *Archaeology* 50, no. 2:44–53.

———, ed. 2000a. *Tales of Five Points: Working-Class Life in Nineteenth-Century New York.* 7 vols. West Chester, Pa.: John Milner Associates.

———. 2000b. "The Rediscovery of Five Points." In *Tales of the Five Points: Working-Class Life in Nineteenth-Century New York.* Vol. 1. *A Narrative History and Archaeology of Block 160,* ed. Rebecca Yamin, 1–14. West Chester, Pa.: John Milner Associates.

———. 2000c. "People and Their Possessions." In *Tales of the Five Points: Working-Class Life in Nineteenth-Century New York*. Vol. 1. *A Narrative History and Archaeology of Block 160*, ed. Rebecca Yamin, 91–147. West Chester, Pa.: John Milner Associates.

———. 2000d. "Appendix A: Archaeological Feature Descriptions, Profiles, and Artifact Tables (Ceramics, Glass, and Small Finds) for Major Analytical Strata Discussed in Chapter 5." In *Tales of the Five Points: Working-Class Life in Nineteenth-Century New York*. Vol. 1. *A Narrative History and Archaeology of Block 160*, ed. Rebecca Yamin, A-1–A-114. West Chester, Pa.: John Milner Associates.

Yoell, A. E. 1909. "Oriental vs. American Labor." *Annals of the American Academy of Political and Social Science* 34:247–256.

Young, Arthur. 1780. *A Tour of Ireland with General Observations on the Present State of that Kingdom made in the Years 1776, 1777, and 1778*. London: T. Cadell and J. Dodsley.

Zimmerman, Larry J., Karen D. Vitelli, and Julie Hollowell-Zimmer, eds. 2003. *Ethical Issues in Archaeology*. Walnut Creek, Calif.: AltaMira Press.

Index

Page numbers in *italics* refer to illustrations.

Charles E. Orser Jr. is Distinguished Professor of Anthropology at Illinois State University and is the author or editor of eight books including *Race and Practice in Archaeological Interpretation* (2004) and *Encyclopedia of Historical Archaeology* (2002).

The American Experience in Archaeological Perspective
Michael S. Nassaney, Founding Editor
Krysta Ryzewski, Co-editor

The American Experience in Archaeological Perspective series was established by the University Press of Florida and founding editor Michael S. Nassaney in 2004. This prestigious historical archaeology series focuses attention on a range of significant themes in the development of the modern world from an Americanist perspective. Each volume explores an event, process, setting, institution, or geographic region that played a formative role in the making of the United States of America as a political, social, and cultural entity. These comprehensive overviews underscore the theoretical, methodological, and substantive contributions that archaeology has made to the study of American history and culture. Rather than subscribing to American exceptionalism, the authors aim to illuminate the distinctive character of the American experience in time and space. While these studies focus on historical archaeology in the United States, they are also broadly applicable to historical and anthropological inquiries in other parts of the world. To date the series has produced more than two dozen titles. Prospective authors are encouraged to contact the Series Editors to learn more.

The Archaeology of Collective Action, by Dean J. Saitta (2007)
The Archaeology of Institutional Confinement, by Eleanor Conlin Casella (2007)
The Archaeology of Race and Racialization in Historic America, by Charles E. Orser Jr. (2007)
The Archaeology of North American Farmsteads, by Mark D. Groover (2008)
The Archaeology of Alcohol and Drinking, by Frederick H. Smith (2008)
The Archaeology of American Labor and Working-Class Life, by Paul A. Shackel (2009; first paperback edition, 2011)
The Archaeology of Clothing and Bodily Adornment in Colonial America, by Diana DiPaolo Loren (2010; first paperback edition, 2011)
The Archaeology of American Capitalism, by Christopher N. Matthews (2010; first paperback edition, 2012)
The Archaeology of Forts and Battlefields, by David R. Starbuck (2011; first paperback edition, 2012)
The Archaeology of Consumer Culture, by Paul R. Mullins (2011; first paperback edition, 2012)
The Archaeology of Antislavery Resistance, by Terrance M. Weik (2012; first paperback edition, 2013)
The Archaeology of Citizenship, by Stacey Lynn Camp (2013; first paperback edition, 2019)
The Archaeology of American Cities, by Nan A. Rothschild and Diana diZerega Wall (2014; first paperback edition, 2015)
The Archaeology of American Cemeteries and Gravemarkers, by Sherene Baugher and Richard F. Veit (2014; first paperback edition, 2015)
The Archaeology of Smoking and Tobacco, by Georgia L. Fox (2015; first paperback edition, 2016)
The Archaeology of Gender in Historic America, by Deborah L. Rotman (2015; first paperback edition, 2018)
The Archaeology of the North American Fur Trade, by Michael S. Nassaney (2015; first paperback edition, 2017)
The Archaeology of the Cold War, by Todd A. Hanson (2016; first paperback edition, 2019)
The Archaeology of American Mining, by Paul J. White (2017; first paperback edition, 2020)
The Archaeology of Utopian and Intentional Communities, by Stacy C. Kozakavich (2017)
The Archaeology of American Childhood and Adolescence, by Jane Eva Baxter (2019)
The Archaeology of Northern Slavery and Freedom, by James A. Delle (2019)

The Archaeology of Prostitution and Clandestine Pursuits, by Rebecca Yamin and Donna J. Seifert (2019)

The Archaeology of Southeastern Native American Landscapes of the Colonial Era, by Charles R. Cobb (2019)

The Archaeology of the Logging Industry, by John G. Franzen (2020)

The Archaeology of Craft and Industry, by Christopher C. Fennell (2021)

www.ingramcontent.com/pod-product-compliance
Lightning Source LLC
Chambersburg PA
CBHW050648270326
41927CB00012B/2934